Masterji

Masterji: A Sansi Saga

Based on a true story

Sewa Singh

(With Susan Mccord)

PARTRIDGE

A Penguin Random House Company

Print information available on the last page.

To order additional copies of this book, contact
Partridge India
000 800 10062 62
orders.india@partridgepublishing.com

www.partridgepublishing.com/india

Contents

Preface

Natha Singh alias Nathu is a retired primary school teacher in Narangwal, a village in Ludhiana district in the State of Punjab. He begins his day reciting from the Sikh holy books, then goes at dawn to the Gurudwara for morning prayers. Stooped and thin, he takes long, slow walks in the village fields, talks to other old men as they pass by and is greeted as "Masterji" by the younger men, many of whom were his students. Not many of them know the story of how he became "Masterji", a respected school teacher.

This story has been written by his son, Sewa Singh.

Natha Singh told us how badly the Sansis, the people of his caste, were treated when he was young. They were at the very bottom of the society, below all the other 'Untouchable' classes and designated a 'Criminal Tribe' by the British. They were very poor and considered dirty by the Jat farmers. They were the only 'criminal tribe' living in Narangwal and the family lived at the edge of the village pond. Neither his father nor any of his relatives could read or write, and most of them made the least part of their living by stealing and hunting wild rabbits, cats and jackals etc.

My family and I lived across the road from him in the early 1970's when my husband was the Resident Director of a Johns Hopkins University Health Project in Narangwal. We became good friends of his second son, Sewa Singh, and often visited each other's house back and forth. We still do, but now between New York and India. I often asked Sewa Singh, 'How did your father, from the Sansi caste, treated as the lowest of the low, become a school teacher?' No one in the family really knew the exact story of his struggle behind it.

In 1995, when I was spending a year in India, we decided to find out about the life of Natha Singh. Sewa Singh was working in Delhi when we first began this project. We went to the village on numerous visits and tape recorded the interviews with his father. He liked the idea of telling his story, but on the first evening when we sat in his room he gave short, factual answers to Sewa's questions. Sewa couldn't get him to elaborate. His explanations seemed succinct and unnatural. Then Sewa suggested that we should switch off the light in the room. As we sat in the dark, Natha Singh talked and talked, just like story telling outside the house, people sitting on their charpoys in the dark, talking and telling stories. After this first session he became relaxed and comfortable in talking. During the day we took the tape recorder to the fields and he spoke relentlessly. Sometimes we sat under a tree by a tube well, sometimes by the village canal, sometimes by the little shrine of the Sansis. If we got hungry, Sewa would pluck a papaya from the tree on the little plot of land Natha Singh's family rented to grow vegetables, or dig up a carrot for us to eat. Generally a man of few words, Natha Singh loved talking about his past, especially his teaching and religious life. His memory of details, names, dates, places, was amazing. Hours would go by talking as we sat in the fields or in his house at night.

After we had made the tapes, Sewa Singh translated them from Punjabi to English on tapes and we transcribed them. Sewa began writing the story of his father. Natha Singh doesn't express much about his feelings in general. When he told us about his first wife he just said that after two years she died. When we asked for details, he said she was sick, nothing else. So Sewa wrote and we sat together going over the manuscript, deciding what more details we needed from further interviews or from background reading about the Sansis and other scheduled tribes and castes.

Life in his comfortable house is busy. His two daughters-in-law get up early to cook breakfast for the family, bathe the four oldest children and dress them for school. Lunch has to be packed for each one. The youngest, Kulbir, often eats his on the way to school, so some extra is put in his older brother, Tejwant's, lunch box. With a typical morning Natha Singh's wife might be sitting on a charpoy, a rope-strung cot, in the courtyard shelling peas and monitoring the work of her daughters -in-law who have many chores, washing clothes, sweeping the courtyard, feeding and milking the buffalo, as well as cooking. On two sides of the courtyard are the living quarters, the two room house built by Natha Singh's father in 1931 and three freestanding rooms built by his sons after they got jobs and were able to contribute to the household. The largest is where his wife sleeps and is the central family room with the TV set and the refrigerator. The kitchen is outside, covered by a roof. Next to it stands the bathing room and the hand pump which is constantly being used to fill buckets for cooking, drinking, and washing. On the far side are the rooms for the buffalo and storage. Natha Singh's third and fourth sons live with him and go out to work, Gurdev on his motor scooter to his teaching job in the high school and Hari to his job as a carpenter at the nearby military base. In the evenings when the children play in the courtyard, a peacock often flies down and eats the grain that they put out for him.

Susan McCord

Acknowledgement

**Special thanks to Miss I.L. Gonsalves
for her contribution.**

**This book is dedicated to Susan Mccord
who had initiated this project**

Reporting to the Police

"One evening a police constable had visited our village and proclaimed, 'Tomorrow the 'Bada Saheb', Superintendent of police, is paying a visit to the Dehlon police station. All Sansi families including children must report to the Dehlon police station without fail. This kind of ominous diktats from the police would invariably distress my elders. That day late in the evening my father Chhotu and his elder brothers, Thaman and Gaata, were sitting on their charpoys, string cots, in the open space in front of our thatched huts which were located on the bank of the village pond. The next day, they had to face the police people and they all seemed to be very dejected. Our area police station was situated in Dehlon Village which was more than seven miles away from our village. I was sitting beside my father and listening to his conversation with my uncles. They were expressing their anguish about the nuisance of reporting to the police station occasionally and recalled a few episodes in the past citing the uncouth behaviour and the high-handedness of the police. Their past experiences held profound torment in their minds. The police staff would yell at them sans any reason and maltreat them like animals. They had to tolerate this viciousness and stay dumb with their heads down. My aunts avoided partaking in the conversation of the elders. This time my father had asked me to accompany him in reporting to the police. I was terribly scared and nervous about my maiden visit to the police station.

Ultimately my father decided to retire for the night as we had to wake up early in the morning to organise a few things at home before our departure to Dehlon. With the first crow of the cock, my father was out of bed, and awakened me too. He tossed some grass in front of the buffalo before he began to milk her. He quickly kindled the fire on the Chula, an earthen stove, and got engaged in preparing Rotis, handmade Indian bread, for the day. I washed my face and got ready with my daily dirty clothes. My father wrapped up some of the rotis and onions in a piece of cloth for our lunch. He quickly milked the buffalo and placed the milk on the fire for boiling. His next priority was to churn the curd and skim butter from it. After churning the buttermilk was ready. We ate some roti with ground red chillies and some fresh homemade butter. He wanted to ensure that all necessary household tasks were completed before our departure. He was unsure about how much time would be consumed at the police station.

At last my father had completed his pressing morning household chores and hinted to his brothers that he was now ready to move. My uncles and aunts emerged from their huts with some paraphernalia, and just before sunrise we all set out on foot to the Dehlon police station. As we came out from the village, we observed that other Sansi families were also on the way to Dehlon. As usual everybody was in their daily dirty clothes, just like us. Generally the men were clothed in a long 'Kurta', a long shirt and a loincloth and the women were wearing a blouse and 'ghagri', a long skirt. Most of their dresses were patched at one or more places. The majority of the young kids had either short pyjamas or a shirt on them. Some families had laden the donkeys with their children and some of the old men carried their hookahs with them.

There was no proper road; just a dusty trail passing through the green fields near the village but the rest of the path was through barren land with only wild shrubs and trees around. After walking for about two miles I felt weary so my father put me on his shoulders and later on my uncles took turns carrying me. My aunts and other Sansi ladies were walking in a separate group from the men folk and were engaged in chatting with each other. When we had travelled for more than half of our journey, the men decided to halt and take a short break. There were no means of public transport in those days. We continued marching after resting for a short time as we were anxious to reach the police station as quickly as possible.

Finally we arrived at Dehlon police station and the men directed the ladies and children to camp under the shady trees away from the main gate. They went inside the police station to report their arrival. Their return was instant as they were asked to wait outside. The Sansis from other villages began pouring in bunches with their belongings. The ladies and men hugged each other with great enthusiasm as some of them were close relatives. The ladies had established their own individual groups and the men folk assembled in small clusters under the shady trees and began conversing among themselves. Some men had carried their personal hookahs with them to pass their time. The bunch of old men felt a strong desire to kindle their hookahs and one of them yelled at his wife to arrange for fire for it. That lady instantly directed some young boys to fetch firewood. The boys collected some pieces of dry wood and she ignited the fire and prepared the embers to light the hookahs. She instructed the boys to bring in the Chillums, tobacco pipe, to replenish them with tobacco and charcoal. Once this was done, she sent them to distribute the Chillums, to the men in waiting. When the Chillums were delivered to the old men, they felt relieved, began smoking and resumed their chatting. Some of the older women also had an irresistible urge to smoke; they headed for the group of older men to share their hookahs. The children had a gala time playing with their newly found companion. All the Sansis were conversing in their own colloquial language. I stayed in the company of my father and uncles who had mingled with the bunch of old men, and silently observed the whole scene around me.

Those Sansis who brought their donkeys had let them loose for grazing in the open space near the police station. All of a sudden some donkeys began braying and a constable surged from the police station and yelled at us to curb this nuisance and drive the donkeys away from the police station. He also warned us to keep the donkeys out of sight of the 'Bada Saheb'. Some boys instantly rushed to the donkeys and drove them behind a wall away from the police station. Most of the Sansis had brought their hounds and sniffer dogs along with them. The men proudly exchanged the tales of their prized hounds, when their animals had chased hare, wildcat or jackal. Each one pompously recounted their hunting contests with their rivals when their hounds had proved their prowess to haul the prey first, leaving behind the other hounds. They highly appreciated the remarkable skills of their sniffer dogs that would get a whiff of the prey and force it to move out from its hiding den to be chased by the waiting hounds. The hounds with the longest tails were considered to be of the finest breed. They contemplated mating their animals to produce the premium breed and requested for pups from each other.

Besides gossiping the ladies often had one important topic to discuss their young children. They enquired about their kids and conferred with one another the possibility of an engagement even while some of their children were still being breastfed. Some men wished to cement their friendship forever on the basis of their pregnant ladies. They committed to get their children engaged if one had a boy and the other had a girl, even though the child was still in the womb.

Our elders noticed that the 'Numberdar', our village headman, was approaching with quick steps, perhaps he was late. Sansis from our village went ahead to bestow 'Salaam', greetings, to him. He acknowledged their "Salaam' but hurriedly headed to the police station. His presence was mandatory at the police station to submit the report about his village and especially about these criminal tribes.

Everybody began feeling impatient now as almost half of the day had already gone by, yet there was no sign of the 'Bada Saheb'. The primary excitement in the camp had turned sluggish, and the men began joining their individual families. All eyes were set on the main road to catch sight of 'Bada Saheb'. Suddenly we heard the sound of a roaring motor car and became alert. For a moment there was pandemonium among the police people. We rushed towards the police station but the policemen prevented us from blocking the main entrance and pushed us away. The car arrived at the main gate, the Police Inspector saluted the 'Bada Saheb' with full tenacity and the constables conferred him with a rifle salute. All the other people also bowed and bequeathed 'Salaam'. He pompously alighted from the car, and the police inspector respectfully escorted him inside the police station. Some other officials also accompanied him. Our immediate anxiety had eased off, and we returned to our place under the trees.

The children were feeling hungry but earlier the ladies had refrained from serving food to them because of the ambiguity of the situation. Now they could safely serve food to their men and children. My father also unfolded rotis and we ate it with onions. One and all were in a great hurry to finish their food as quickly as possible because we were afraid that the 'Bada Saheb' might summon us anytime. The elders were more nervous as they had to face the 'Bada Saheb' now and the ominous feelings of uncertainty had permeated their minds. We were all waiting for the call now.

Perhaps the 'Bada Saheb' also had his lunch, and after a long wait a constable appeared from the police station and commenced calling the Sansis from each village. When the Narangwal Sansis were summoned in, all men, women and children swiftly entered the police station. We bowed to 'Bada Saheb' and all other officials. Our village 'Numberdar' was present there and testified to the 'Bada Saheb' that the Sansis from his village did not create any serious trouble. He had a special characteristic that he may be unkind to the Sansis in the village but he would never criticise them seriously at the police station. The 'Bada Saheb' verified it from the Inspector if there were any serious complaints from Narangwal. The Inspector informed him that the Sansis from this village were barely caught up with any grave crimes. My uncles, aunts and my father were standing in one corner. Seeing lots of policemen around I was terribly scared and clinging to my father like the other children to their parents. Now the 'Bada Saheb' set his piercing gaze on the young children.

He pointed out to me and asked, "Whose child is this?"

My father cautiously replied, "Saab, he is my son."

The 'Bada Saheb' retorted, "How old is he?"

"About six years."

"Does he go to school?"

"No."

The 'Bada Saheb' then thundered, "Why? Send him to the school without any further delay. Don't you know that as per the law all children of this age must be admitted to school for primary education?"

My father was dumb struck for he had never thought of me sending to school. He was apprehensive and meekly responded, "Saab, I am raising him single-handedly as his mother passed away long back when he was very young. He is my only child, and there is nobody else to take care of him. It would be impossible for me to send him to school."

Before my father could complete his sentence, the Police Inspector immediately was up on his feet and shouted at my father. He grabbed his arm and twisted it. I witnessed my father writhing in pain. The Inspector shouted, "How dare you to open your mouth in front of the 'Bada Saheb' and rebuff him instead of complying with his order? I will teach you a lesson later on."

This horrifying scene made me frightened, but my uncles and aunts with folded hands begged the 'Bada Saheb' to protect my father from a beating. They apologetically pleaded with him repeatedly saying, 'Saab, please spare him, we will persuade our brother to admit his son in the school.'

The 'Bada Saheb' signalled to the Inspector and nodded. The inspector ultimately released my father and threatened him to face the dire consequences if he ignored the order. The 'Bada Saheb' thundered to the other Sansis to send their children to school without fail. They immediately concurred because they had witnessed the brutal consequences of making any excuse. My father was a living example infront of them and thus they remained tight lipped. Then the 'Bada Saheb' directed the Inspector to dismiss us and call the Sansis from the other village. We all returned home before evening.

Susan was curious to discover the life of my father Natha Singh alias Nathu. She would often enquire about his early life which he had seldom uttered a word to me. It had never crossed my mind to ask him to enlighten us about his early days. Ultimately both Susan and I decided to explore the hidden mysteries of his tacit life. I spoke to my father about our project that Susan is fascinated with his way of life and wishes to delve into his bygone days. Perhaps he was shy to divulge about the painful episodes that had occurred in his life. He had a high esteem for Susan and ultimately consented to oblige her. Susan was elated about this project and purchased a mini cassette recorder to record the conversations of my father. Since I was employed, we had to synchronize our timings jointly to be with my father for recording. After her periodic visits between India and USA, finally we commenced recording the life story of my father right from his childhood.

Admission

"After returning from the police station my father was traumatized with the diktats from the 'Bada Saheb'. He was now perplexed as how to manage his daily chores if he admitted me to school. On the other hand, he was frightened about the orders of the 'Bada Saheb'. He made up his mind determinedly to admit me in the school. For this purpose now he had no authentic proof of my date of birth. In the olden days people hardly bothered to maintain any birth records of their children. If need be then they would associate the child's birth with some significant event or incident which had occurred at that time, such as an epidemic or heavy floods etc. The teacher would deduce that the child was born around that time, and consequently would establish the date of birth. Life was not based on watches and calendars then. Life flowed in its natural course and people would not seriously stress about it.

One day my father took me to the Government primary school in our village for my admission. He told the teacher in-charge to admit me in the school. The teacher gazed at both of us but reluctantly pulled out an admission form from his desk and began filling it. He asked my father several questions while filling in the admission form, "Chhotu, what is his name?"

"Nathu", my father replied.

"How old is he?" the teacher enquired.

"About six years." My father replied hesitantly.

"When was he born?"

"I don't exactly remember."

"Do you have any idea in which year?"

Then my father quoted the incident when heavy floods had submerged the entire village. Then the teacher thought for a while and counted something on his finger tips. Subsequently he successfully ascertained my auspicious date of birth as June 13, 1921.

After completing the admission form, the teacher asked my father to provide his thumb impression on the form. Thus I was now enrolled in class one. Other Sansi families were equally petrified about the episode in the police station so they also followed the example of my father. Soon after my enrolment, six other Sansi boys got admission to the Primary School. There were two Sansi boys who were already studying there when I joined the school. One was Nigahia from our village, and the other was Karam Chand from another village called Lohgarh. Bhagat Ram was the then headmaster at the school alongwith other two teachers Shaadi Ram and Polo Ram. There were about a hundred students in the primary school.

The school was not absolutely liberated from discrimination towards the lower castes students. Being a Sansi, the teachers in the school seldom treated me at par with the children of the Jats and other higher castes. Even so they were less discriminating when they apportioned punishment to all the students. While teaching in the class there was no disparity but occasionally they would use loathing language towards me. I would silently digest this perennial insult as this was the price to pay for being an untouchable Sansi.

My uncles and father were pleased that I was progressing satisfactorily in the school. They hardly understood anything about education but the fact was that I was getting promoted to the next higher class every year. I was very regular and never missed school until class six. My father hardly ever asked me to stay home for any sort of domestic work. He solely managed all the domestic chores. Perhaps my father now had some sort of aspirations about educated people having a better status in society. He had noticed that educated people achieve a unique status and everybody considered them with more respect.

From my batch, the other six Sansi children gradually dropped out from school but I continued with my studies. The Government was interested that all school age children must get registered in the Primary School. However nobody really cared whether they continued their schooling or not.

All the children of the lower and higher castes would sit together in the class, but they never shared their food with each other during the lunch break. Some students would return home for lunch, but I would sit alone and eat my roti in the school because I was never sure whether my father would be at home or not. Because of my solitary nature and being a low caste, it was hard for me to establish companionship with other students.

Being the only child in the house, my life had been monotonous right from my childhood. Unfortunately, my uncles also had no children at that time. There were hardly any children of my age around in the neighbourhood to play and be friends with. My father remained occupied most of the time to survive and take care of me within his very limited resources. My aunts and uncles always adored me but my eldest aunt, Kakko, loved me the most and she would often invite and proffer buffalo milk to me. My life continued rolling under such high and dry environment.

*   *   *

Demobilising the Criminal Tribes

"Like Sansis, the other tribes the Harnias, the Baurias, the Bangales, Bhedkut etc. were nomads from ages. There used to be plenty of non cultivated land and these wandering tribes would set up their camp with their ragged tents at any open space outside any village. They could obtain the basic essentials from begging and hunting to run their carefree life style. After a fortnight or so they would move again because they would not find adequate supplies for living at one place. Some petty stealing from the fields would also instigate the villagers to suspect them. Five to six families together used to wander in small groups. They would transport all their limited belongings on donkeys or ponies accompanied by some goats and hounds.

Gradually the crime was on the increase and the law enforcement authorities were drastically attempting to curb it. They hardly had any grasp on these wandering tribes. To track down the nomads was almost impractical as they were constantly on the move. The police department could not trace them if they committed any crime as they would vanish from the scene over night. Ultimately the British authorities concluded that the majority of the nomads were largely responsible in committing most of the crimes. Thus the British government designed to rein in these tribes and keep them under their paws all the time. They enlisted them as 'Criminal Tribes' and passed a stringent Criminal Tribes Act in 1871. This law had permanently clipped their wings and coerced them to inhabit in any village. They were callously caged in a very constricted sphere of their own village boundary.

Now with the laid down stringent law, the criminal tribes had no other alternative except to settle down wherever they found it convenient. While roaming around they were well aware of the convenient spaces accessible for them to settle down. Every village generally had several unoccupied free spaces called 'shamlat', a village common land or uninhabitable land. These nomads ultimately established themselves on such places near or around the village ponds or marsh land. Generally the villagers would not object if anybody occupied such useless space. Such waste land was not documented in the government land records. These wandering tribes would verbally request the village headman to allow them to raise their tents on such worthless land. But the village Numberdar, would then notify in the area police station that such people had established themselves permanently in his village. Sometimes the people from the village would object to it fearing that these nomads could be a nuisance in the long run as they were notorious for larceny and other criminal activities. At that time the populace was sparse and plenty of fallow land was available in the villages. So one way or the other they could manage to settle in such places.

According to the law if any individual belonging to any criminal tribe was apprehended beyond the boundary of their village, he was instantly punished for six months in jail. There was no scope for them to present any kind of justification. Even if anybody appealed in the court against this punishment, the magistrate would not listen to any argument and uphold the sentence.

Any male child attaining the age of eighteen years was automatically covered under the Criminal Tribes Act."

*   *   *

Settling in Narangwal

Now I could envisage how the different families in Narangwal and our other nearby villages were closely interrelated with each other and how they had settled at various locations. From the descriptions of my father, I could evidently envision how our ancestors had set up their roots in and around Narangwal. My father's childhood and youth had witnessed how our families had gradually improvised in establishing themselves on the bank of our village pond. Both Susan and I rejoiced at recording and listening to my father.....

"My father Chhotu would occasionally mention about our ancestors, how they had captivated the space to settle in and around Narangwal like the other wandering tribes. It was obvious that my forefathers had no money to buy a piece of land and then they had no choice but to perch at any uninhabitable available space. It was said that our ancestor Budhu had erected his ragged tent on the bank of our village pond. My three uncles, Thaman, Gaata and Chhotu, gradually converted their tents into three small mud and thatched huts. As they got married, gradually they began living separately with their families in the same space. During that period not a soul from the village demurred about it. These thatched huts were situated on the bank of the village pond which was the village shamlat. Since the shamlat was the common land of the village hence no individual could stake any personal claim over it. Nobody could pursue any legal action over its jurisdiction. At the same time anybody who occupied or developed such space could not put it up for sale. As a result anybody who developed it would turn out to be its owner without official authorization.

During summer season my uncles and father slowly commenced reclaiming more and more area around their huts by filling up the banks of the pond with the mud from the pond itself. Some farmers in the village could not digest this remarkable expansion and it irked them quite frequently. Finally the Jats openly objected to it. Our forefathers declined to budge and held up against them. They incited the farmers that if they wished, they could come and stay there and develop the place. This aggravated the farmers but my forefathers stood their ground. Finally circumstances became as tense as some of the farmers invaded to demolish the huts. They partially damaged the huts. Somehow our forefathers managed to register the case against the farmers in the court. The magistrate was a Muslim. He briefed the Sansis that 'he would listen to their case but would be incapable to take any stringent action against the Jats' without proper witnesses in the courtroom. He had strong apprehensions that no witness from the village would turn up in their favour.

To settle this issue amicably, the magistrate questioned the Jats' as to why were they harassing these poor Sansis. They also needed a place to live and secondly they were not tresspassing into anybody's personal property. Why were they constraining the Sansis only? It would be desirable for both the parties to have a mutual understanding and let the Sansis live peacefully. The Sansis also highlighted to the magistrate that some of the Jats' in the village too had occupied the 'shamlat'. Why were the Jats opposing the Sansis only? Having no other choice, thus the Jats' executed a written agreement with the Sansis that they would allow them to live there peacefully in future.

Now three huts had emerged in a row distinctively. My eldest uncle, Thaman had erected wooden beams to support his hut and covered its top and the sides with thick thatch. My second uncle, Gaata, had low mud walls to support the central beam and covered the roof with thick layers of thatch. My father had also constructed mud walls about four feet high with a thatched roof above it. Comparatively our hut was bigger in area than my uncles. We managed to squeeze in one portion for living and the rest of the area was for our buffalo. We had nothing in the name of furniture except one or two string cots for our versatile use. My father had built up a hearth in one corner for cooking. Since our cooking was sparse, my father had very limited clay utensils for cooking and eating food. He had stretched a string between the two beams of the hut to hang our clothes. There were two tall clay pitchers to store the grains. An oil lamp dangled in the middle of our hut. With one glance, anyone could easily gauge the level of our naked poverty. We scarcely had any other possessions except our buffalo. My other uncles too had very limited belongings in their hovels. We were at the lowest ebb of our life.

The summer season was at its peak and I was sitting under the shady tree in front of our huts. My second aunt was occupied in cooking lunch in her hut. My uncles and father were out at that time. My aunt had just finished cooking and I noticed that she was trying to scare away something inside the hut with a piece of cloth. I was aware that there was a wasp's nest in their hut and she was always frightened of it. She attempted to chase away the wasps and drive them out. But the wasps kept on encircling inside the hut. She got agitated and suddenly in a fit of rage, picked up a burning stick from the hearth and chased the wasps from corner to corner perhaps to burn them. In that process she accidentally torched the thatched ceiling with the burning stick. The whole hut was instantly up in flames. She ran out of the hut and cried for help. With a few gusts of wind the fire engulfed the two adjoining huts as well. I made a futile attempt to throw some mud on the fire but it was in vain. My aunt was crying and stared helplessly at this scene. The neighbours rushed to our rescue when they heard the piercing cries of my aunt but in the mean while our huts had already been reduced to ashes before the people could make any effort to extinguish the flames. Our limited belongings in the huts had also been reduced to ashes. Everything was over in a short time leaving behind only the roasted mud walls. Fortunately our buffalo was outside the hut at that time. We were now under the open sky.

My uncles and father were stunned when they discovered that their huts had been reduced to ashes. They began gathering the new raw material to reconstruct their huts. They first washed the walls with mud, then fixed wooden planks over it and finally roofed it with thick layers of thatch. Gradually in a few months time once again the huts came into existence. The open space around the pond was more beneficial to our families. During summer time our families managed to cook as well as sleep under the open sky. At dusk my father and uncles would put the string cots in the open space to sit and chat together. During the winters we would utilise this open space to bask in the sun.

Every year during the summer, my uncles and father would dig the mud from the pond and reclaim more area in front of our huts. Other people from the village too would dig mud to wash their houses with it, but not to reclaim the area like us. The regrettable part of this hard labour was that every year during the monsoons, the floods would wash away most of this reclaimed area. It would plunge like an avalanche into the pond again during the heavy rains. There was a large open space on one side of the pond but it was at a lower level than our huts. During the dry season, the children from the village would gather there to play every evening in this open space. A big banyan tree in front of our huts provided shade for us and our buffalo as well. A carpenter from our neighbourhood would sit and work under this tree and chat with my father and uncles. Unfortunately this tree was uprooted by a storm in 1950.

Once during summer when the pond had dried up again, my father was on his annual mission to excavate the clay from the dry pond and fortify the area around our hut. Suddenly he noticed that our hut was up in high flames. He dashed to put off the fire and called for help. First of all he made desperate efforts to salvage anything from the burning hut. He could just retrieve two string cots but one got slightly burnt. He helplessly watched the rest of the things go up in smoke. He made futile attempts to put some mud on the fire but it was in vain. Some other people rushed to assist him but our thatched hut had already been reduced to ashes. I was at school at that time. When I came back from school, I was stunned to see that our hut was missing and instead some ash was flying around. My father described to me what had happened. The actual cause of this mysterious fire could not be ascertained. My father was feeling irritated and miserably depressed about the loss of our hut and few belongings.

My father was now determined to make a sturdy house with bricks and cement. By selling buffaloes he had saved some money over the years, which was now sufficient to construct his dream home. During those days one could sell a class buffalo for thirty to fourty rupees in silver coins. He contacted the mason to obtain an estimate on the approximate expenditure to build his dream house. Now there was sufficient safe space where he could think of constructing two rooms, one room for our living and other for the buffalo. He decided to construct a single unit of two rooms measuring sixteen by twelve feet each with one main entrance. The mason had demarcated the foundation line and my father had dug the foundation himself. He would fortify the base by pressing pebbles in it. The cost of the bricks was seven rupees per thousand. He had purchased sixteen thousand bricks to build two rooms. The iron girders had been purchased for one rupee per foot. A mason from Ballowal village constructed our house. Just two small spaces of four inches each were left open near the ceiling for ventilation. My father had avoided having windows in the house as he would accumulate the filched stuff from the fields and sought to ensure that nobody could peep into his house. Generally he would pile up the stolen stuff in the rear room and used the front room for cooking and keeping the buffalo. Actually we had to fasten our buffalo in the room during the winters only otherwise she would stay outside most of the time. The woodwork of merely two doors was undertaken by our village carpenter Ram Singh and his son. Our house resembled a mini fortress where not even the ray of the sun could penetrate except through the main door. Our house was completely ready in the year 1932.

My second uncle Gaata had managed to construct a single room house with bricks and iron girders earlier than us but my eldest uncle Thaman continued residing in the thatched hut."

*   *   *

The Sansis in Narangwal

"Generally the Sansis in Narangwal had large families and it was not easy for them to even manage two meals a day. They had no regular source of income to support their families. Basically their living was based on begging in the village and occasional stealing from the surrounding fields. Due to this reason the farmers would yell at them if they found a Sansi loitering around their fields. Sometimes the Sansi men would go hunting during the day to supplement their meagre meal.

Some Sansis were opium addicts and their families suffered severely. A few of them would immerse dry poppies in the water and leave it to soak for two to three hours. Later on they would filter the water and drink it. There were some Sansis who indulged in brewing country made liquor at home not only for their own consumption but to sell it too. The majority of the Sansis usually smoked the hookah or cigarettes. Now I appreciate that my father and uncles were not addicted to the other things except the hookah.

The Sansis were so critically poor that they could not even endow their children with proper clothes. Generally their young children ran around naked and the school aged children usually wore either a shirt or short pants but not both. Their parents would beg for clothes from the village. First of all they seldom wished to send their children to school and secondly they were unable to pay their school fees. Their primary aim of life was survival. They had no assets except their thatched huts or a few utensils. As a youngster, I hardly remember my father ever purchasing new clothes for me. He too would wear the same torn or patched long dirty shirt daily. People would donate half torn clothes to the Sansis, which they would patch and reuse. My aunts would go begging and later my wife too joined them.

When any girl from our village was getting married, the Sansi ladies would beg for one or two paisa from the groom's marriage party. They would also seek food from the girl's house. In those days the marriage party would often stay at the bride's home for three to four days. The Sansi ladies would go there to sing folk songs, dance and beg from the men who would often use indecent language to the begging women. These women would often disregard their filthy annotations because they sought the money from them. At the departure of the bride, the groom's father would shower coins over the married couple. The poor people including the Sansis would do their best to gather the maximum coins. A few individuals would try and deploy a 'jhalli', a piece of cloth fixed on two sticks, to grab most of the coins. Others would strongly object to it and even pick a fight with the person deploying the 'jhalli'.

Normally during an eclipse, the village people considered it inauspicious to move outside. Most of the Sansi men and women would go for begging in the village. They would often use a standard phrase while begging, 'Anne ghode da daan, pate purane da daan.' (Please bequeath old shoes and torn or old clothes). In the old days people especially the pregnant women were more petrified during an eclipse because of the many superstitions attached to it. Willingly they would offer more alms generously to ward off any ill luck to their families. Begging people would accept anything like grains, money, old clothes etc. When somebody donated something to them, they would always bless them by saying 'May God bless you'.

The Sansi men had a different way of begging than their women. They would play a few instruments like 'bansuri', flute; 'dhol', drum; 'duff', an earthen tumbler with skin on one side; 'shainay', a jingling rattle-like instrument and 'tasa', an iron triangle. They would also beg by entertaining the people at weddings and other occasions of the higher communities. But they would never beseech at any event within their own community or other lower castes like them. My uncle Gaata and another man would play the instruments and dance for money and food during weddings and other celebrations in the villages.

In the olden times at any function people would serve food in reusable clay plates called 'Sanaks'. People would sit down in rows on long sheets of cloth. A standard procedure was observed while serving food at any function. At first they would serve boiled rice followed by powdered sugar and then Desi ghee, clarified butter, on top of it. One could eat as much as one wanted. After this course they would serve dal and roti. Black dal, 'lentils' and roti was offered to the guests only. If any rich family served up ladoo and jellabi, Indian sweets, it was called 'pakki roti'. Such food was very expensive to afford at that time. People would appreciate if any family served 'pakki roti' and it was considered a matter of great pride. Only the wealthy families could afford to serve meat to their guests.

At times after attending to the guests, the family may offer food to the beggars to take away. Well-to-do families may possibly permit the beggars to sit down and eat. However, they would not provide Sanaks to the beggars to eat their food. The beggars would have to spread their own cloth or utilize their own begging bowl to eat food.

Like other sansis when my uncles Thaman and Gaata had an opportunity to be gluttonous at any place, they would compress the boiled rice before the powdered sugar was served. The same way they would pack down the sugar before the ghee was poured on top of it. As a general tradition if somebody requested for more sugar then he was served ghee as well. My uncles would not eat much of rice but smartly devour most of the sugar and ghee from the top.

The Sansis seldom worked as labourers at the time of my grandfather. Some reforms were taking place among the Sansis and their living conditions were improving but at a very slow pace. A few Sansis in Narangwal now embarked on raising their own buffaloes, goats and sheep. To enhance their income, they also began grazing cows and buffaloes on a contractual basis for other people. Sometimes my uncles would work with the farmers in the fields to earn twenty paisa for a half day. At that time one could purchase forty seers of maize or grain for one rupee.

Occasionally, especially at night, the Sansis in our village would filch cotton, maize and grains etc., mainly from the fields of nearby villages. They avoided stealing anything from the fields of their own village. Once my father had gone to pilfer maize from a nearby village in the night and unfortunately the farmer trapped and caught him red handed. My father tried his best to flee but the farmer was also physically very strong. When my father could not unshackle himself from his grip, he eventually clutched the farmer's thumb and fractured it. The farmer cried with pain and let go of my father. In Narangwal my uncles and father were the strongest men among the Sansi community.

The Sansis in our village always avoided crossing paths with the stubborn farmers who would occasionally yell if they discovered them loitering around their fields. The Sansis were skilled in stealing grain from the fields especially in the night and operated in small groups. They would rob the maize from the corn stacks very tactfully. The stacks would appear intact from the exterior as if nothing had happened, but when the farmers would open it up, they would discover that all the ears of corn had vanished. In the night they would dare to steal it under the very nose of the sleeping farmer. During the harvest season the farmers would guard their grains in the night. He would wrap the grains with a wide piece of cloth and tuck all the ends under his charpoy so that nobody could pilfer the grains sans disturbing him. But the Sansis would quietly hoist the string charpoy of the sleeping farmer with their shoulders and pull out the tucked corners of the cloth and pilfer the grain. They would filch enough to have ample stock of grains for the whole year.

Unfortunately if someone was caught stealing red handed, they would evade handing him over to the police. They would abuse or beat him and warn him not to repeat it in future. Suppose if someone had filched twenty ears of corn, they may penalize him twenty five paisa or so which was the going price then.

Many fields belonging to the Aassi village farmers were located closer to Narangwal. The land was fertile and the Aassi village farmers would often grow seasonal crops in these fields. But the farmers had no solution to guard their crops all the time. When the crops were ready, the Sansis of Narangwal would pillage it at their own will. The farmers endeavoured their best to protect their crops from being plundered on a large scale every year. Consequently they suffered immense losses. Ultimately after suffering over the years, the farmers of Aassi got exasperated and sold their land at throwaway prices to the farmers of Narangwal.

On one occasion a farmer from Narangwal was bragging about being a big landlord to my cousin Gurdial. His ancestors had purchased the land from the farmers of Aassi village. With a straight face my cousin diffused his pride, 'you need not brag about your land, rather be thankful to the Sansis. Our ancestors had compelled the farmers in Aassi to sell their land to you at throw away prices.' The farmer was speechless and walked away dumbfounded.

In Narangwal some Jats and Sansis including my cousins would illegally distil country liquor at home and sell it in the village. The police would often raid their homes and arrest them if they found the stuff in their possession. They would confiscate their distilling equipment too and file a case against them in the court. If the judge found them guilty, he would either send them to jail for a short duration or impose a fine on them. After returning from the jail, they would discreetly resume their brewing operations once more. Such insignificant punishment did not deter them from playing the hide and seek game with the police. Ultimately the police began maintaining the personal records of notorious lawbreakers who frequently offended the law. Habitual criminals were declared as 'Dus Numberi', Number 10, an exclusive category of proclaimed offenders. The police would display their photographs in the police station and preserve their hand and foot prints in the police records. If any serious criminal activity occurred in the area, thus the police would primarily suspect these dus numberis and interrogate them. A few of them had turned as the police informers. Some sansis in Narangwal were in the list of 'Dus Numberis'in the police records".

*　　*　　*

Pass System

*S*usan was stunned at the restrictive living of the Sansis and other tribes in old times. As my father was unable to hold a conversation in English, Susan asked me to enquire from my father about the movement of the Sansis in this absolutely controlled environment imposed by the British Government. I prompted several queries to my father as to how the criminal tribes would get in touch with their relatives or friends at times. There could be several reasons when these people had to call on each other. Then my father revealed about the intricate pass system which was then regulated by the Criminal Tribes Act. We began recording my father with utmost curiosity......

"We the 'Sansis', were the only criminal tribe that inhabited the village Narangwal while some of the other Sansi families had established themselves in the nearby villages. The life of the Sansis was miserable beyond description. Their whole tribe had been declared outlaws by the British Rule. They were oppressed by the law as well as the higher castes. Everyone stared at them suspiciously when they were around. They had become so notorious that people would unnecessarily allege them for any mishappening. In the event of any unlawful activity, they were always the prime suspects for the villagers as well as for the police. Whenever any theft or other criminal activity had occurred in the area, invariably they were subjected to be summoned to the police station.

The animals and birds could cross any boundaries without any restraint but the Sansis no longer could do so. Their wings had literally been clipped by the Criminal Tribes Act. They were not even authorized to cross the boundary of their own village without prior permission from the police. The Sansis had to keep their heads down and bow, to bestow 'Salaam' whenever they came across any higher caste person. Poverty seemed to be their ultimate destiny. They were labelled as 'untouchables' too.

The village 'Numberdar', the headman, was the prime focal point for 'Criminal Tribes' to obtain any kind of permission to cross the bounds of their village. For a certain reason if any person belonging to the 'Criminal Tribes' had to get out of his village, he had to approach his village 'Numberdar' first. He would have to provide comprehensive justification where and why he had to go. Initially the 'Numberdar' would generally refuse the request on one pretext or the other. However after a good deal of pleading and persuasion, if he thought it to be a genuine case then he would furnish the permission in writing, called 'Parcha'. This permission was valid only for a day i.e. departing and returning the same day.

After receiving 'Parcha', the person would begin his journey. He would present the 'Parcha' to the Numberdar there once he reached the other village. Numberdar there would inquire why he sought to meet the person in his village. After he was satisfied, only then he would permit to meet the concerned person. He had to inform the Numberdar on his return that he was leaving his village after meeting. After reaching his own village, once again he would then have to call upon his own village 'Numberdar' to inform his return. This procedure was applicable to both men and women.

It was said that during the Jubilee celebration function, Queen Victoria had voluntarily asked the delegates there if women at any place in her Empire were heavily oppressed. It was stated that an Indian representative had conveyed to her that there are 'Criminal Tribes' in India where the women were not allowed to get out from their village without proper permission. The Queen then made a declaration there to abolish the 'pass system' for women. During that time my grandfather got married to my grandmother. She had applied for police permission to leave her village as she was getting married. She arrived at my grandfather's house with the police permission. The Queen's declaration came into effect just after her marriage.

The process to obtain overnight stay authorization from the police was more cumbersome. A set procedure had to be followed to get permission in advance. As usual the person would initially request his village Numberdar for his written permission. If he granted the permission, then the person would approach his area police station and present the permission from his village Numberdar to the police inspector. If the police inspector was convinced, then on the recommendation of the village Numberdar, he would issue a certificate for an overnight stay. He would also sternly warn the person that if any crime took place there during his overnight stay, he should be prepared to face the consequences. On the day of departure, the person would commence his journey but he could not set off directly to the concerned village without informing the area police station. The police inspector would stamp on the certificate 'Reported'. That area police station could be very far away from his village but he had to show up there first.

He would then travel to the concerned place and his host there would inform his village Numberdar that such-and-such a person had come to stay with him for so many days. Before departure from there, then the Numberdar there would specify on the certificate that this person had spent so many days and nights in his village and returned. After departure from there the person could not proceed directly to his own village, but instead he had to report to his own area police station again. The police inspector would remark on the certificate 'Returned'. After reaching his own village then he would inform his own village Numberdar of his arrival.

If the person visited a place falling under the jurisdiction of another police station the same procedure of reporting had to be adopted. Only the Superintendent of Police at the district headquarters could authorise to stay away for more than three days.

This arduous procedure would ruin two days of one's visit but nobody could afford to violate the law. At that time there were barely any reliable means of transportation. Generally one had to walk from one village to another. Overstaying was considered illegal and punishable under the law. The permission for an overnight stay was seldom granted especially during moonless nights.

I remember after 1940, a circular was released that only the Sansis of Narangwal were 'exempted' from the obtaining permission to visit other places. Thus all Sansis of Narangwal were issued exemption certificates. Under present conditions it had brought immense relief to us from unlimited restrictions. This exemption certificate was issued by the District Magistrate but authorised by the Governor of the State. Probably the Sansis of Narangwal were inactive in any hard core criminal activities. There might be some basis for this exemption. I do not know the basic reason behind it or under what circumstances this exemption had been granted. Who had recommended this exemption was a mystery to us. In a way this was our first freedom before the freedom of India. We could now freely move wherever we wished. The Sansis in other villages were astonished at the exclusive relaxation for the Sansis of Narangwal. Because the source of this exemption was unknown, they could not approach anybody for such relief for them. They remained shackled and confined to their own village boundaries. I had kept a copy of that circular but afterwards it was misplaced. But I have an original exemption certificate which was issued to my father.

*   *   *

Exemption Certificate

Translation:

(For exempted person)

Identity certificate for the exempted person from the Criminal Tribes Act under penal code 25.

1. Name: Chhotu
2. Farther's Name: Mataba
3. Caste: Sansi
4. Village: Narangwal.   Police Station: Dehlon.
   District: Ludhiana.
5. Appearance: Dark brown colour, Round face, one
   mole on the thigh, one mole on the right shoulder,
   boil mark on the left knee.
6. Criminal act abolished under notification code 13
   by the order of Punjab Government.
7. Left thumb impression:
   Date: April 3, 1945   1824-j-45-/20305
                 3, 1945   1824-j-45-/20306 H-Judl
   Date: April 25, 1945   1824-c-T/45/2712 Ct
   Issued on May 15, 1945

   Dy Commissioner Criminal Tribes Punjab

   For District Magistrate, District Ludhiana 17.1.9

Besides the Sansis, there were other 'criminal tribes' like
the Baurias, the Harnias, the Bhedkut and the Banjaras
etc. Each tribe had its castes and sub-castes which were
more than twenty. The Baurias and the Harnias were in
larger numbers than the Sansis".

*   *   *

Lifestyle

While doing manual labour in the fields with my uncles Gurdial and Jeet, once I enquired from them to explore how people washed their clothes in the olden days. Both of them laughed at my curiosity but my elder uncle Gurdial answered in a satirical manner. He commented, 'who bothered about washing clothes regularly in the old days. The Jats' would sluice their clothes while running the oxen well. They would pick up the mixture of oxen dung and urine from the oxen's path and rub it on their dirty wet clothes. They would leave the clothes to soak for some time and then rinse it in the running water from the well. The clothes would appear to look clean irrespective of the mild stink emanating from it. Some people considered another way to wash their clothes with the ash of the dry corn plants. They would dip their clothes in the mixture of ash and water, then rub and rinse it in the running water. This process would give the impression of clean clothes. Ladies at home would occasionally dip the dirty clothes preferably in hot water *for the time being and afterwards they would rub and rinse it to dry. For the really dirty clothes, they would immerse them in the hot water mixed with caustic soda, sodium carbonate. Later on they would beat it with a wooden stick, rinse and dry it. Nobody really worried about the odour of their clothes. People were not fashionable in the old times but satisfied with the bare minimum clothes available to them for their daily use. When I was young I could observe some old people regularly using the daily dirty clothes. The new generation had now begun utilising country made washing soaps and detergents to wash their clothes.*

My Father carried on describing the general lifestyle of the people depending upon their economic conditions.....

"My father and I mainly survived on staple food. We would eat roti with mashed onions, salt and chillies almost every day. Occasionally my father would cook grams dal, a lentil, along with a brinjal or tomato or ghia, a kind of gourd. We could not afford to have dal every day. Plenty of milk was available as my father raised a milching buffalo which would yield plenty of milk most of the time. There was no practice of selling milk in those days. To prepare 'Makki-ki-roti', corn meal bread, was tough but my father could skilfully prepare it. Quite often we would simply add red chillies and salt in lassi, buttermilk, and add mashed 'makki-ki-roti' in it as a meal for the day. Generally people prepared thin rotis from wheat flour but my father prepared thick ones. There was a scarcity of vegetables as the farmers grew limited seasonal vegetables due to the lack of storage facilities. At that time to cook a potato dish was considered to be a delicacy and people cooked it only on very special occasions. Cooking vegetables were more expensive than regular dal because it needed more ingredients.

In the olden days people had insufficient money most of the time and they drastically restricted their needs. They would always refrain from purchasing unnecessary things which had no regular utility in their daily life. Expensive things were not often displayed in the homes for boasting about their standard of living. People had become habitual in controlling their necessities of life. Farmers also hardly had any regular source of income except from the fields. People having jobs would obtain just sufficient remuneration to make ends meet. This simple way of living was embedded in their basic life style. Like the other people my father and I would often wear a khadi shirt made of rough cotton cloth. 'Kalam' brand cloth was most popular then and it would come from the cloth mills in Delhi. One could buy one yard of cloth for two 'Annas', one eighth of a rupee. Ladies would also spin cotton at home and make hand woven 'Khadi' cloth out of it. People bought little more expensive clothes mainly at the time of a wedding, especially for the bride and groom. For daily use one cotton shirt would last about eight months to a year. Most often the poor people would not buy a new one until the old one was completely worn out. They would put patches over and over again and reuse it for the maximum time. My father would often use a patched shirt. During the winter time people would put on two kurtas, shirts, and wrap themselves with thick cotton sheets. People would sit in the sun to warm themselves. Purchasing of woollen clothes were beyond the capacity of the rural people. I had seldom noticed anyone dressed with woollen clothes in the village during winters. Only the very rich people could afford to wear thick quilted jackets during winters.

Irrespective of it being summer or winter, most of the school children as well as other poor people in the village hardly owned a pair of shoes. One had to shell out at least one rupee for a pair of shoes which was considered to be very expensive to afford for an ordinary person. If someone bought a pair of shoes, he would not easily discard it after it had worn out completely. He would repeatedly get it repaired until such time it could not be repaired anymore. Ultimately he may end up donating it to the poor people like the Sansis. My father had purchased my first pair of new shoes with extreme difficulty when I enrolled in class five in the high school. Shoes were made to order by the cobblers in the village. The cobblers would often use the leather of buffalo, cow or camel. Comparatively it was inexpensive and more durable as compared to the shoes made of goat or sheep skin.

People had no yearning to expend money on clothes to maintain an exclusive set of clothes for any special occasions. If per chance someone had to visit his relatives or grace any special function, he would scrounge a shirt from one person, a pyjama from another and shoes from yet another person. People could not comfortably afford to purchase a complete set of decent attire.

The underlying reality was that all Jats' were not rich. They also lived in poverty like the other low caste poor people. Their clothes would also be as dirty as the other poor people. Because the Jats' owned a piece of land, they considered themselves to be superior. Some of the Jats' in our village did not even own a piece of land and survived on doing some minor chores. From a distance anybody could recognise the low caste people because of their shabby attire. The stench of their daily dirty clothes was unique. The tanners' in the villages wore stained clothes most of the times.

Way back then Life was not dependent on clock and calander. During that period wrist watches did not exist and clocks were exceptional. Some of the wealthy people in the cities would install tower clocks in their homes as a matter of pride otherwise the common man in the villages guessed the time from the lengthening of the shadows. I never had a glimpse of a clock in any house in our village. People were dependent on various means devised by some institutions to notify the time to the public only at a specific hour. At noon in certain areas they would beat the drums or sound heavy gongs indicating the time at 12 o'clock. In our area the Nawab of Malerkotla town would fire a gun at noon which was heard in the neighbouring villages. In our village Gurudwara, Sikh temple, they would sound a gong at 12 o'clock noon. This exercise was very helpful for the people in the village, especially for the labourers working in the fields."

*   *   *

Days in the Primary School

"I was gradually progressing in the primary school. My father hardly ever asked me about my studies in the school. But whenever I progressed to the next class, I would convey it to him. The primary school was up to the fourth grade only.

During the final year of my primary school, our class teacher had alerted us regarding the State level competition in mathematics for class four. He designed a question paper to evaluate the aptitude of those students who would be intelligent enough to compete in this tough contest. He organized a test in the class and selected the students on merit basis who would participate in the State level exam. With the consultation of the headmaster, he selected eighteen boys who were considered to be excellent in Mathematics to compete at the State level exam. Fortunately I was one among them. Master Bhagat Ram was assigned to coach us in mathematics for the contest. He would pick up assorted questions from three different mathematic books for our preparation and made us practice rigorously. He would personally arrange extra classes for us and recommend various types of questions for our practice. With the prolonged sessions of practicing, he was confident that some of his students would definitely win the scholarship.

After the preliminary knock out round, only nine of us got qualified for the finals. In the last round I had accurately answered all the questions in the written examination but unluckily I had overwritten one of my answers. Due to this overwriting the examiner had deducted some marks. I had answered all the oral questions very well. When the result was declared, they did not disqualify me directly but I could not become eligible for the scholarship on merit basis. In the end five students from our class emerged as winners of the scholarship.

In those days the students were not overloaded with many books and home assignments, as our teacher would make us practice enough in the school itself. We had three books in our curriculum, the Urdu language, Mathematics and Geography. There was no school uniform for the students. I would wear a simple cotton shirt and a pair of shorts for school as well as home. Our teacher would give more emphasis to keep our clothes neat and clean. I used to wash my own clothes every week rinsing them in plain water and drying them. Affordable detergents were not available at that time. When my clothes would really appear too dirty then I would request my father to purchase some caustic soda. I would add caustic soda in the boiling water and dip my dirty clothes in it. Sometimes my father would also immerse his only dirty shirt in this exceptional washing exercise. After soaking them for half an hour, the heavy grime would come off from the dirty clothes. I would not receive a new set of clothes until the old ones were about to wear out. Though the children of the Jats' were slightly better off than the poor low caste people but the state of their clothes was more or less the same.

In the primary school the teachers would sketch a sun dial on the ground and erect a stick in the centre of a circle. They would guess the time from the shadow of the stick on the sundial. Perhaps the quality of the teaching was better at that time because the teachers were not time conscious but rather they concentrated more in improving the efficiency of the students. They would continue teaching until they felt satisfied that students had learned their lesson well. There was no bell to remind them that the period was over. The teachers proffered to report early and left late from the school. The same class teacher in-charge would impart lessons to the pupils on various subjects assigned in their syllabus.

The teachers would ask the students to memorize the verses from our Urdu syllabus book and listen to the poems in the class. When an officer would visit for inspection, he would also ask the children to recite poems orally. There were no games, no physical exercises or any other extracurricular activities. In our school, three maps had been painted on the walls, the district map, the state map and the country map. If the teacher-in-charge observed that the students were getting bored, he would advise them, 'Go and see the maps'. The children would rush to see the maps as later on the teacher would question them about the maps.

During old times physical punishment to the students was very recurrent in schools. The teachers would not vacillate at all to utilize the cane if the students did not behave properly. Parents never protested to the teachers in meting out punishment to their children in the school. Sometimes it was rather the other way around. They usually believed that if the teacher had punished their child then certainly their child would have been at fault or he may not have been studying properly. Parents wanted their children to study for their own bright future. Generally the teachers worked on the basic principle, 'spare the rod and spoil the child'. Sometimes if the child was naughtier at home too then his parents would visit the teacher in-charge in the school and request him to straighten up their child.

Before Independence in the province of Punjab, primary school education was compulsory for all children in the sixty villages. Narangwal was one among them. After Independence, in 1957 the Punjab State Government made primary education compulsory for all the villages in the state. In reality they had developed a suitable system to monitor compulsory education to all children. They had established a committee in each village to monitor the progress of the primary education. Mostly the committee members belonged to the Jat community. If a child dropped out of school, the headmaster would intimate the committee and in turn they would persuade the family to encourage their child to attend school. If the family rebuffed the committee then they would refer the case to the district court. But such action was taken by the committee only in extreme cases. The court would summon the parents along with the youngster. First and foremost the magistrate would impose a penalty of five rupees and instruct the family to send their child to school. He would not listen to any arguments of the parents with or without an advocate. I remember only one person, Sucha Singh, from our village who had to appear in the district court for his son. Similarly the compulsory education rule was obligatory for the girls too but the government was not very strict in the case of girls. Luckily our village had a separate school for girls.

The village committee barely had any special interest to compel the children of the Sansis to pursue compulsory education. They had formed their personal opinion that the Sansi children would not continue their studies. Their basic purpose was to get them registered in the primary school at least for the record purpose. Nobody made any sincere attempts to follow up after the Sansi children were enrolled in the school. The higher caste people rarely encouraged the children of the poor to continue going to school. Sometimes they would rather discourage them and even taunt a poor man if his child continued his studies, saying 'If your child continues attending school, he is not going to become a District Collector.' But on the contrary they would make all efforts to send their own children to school. The Jats' regularly required help from the lower caste children for labour at their homes or in the fields, for a paltry amount of money or sometimes just for food. If the majority of the poor people remained uneducated, it was in the interest of the Jats to have more inexpensive labour easily available to them. If every child pursued his studies then who would work for them? In the first place Sansis rarely admitted their children to school, and even if they did, then they would drop out after class one or class two. Generally the Sansis hardly had any concern in educating their children as a priority in their life.

I was fortunate that my father had not forced me to abandon my studies and indulge in activities like the other illiterate Sansi families. He struggled alone but despite all odds I completed my Primary school education in 1932."

*   *   *

Our Lineage

*S*usan's curiosity was now delving into the genealogy of our family. Astonishingly it had never crossed my mind to solicit it from my father and create a genealogy chart. When we raised this subject with my father, unbelievably he revealed to us his deep quest to maintain the track records of our ancestral history of our village Sansis and our family. When he began narrating the background of the Narangwal Sansis, I was astounded with his amazing memory for minute details about the genealogy of our ancestors. He distinctively remembered the names of every family by heart right down the line. I believe that there would be no other Sansi in our village who had such comprehensive details of our ancestors. His vivid explanation made it evident to us how the Sansi families had settled down in and around Narangwal. We asked my father to verbalise the history of our ancestors and I switched the tape recorder on.....

"As far as I was informed by my father and uncles, long back our ancestor was Bhaga. In the early stages he had settled down along with some other Sansi families near village Gharuan which was then said to be a remote place. These Sansi families had gradually established themselves. Another Sansi named Gond got into a serious rift with Bhaga over some critical issue. They would often clash with each other and their enmity was taking a serious turn day by day. One day it crossed all limits when they ferociously fought with each other. To defend himself Bhaga injured critically Gond during the fight. It was said that Gond had hardly any chance of survival. There was panic among all the Sansi families. Now the situation had become critical and all the Sansis were appalled and wanted to escape from there to avoid any police investigations. They had no other option except to flee from there. In the night Bhaga along with his wife fled from there and finally arrived at Kalakh village which was about sixty to seventy miles away from Gharuan. Consequently other Sansis also ran away from there and headed towards a place called Samana which was more than a hundred miles away. Thus the families quietly evaded the police case and kick started a new life in this village without potential fear of arrest. It was believed that the Sansis in Samana are close kinfolk to the Sansis of Narangwal.

After Bhaga and his wife landed at Kalakh village, they decided to settle there. Their first son Nikku was born. Nikku was still very young when his mother had fallen critically ill and ultimately passed away in a short span of time. Now Bhaga struggled to handle this young child but frantically found it complicated to raise him alone. Bhaga was in his youth and decided to remarry at least for the sake of his son. He soon tied a knot with another girl considering that she would now take care of his young child. While living there Bhaga had five more children from his second wife. As time passed by his children grew up. Since Nikku was the eldest child among the other children, he could not adjust with his step brothers. Bhaga arranged his marriage but Nikku considered it necessary to live independently with his wife. He decided to walk out from Kalakh and settled in Narangwal. He alighted on the west side of our village. Nikku and his wife had three sons after they had shifted to Narangwal.

Bhaga continued living with his wife at Kalakh and organised the marriages of his other sons one by one. His other sons also expressed their desire to live independently with their respective wives. His son Boota wished to move out from Kalakh and settled in the Chhota Narangwal village which is just adjacent to our town. After Boota had permanently settled in Chhota Narangwal, he had two sons. Gradually Bhaga's three other sons, Taru, Godhan and Bhola also departed from Kalakh and they found a place to settle in the nearby Lohgarh village which is located between Kalakh and Narangwal.

Finally Bhaga's fifth son Budhoo also got married and continued residing with his parents. But a few years later he also moved out from Kalakh and shifted to another village Mehma Singh Wala which has proximity to Kalakh. During his stay he had a brawl with someone there and hence headed towards Narangwal. Nikku was already residing in Narangwal but there was no space available around his place. Ultimately Budhoo along with his family managed to establish himself on the bank of our village pond which is on the east side of the village.

We are the descendents from Budhoo who had two sons Mataba and Zhaba. After Zhaba got married, he had only one girl child but no son. Hence he had no further ancestry. But Mataba had three sons Thaman, Gaata and Chhotu from his marriage. My eldest uncle Thaman had only one daughter but no son. My second uncle Gaata initially got married to Tabbo early in his youth. They lived together for few years and had no issue yet. Tragically my aunt Tabbo gradually fell seriously ill and did not survive. My uncle was still young and after some time he intended to re-marry. He would frequently visit his relatives in a village Kasapur. There was a beautiful lady named Bachni and unfortunately her husband too had died. Bachni had two sons, Kulu and Dalu, and one daughter Bibi from her marriage. She was still young and my uncle fell in love with Bachni. After some time he proposed to her and her relatives gladly accepted this proposal but decided to retain her children with them. Bachni was also pleased as she was not carrying any liability to my uncle Gaata. They had a simple marriage ceremony. Then after her marriage they got blessed with two sons, my cousins Gurdial and

Jeet. My uncle Gaata was an open minded person and he never forbade the previous children of Bachni to visit Narangwal and stay with them. Her children also had a very cordial relationship with my uncle Gaata and my cousins. They would address my uncle as Bapu, Father. Bachni's daughter, who had been married, would also visit Narangwal with her husband and children and spend considerable time with the family.

My father Chhotu, the youngest son of Mataba, also got married. My father later on disclosed to me that my mother passed away shortly after my birth.

The Sansis in Narangwal born from the first wife of our ancestor Bhaga, are called from 'Baddike', means the child from the Bhaga's first wife. The children from the second wife are called from 'Chhotike, means from the second wife."

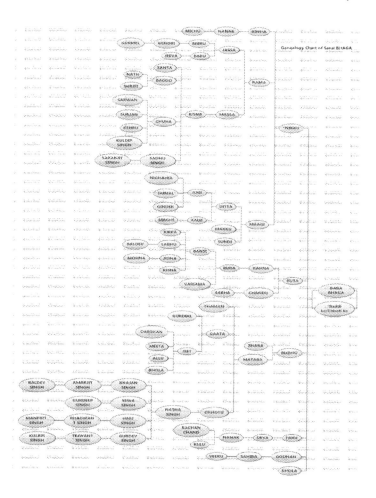

Genealogy Chart of Sansi BHAGA

This was an incredible experience of my life to unwaveringly hear about our ancestors from my father. Occasionally I would not comprehend when the elder Sansis in our village addressed our family with our ancestor's name Mataba. I was curious to find out about it but would push it aside for the time being. I hardly had an open opportunity to pose any questions to my father why the Sansis addressed our family like this. We were studying and he was teaching so there was hardly any possibility to unwrap such issues with him. But after listening to the full episode about our ancestors, all my misgivings had absolutely vanished from my clouded mind. The whole image was vivid with a deep insight about our ancestors. There were some other close relatives who would often visit my uncle Gaata but I seldom understood our actual relationship with them. This way I acquired an overall background of all the Sansis existing in Narangwal and other nearby villages.

I assessed that our genealogical record corresponds to the dates back to my father's great, great, grandfather, which is probably around the early nineteenth century. The significant feature of our genealogy ladder represents that this lineage was followed by the son's only and conveys the veracity that the daughters were perceived as becoming a part of their husband's family after marriage. When my father described that an ancestor had no issue, it meant that the person had no male child but may have had a daughter.

* * *

My First marriage

*W*hen I was young I could not grasp why Maghi and his sister Lalo would always address my mother 'Maasi', like mother. Both brother and sister were living across the road. Their mother had expired but their father was still alive at that time. Whenever they required anything they would approach my mother for help. My mother would help and treat them affectionately. I could not ascertain the background behind this link. I rarely paid any attention or bothered to inquire from my mother or father about the mystery behind this bond.

I had no knowledge about the first marriage of my father even though it was short lived. Later on when he enlightened us with the episode of his first marriage then the connection of Maghi and Lalo became evident to me. The fact was that Maghi and Lalo's mother was the real sister of my father's first wife. After their mother had passed away, they had nobody else close by except their father to look after them. In the meanwhile after the *death of my father's first wife, he married my mother. But because of the old relationship of my father's first wife, Maghi and Lalo considered my mother at par with their mother's sister and consequently called her 'Maasi'. They esteemed and behaved with my mother like they would with their own mother. I had not seen Maghi's mother but their father was alive as long as I remember. My father carried on with his tale of his first marriage.....*

"My father had to spend the whole day grazing the buffaloes; he had a tough time in managing the household errands at home. He would rise early in the morning and sleep very late at night. He drastically needed an additional helping hand who could manage the household chores daily. He had never revealed his intentions to remarry and the only other option was to get me married. Though I was not of marriageable age, he took this decision under the extremely compelling circumstances. He looked for a girl for me in Chak village through his relatives and arranged my marriage. I got married when I was studying in the fourth grade in the primary school. She was around fifteen or sixteen years old and I was about ten. Only my father and my uncles accompanied me to her village for the wedding. My father was aware that it was no match for me but got me married just to bring home a helping hand. She joined us six months later after our marriage. My father had some relief after she came to live with us. My wife started managing the household work but she remained physically in poor health most of the time. Gradually her condition worsened and she fell seriously ill. We tried to treat her with home remedies and some medical assistance but her health did not improve. Eventually she became so ill that she was unable to move out of the bed. She lingered on for some time but ultimately she too succumbed to her sickness within two years of my marriage. Her assistance to my father was short lived and my father began reeling under the house hold pressure once again."

*   *   *

The Jagg

66"I recall a very disheartening incident when I was still studying in the primary school. We owned a class buffalo, and she was very precious to us for our survival. Unfortunately the animals were infected by a contagious virus in the air. This disease was called 'galghotu', Haemorrhagic Septicaemia. This virus had infected the animals at large in many villages around. Dozens of animals had succumbed to this disease and we too were petrified and worried about our buffalo. My father made efforts to isolate our buffalo but unfortunately she got infected with this deadly virus. She stopped eating and was no longer able to stand. She was lying flat on the ground and we watched her die helplessly. On her death I felt very poignant and began crying. My father was also feeling utterly miserable but contained himself. He mustered the courage and comforted me, "Son why you are crying? Don't worry; we will raise yet another buffalo."

In olden times there were no means to deal with such natural calamities due to the lack of medical facilities.

People were solely dependent upon the mercy of God. They would adopt various ways and means to defend themselves against the natural disasters. The clamities like incessant heavy rains or raging contagious diseases among the cattle or severe drought, plague etc. were uncontrollable. People believed the only way was to pray and perform the 'Jagg'. The villagers especially the farmers would choose to carry out the 'Jagg', community meal for one and all on a large scale, with prayers to repulse the natural calamity. During the 'Jagg', this process would continue for two to three days at a stretch. The farmers would collect voluntary contributions from the villagers to organise the 'Jagg'. Some people would also donate rice and gur, jaggery.

They would proclaim the date of the 'Jagg' in advance in their own village as well as convey this message in the nearby villages also. Generally during the 'Jagg', they would cook an enormous quantity of rice with gur in it until it converts to a semi-dry state. People would gather at a common place and pray to God to protect them against the natural calamity before serving the food. No family in the village was allowed to cook food in their homes during the 'Jagg' period. It was obligatory for every family in the village to eat at that common place. The food was never served on plates. The people would bring a piece of cloth from their home and spread it on the ground, and the semi-dry preparation was served on it. A group of people would make the rounds in the village to ensure that nobody was cooking food at home. If they discovered any family doing so, they would request them to stop it. The poor people from other villages too would come to eat the food as much as they could.

If the 'Jagg' was performed because of the epidemic affecting the cattle, then the people would prepare Holy water and pray to God to protect their animals. People from all the sections of society, rich or poor, would bring their cattle to a common place in the village and the Holy water was splashed on them one by one with the bough of a neem tree".

*　　*　　*

High School Escapades

"In 1932, I had passed out of primary school and sought to pursue my studies in high school. Most of the other pupils, who had also passed out from the primary school, were planning to seek admission in the Government High School in Gujjarwal which was about four miles away from my village. I conveyed my intensions to my father that I was looking forward to get admission in the high school. He barely had any knowledge about the high school so he did not object and willingly agreed to pay my school fees. I secured the school leaving certificate from the primary school and visited the high school. There was no difficulty in getting admission there and I deposited two rupees as my school fees. The school had fixed slabs for the payment of fees, two rupees per month for the fifth and sixth class, three rupees for the seventh and eighth class and four rupees for the ninth and tenth class students. The total strength was more than three hundred students in this school.

Since I had taken admission in the school in a different village, I had to cross over the boundary of our village.

For this reason I had to acquire a special 'pass' which was issued by the Superintendent of Police. I applied for it through our village Numberdar and he testified for the issuance of this special pass which was issued in a short time. The Sansi children who were pursuing their studies were allowed to attend school with this special pass and exempted from reporting to the police station.

Most of the Jat boys who had completed primary education from Narangwal got admission in Gujjarwal high school. New admissions were over and our classes had begun. There was no school uniform for the students here too. I would saunter to school every day along with the other students and it would take more than an hour for us to get to school. There was a tower clock in the school which was wound weekly. Here the teaching process was poles apart from the primary school. There was period system and a bell would sound at the end of each period. Here the teachers were qualified for specific subjects.

Niranjan Singh was the headmaster in the high school Gujjarwal and he belonged to our village Narangwal. Like us he would also walk from the village but we seldom dared to walk along with him. He was intelligent and believed in very strict discipline in the school. The teachers from the neighbouring villages would also walk to school. Generally they dressed in simple cotton clothes when they attended school. There was only one fashionable teacher who would change his clothes twice a week. He would dress in half pants and a shirt like the British. There was no other high school in the vicinity of

Gujjarwal. This school had the facility of a hostel for the students and teachers who belonged to faraway places.

One day, after the Morning Prayer the students were marching from the school ground to their respective classrooms. One of my classmates, Pal, was marching behind me. He was good in studies but naughty and defiant in the class. Our new Physical Training teacher, Bisakha Singh was monitoring the students. While marching, Pal intentionally tripped me and I suddenly fell down to the ground. Luckily I wasn't hurt much but the march past came to an abrupt halt. Bisakha Singh rushed to me and had noticed this mischief of Pal. Another teacher Mr. Mehta, also came running to check if I was hurt. Both the teachers asked me "Nathu, what happened?"

I replied, "Masterji, I cannot figure out but Pal must have deliberately tripped me."

The PT teacher sneered at Pal and ordered both of us to step aside and wait. When the rest of the students had gone into their classrooms, he directed us to go to the headmaster's office. I was cursing Pal because he had forced me into trouble too. We were aware that the headmaster would not spare us. When we reported to the headmaster, he stared at us and glanced at his cane. He believed that we must have done some mischief and that is why we were directed to his office. He got up from his chair, picked up his cane and bellowed, "Yes, Nathu, what is the matter? What wrong have you done with Pal?"

Perhaps he deemed that I was at fault. I was trembling with fear but replied, "Masterji, during the march past Pal tripped me."

At the same moment the PT teacher Bisakha Singh entered the office and complained to the headmaster against Pal. He disdainfully ogled at Pal and commented, "Pal, I spare you this time but don't fool around with Nathu. Even though he is a Sansi, his father is richer than your father. Your fees are exempted but he has paid full fees."

I had only one best friend Harbans Singh, in the high school. He was the eldest son of our headmaster. His house was not far away from my house. In fact he was one year ahead of me when I joined high school. Unfortunately he got a severe eye infection which did not heal for a long time. Eventually he had to undergo a critical operation for his eyes. But after the operation, the doctor had seriously cautioned him not to read anything for at least one year. As a result he had lost one academic year. Thus we became classmates in grade seven.

In the high school the teachers would assign home work on a regular basis and I had to dedicate additional time at home. I would finish off my homework at night by the light of an earthen oil lamp especially in the winters. My father would see me struggling to study in the poor dim light but could not spare money to buy a good lamp. Finally when I was in class nine, my father managed to buy a kerosene oil lantern for one rupee. I was thrilled and contented with it. To think about a table and chair for studying was beyond my wildest dream. I would sit on the string cot and finish my homework.

I was not too brilliant a student but I could manage my studies at home without any additional help. There was no tuition system at that time and the teachers would voluntarily take extra classes if need be. There were hardly any other activities in the school but physical training (PT) was compulsory for every student.

Our school had a champion band comprising of flutes, drums and bugles. The students in the band had a very impressive uniform. Our PT teacher was the in-charge to coach students for special marching drills. The students would create exceptional patterns by marching from various directions. Every year our school would participate in the annual competition held at the State level and would win the contest most of the time. There was hardly any other real challenger except Arya School in Ludhiana city. Our headmaster would make it a point to display these impressive drills to the Education officer whenever he visited our school for inspection.

My father had financial constraints to pay for my school fees, books and notebooks etc. I would understand from his cold response that I had to wait for days until he received money from somebody. Sometimes my school fees were delayed and I had to request for a waiver of penalty as our headmaster was aware of our financial limitations. When I was in class seven, our headmaster made efforts for the exemption of my school fees. The DEO, District Education Officer was visiting our school for an annual inspection. I still remember that the name of the DEO was Mr. U. Kramat. A day before the inspection our headmaster had asked me to bring my father along the next morning. The next day my father and I came to school and he kept on sitting and waiting in front of the headmaster's office. I headed to attend my class and advised him that I will join him later. The DEO and his personal assistant arrived at the school and finished his customary round of inspection. After the review of our class, I joined my father. The DEO then returned with the headmaster after inspecting the PT parade.

The headmaster called us in and my father bowed to bestow 'Salaam'.

"Who are they?" the DEO enquired from the headmaster with a grin on his face.

The headmaster introduced us to the Officer, "Sir, We have this student Nathu belonging to a criminal tribe and they are extremely poor. His father has approached for aid from you for free books and a waiver of school fees for his son."

The DEO was taken by surprise with such an unexpected demand and instantly reacted, "Headmaster Saab, I cannot promise any help. I am already falling short of funds and there are many students who are seeking aid. I cannot help everybody like this."

My father and I watched them helplessly. The headmaster struggled to convince him that my father desperately needed the aid but the DEO refused to relent. Finally the headmaster got irritated and contended, "DEO Saab, I am truly amazed that you are unable to provide assistance even to a single student from my school! If an officer like you does not come forward then who would help the poor people? His father is illiterate and does not have any regular source of income. But he intends his motherless child to continue his studies. That you are incapable to help him is beyond my comprehension."

The headmaster and the DEO had a heated argument and finally the DEO's personal assistant intervened at one stage and requested the headmaster, 'Sir, please forward your written request to his office for his reconsideration.'

The headmaster asked us to leave saying that he would endeavour whatever was possible. We were not very optimistic for any assistance but to my revelation I was provided books and a grant of two rupees every month for my fees which was a tremendous relief to my father. But I do not know if my father ever thanked the headmaster or not. This unexpected aid continued only for that academic year.

The following year I advanced into class eight and admissions had begun for the new academic year before the summer vacations. When I went to join my new class, they demanded full fees from me for the current academic year. I was informed that last year the grant was sanctioned from the 'Red Cross' fund of the school granted by the headmaster. Now the 'Red Cross' fund had dried up and there was no other substitute to waive off my fees."

I was not allowed to join the class. I returned home from school and broke the bad news to my father that I needed money to pay my fees. He was taken aback by this shocking news, perhaps he had taken it for granted that my fees were permanently waived off. I explained the entire story to him. Now my father was fuming and holding my hand led me to the headmaster's house. When we reached the headmaster's house, he called out to the headmaster and asked, "Headmaster Saab, why have you reinstated Nathu's fees? We are helpless poor people and on top of it you have withdrawn the aid. It is people like you who do not wish my son to study."

The headmaster embarrassingly replied, "Chhotu, it is not in my hand anymore to waive off his fees. I am extremely helpless."

The headmaster made futile attempts to convince my father and explained that now the situation was beyond his control. But my father wouldn't listen to his point of view. My father felt dejected and declared that after the summer vacations, he would not send his son back to school. The headmaster looked at my father leaving in a huff. Back at home my father seriously proclaimed that there was no need for me to go to school anymore and I should now look forward doing something else. I was about thirteen years old at that time.

Ultimately my father even stopped speaking to the headmaster anymore.

The summer vacations had begun but it appeared to me that this was the end of my schooling. I dared not to persuade my father to reconsider his drastic decision. I was fully aware that he was a stubborn man and would not easily listen to anybody. I thought that he was not going to change his mind and I should look for some sort of occupation. There would be no point to sit at home anymore. There was hardly any work available in the village but the only option was to graze buffaloes along with my father.

Ultimately the summer vacations had come to an end and I had not mentioned anything about school to my father. There was hardly any question of me going to school right away. My uncles also maintained silence about my schooling but my aunts would sometimes raise questions as to why I had stopped attending school. I would evade my reply and ask them to directly discuss the issue with my father.

More than a week had passed after the school had reopened and the headmaster must have noticed that I was missing from the school. One day he came across my uncle Gaata and explained him, 'Gaata, I want to speak to you regarding Nathu. I have noticed that Nathu has not been attending school since its reopening. I understand that Chhotu finds it difficult to pay the school fees. The waiver of his fees is not in my hands now like the previous year. Chhotu would not perceive my situation and I wish you to put pressure on him to send Nathu back to school.'

My uncle was cautious and avoided taking any chance in advance before making a commitment and asked the headmaster, 'Headmaster Saab, what would happen if Nathu refused to continue his schooling?'

The headmaster was confident and said, 'Gaata, I am certain that Nathu will not refuse because he is interested in studying.'

My uncle contacted my father and had an argument with him on this subject and complained, 'Chhotu, why have you not listened to the headmaster and behaved very rudely with him? Last year he was able to lend a helping hand without asking you but now he has limitations to extend that help. Why are you so ungrateful? Was it his fault if he helped you last year? Why did you stop Nathu from going to school? On the top of it you have snapped ties with the headmaster. I advise you to send Nathu back to school without wasting any more time.'

My father silently listened to his elder brother without any counter reaction. Being the youngest, he appreciated his elder brother's concern and as a mark of respect he ultimately submitted to my uncle's wish and agreed to send me to school once again. I was around and my father asked me, "Nathu, do you want to attend school again?"

I promptly replied, "Father, if you wish then I will go."

He instructed me, "Then start going to school from tomorrow, I will give you the money to deposit the fees."

I was in the eighth grade now. In that year I witnessed a serious brawl between two teachers in our school. During the recess a majority of the students would enjoy watching the volleyball match among the teachers. We would finish our lunch quickly and gather around the volleyball ground. Our teachers would divide themselves into two teams and commence their volleyball match. The students would often applaud whenever any team scored a point over their rivals. It would always trigger high passions in both the teams.

One day while the volleyball match was in progress, suddenly a fight erupted between two teachers. There was some enmity between the Science teacher and the Drawing teacher and they would always play in the opposite teams. Both the teachers belonged to the lower caste communities. The Science teacher was a 'Ghumar', a potter, and the Drawing teacher was a 'Chammar', a cobbler.

Amid the match, the Drawing teacher volleyed the ball and challenged the Science teacher, 'O, Ghumara, you return my volley if you have the strength.'

The Science teacher as well as the other teachers was taken aback at this unwanted call, but the Drawing teacher returned the volley and reacted instantly saying, 'O, Chamara, now you return my volley.'

This was the flash point as both of them felt affronted being publicly addressed by their castes. The Drawing teacher immediately assaulted the Science teacher and then they furiously began punching each other. The Science teacher started bleeding profusely through his nose when they grappled with each other. There was turmoil on the volleyball field as other teachers swiftly struggled to disengage them.

In the meanwhile the recess was over; all the students and teachers returned to their respective class rooms. Unfortunately these teachers had their classrooms just opposite each other. The Drawing teacher generally carried a cane from home to the school every day. He picked up his cane and hurriedly darted to the Science teacher's classroom. He struck the Science teacher on his head from behind with cane. The Science teacher was stunned for a moment but managed to bear the shock. Before the Drawing teacher could strike again, the Science teacher battered the Drawing teacher as he was physically stronger than him. Again there was a great hue and cry and the other teachers heard this commotion and dashed to separate them. I witnessed this scene being in the Science teacher's classroom.

This matter had already been reported to the headmaster. The other teachers had thoroughly briefed him what exactly had taken place during the recess and in the classroom. The headmaster summoned both the teachers to his office. He was feeling disgusted with such a shameful act displayed by both the teachers. He questioned them,

'Why did you fight in the school? If you had any personal rivalry then you should have settled the scores outside the school premises. Don't you realise what would be the impact of your clash on the students? You have put up the worst possible example before the entire school.'

Both the teachers tried to put forward their point of view to defend themselves but the headmaster was so annoyed that he was not prepared to listen to either of them. He was very upset and exasperated with the behaviour of these teachers. The headmaster prepared his report about this incident and forwarded it to the Education Department. A Departmental inquiry was directed against both the teachers. Within two days an Education Inspector visited our school to inquire about the case. He listened to both the concerned teachers and obtained detailed information from the other teachers who were present during the match. The headmaster had also formed his strong feeling against the Drawing teacher. He asserted that the Drawing teacher must be transferred from the school without fail. We students gathered part of this inside story from the other teachers while they were exchanging the latest developments on this subject.

The Inspector made his investigation report and submitted it to the DEO's office. The drawing teacher was immediately transferred from the school.

When I was in class ten, the final year of my schooling, we had major subjects like Mathematics, Science, English, History, Geography, Hindi or Pharsi (Persian). After I passed my eighth grade, our medium of instruction for some subjects had changed, which was decided by the British Government. In the ninth and tenth grade we had studied Mathematics and Science subjects in English but History and Geography subjects were taught in Urdu. Surprisingly during the final exam, the History and Geography question papers were set in English but we had the option to answer in English or Urdu. For Mathematics and Science subjects, the question papers were set in English and we had to answer in English only. Though we studied the subjects in English but we were unable to speak or write in English proficiently. For our convenience the teachers would elucidate the questions in detail in Punjabi or Urdu. We struggled to comprehend the questions as well as to furnish the answers in English. The only option was to memorize the answers in English for various questions otherwise there was no other way.

Finally I passed Matriculation, class ten, in the second division. My father was very glad that his son had successfully passed Class ten. Being a Matriculate was considered the first benchmark of an educated person."

*   *   *

The Phantom of Caste

My father being an untouchable, the shadow of his lowest caste chased him ubiquitously. Most of the time he seemed so susceptible that anybody could easily hurt him. Without showing any resentment he had accepted this ache as an integral part of his daily life. He had to ingest discrimination quietly with deep anguish. When we sought his opinion on this subject, he appeared to have instantly gone into a shell and was unenthusiastic to speak much about it. I felt that we had suddenly reopened raw wounds of his past. We coaxed him slowly but painfully, he began conversing about this ominous subject.....

"When I was young, I always felt affronted when someone addressed me as 'Hey Sansi.' But I could never muster the courage to openly begrudge them. I was very poor and belonged to the lowest caste with the tag of an 'untouchable'. The lowest caste people would always bear the insult if they were abused or called names. Addressing them by their caste was even more offensive and these people would easily fight over this. If the lower caste person happened to perpetrate any slightest mistake, offhand the higher caste people would yell at him and address him by caste but not by name. The low caste individuals would remain subdued most the time. But on the contrary the Jats' and other higher caste folk would feel proud if they were addressed by their castes.

During my high school days I hardly had any friends except Harbans Singh. The other Jat students maintained an imperceptible distance from me. Sometimes I would play cards with Harbans Singh in the afternoon not in his house but in their buffalo shed. One day another Jat noticed us playing cards and he complained about this to Harbans Singh's father. That was the end of our card playing sessions in the buffalo shed. We found another secret spot near the village common place and continued playing cards there. I rarely visited Harbans Singh's house and I would avoid touching anything there. If by mistake it happened, they would purify the object later. They would scour it with hot ash or scrupulously wash it. Otherwise the higher caste people would not permit us to go into their homes. The children of the higher and the lower castes would play together at a common place in the village which was now acceptable up to a certain extent but otherwise nothing beyond that.

If we had to make contact with a higher caste person at his home, we would shout from outside his door. He would emerge and ask the purpose of our visit. He would hesitantly allow our entry only under inescapable conditions. Middle caste people like carpenters, iron smiths, tailors, masons, potters etc., were much better off than us. They could go into the house of a higher caste man without restrictions. But at times the higher caste individuals would not even spare them if something went wrong. At times they would not desist from insulting and criticizing them too. High caste people were more dependent on the middle castes so they had a little better status than us.

Once the Government had planned some development schemes especially to ameliorate the living conditions of the people belonging to the low castes. They wanted to establish a village development committee in each village. Word had spread in the village about this working group in advance. A Development officer arrived from the district headquarters to form this committee. Initially he discussed this issue with the higher castes especially with the Jats' as they were in the majority. The officer counselled them that in order to work together, a representative from each community would be incorporated in the development committee. The Jats' became highly infuriated with this condition and could not swallow this proposal. They strongly opposed the establishment of such a committee and considered it as an insult to them to include low castes in it. How could the government include the untouchables in the committee when the same people 'bow' to us daily? In the committee they would sit with us to discuss the village development. There was a lot of resentment about this move. The Jats' raised many objections especially by one Nagina Singh. He satirically commented in the meeting, 'Sade nefe the joon hun sade sar te baithu.' (The lice from the waist band of our underpants would now sit on our head). (A proverb in the Punjabi language). They even threatened to boycott such a proposed committee. The Development officer was helpless under such critical conditions and reported this state of affairs to the district headquarters. Thus such a committee never came into existence.

The phantom of the Castes was intensely impregnated in the psyche of the Jats' and other higher castes that the majority of them would always consider themselves to be supreme. To a great extent they had hardly considered the Sansis and the other lowest castes as human beings.

I vividly remember a common scene at one of our village Gurudwaras, a Sikh Temple, located near the hospital where they frequently held religious functions. The Sansis and other lower caste poor people would throng there in anticipation to obtain some Prasad and food. In the first place these poor people were not even allowed to enter the main gate of the Gurudwara. They were expected to remain outside. If someone endeavoured to trespass then he was unceremoniously instructed to remain outside.

Prasad, is a sacred offering prepared in every Gurudwara. It is made from wheat flour, sugar, ghee and water. When the religious ceremony is over, the people from the Gurudwara would serve Prasad to everyone who visited there. These poor people would keep on waiting impatiently as they were generally served last. Normally Prasad was served by two persons within the Gurdwara;

one person would hold the Prasad container and the second person would serve it to the people. But for these poor untouchables, the serving people would add a third person to serve them. The second person would hand over the Prasad to the third person and he would further distribute it to these feverishly waiting low caste people. Before they began distributing the Prasad to the low caste people, these serving men would cover their mouth and nose with a piece of cloth to avoid their stench. They would often yell at the poor because there used to be a stampede to receive the Prasad first. But the lower caste people hardly bothered about their shouting. The Sansis had no yearning for Sikhism but undoubtedly they were interested in obtaining the Prasad.

Some communities among the low castes also practised Sikhism with full faith and austerely followed its rituals by the book. Initially these low caste people had no Gurudwara in their vicinity for their own convenience but later on they constructed a Gurudwara in their own neighbourhood. They displayed a copy of the Sikh's Holy Book 'Sri Guru Granth Saheb' with full fervour. Like all other Gurudwaras, the Jats' also had the same copy of the Holy Book in their Gurudwara. But the Jats' detested visiting the Gurudwara of the lower caste people. They asserted as well as affirmed that it was below their dignity to bow in front of the Holy Book there. Outwardly they would pretend that all human beings are equal in this world, which is the basic philosophy of the Sikh religion but practically, the picture was poles apart.

Once a religious and political leader Gopal Singh Khalsa sought to gratify and demonstrate to the lower castes that there was no disparity between the Jats' and low castes Gurudwara. He visited our village and contacted some Jats' who were considered to be religious and influential in the village. Perhaps these prominent people had some self interest to oblige Gopal Singh to obtain special favours from him in future and consented to accompany him to the lower caste's Gurudwara. Previously they had seldom visited there in general or attended any religious function. These Jats' informed all the low caste people that Gopal Singh Khalsa would visit their Gurudwara and they should bestow proper respect to him.

Finally Gopal Singh Khalsa along with his group paid a visit to the low caste's Gurudwara. This visiting party bowed there in front of the Holy Book and settled there listening to the chanting of holy hymns for some time. After a short while they were served Prasad as a normal ritual in any Gurudwara. They were even more contented when lower caste persons presented them 'Siropas', a robe of honour. They came back from there with a look full of satisfaction on their faces as they had proved a point to the lower castes. But this contentment was short lived, since this drama was talked about throughout the village that these people had visited the low caste's Gurudwara and accepted Prasad from there. The Jat community in the village acrimoniously condemned and criticised this group. They even decided to shun those few prominent people who had escorted Gopal Singh Khalsa.

As a consequence, Gopal Singh never showed his face again in the village.

There was an unbridgeable gap in preaching and practicing the Sikh religion among the Jats. The hate against the low castes was truly too heavy in the air."

*   *   *

The Sikh religion does not promulgate the Caste system and the Sikh Gurus have strongly condemned it. They have sermonized that all human beings are born equal and the creation of one God. As a principle everyone could visit the Gurudwara without any restriction irrespective of caste and creed. In reality the Jats' always remained in the delusion that they are the sole custodians of the Sikh religion. There are many holy hymns in the Sikhs' Holy Book which were composed by Saints of the different low castes. Paradoxically the Jats' would recite those hymns with dedication but still they would hate the low caste people all the time.

Low caste folk had no guts to question the Jats' why they abhorred them. Sansis being one among the lowest caste were incapable to harm the Jats in any respect and remained at their pity most of the time but still they were subjected to hate. These untouchables were not allowed to touch anything in the Jats' homes but when they returned the money, the Jats' would gleefully accept it with their hands! Money never turned polluted nor had to undergo any special purification process of being treated with hot ash. Right down the ages, the Jats' and other higher castes had dominated the lower castes to retain their supremacy. Their mind-set towards the lower caste had turned so inflexible that it had become impractical to amend their attitude. Revulsion was embedded so intensely in their hearts and minds that it would not fade away so easily. Perhaps it would require a significant time and number of generations to steadily modify their psyche towards the lower castes.

Only selective Jats and higher caste persons were branded in the village who would openly articulate their hate against low castes but the others would remain subdued and maintain a reasonable distance all the time. Presently the low caste people are somewhat better off economically. Their standard of living has now slightly improved. The low castes occasionally participate in the religious functions in the Jats Gurudwara but still they would evade breaching the rituals in the sanctum Sanctorum. If they contravene the specific order of the rituals then the Jats would criticise or may even prevent them from executing those rituals. In general now they can touch utensils in the Gurudwara's kitchen and perform other customs without hesitation. Still the majority of the Jats would not visit the low castes' Gurudwara. When my father wished to visit the Jats Gurudwara, he was taken there but he would prefer to participate in the basic services which would not hurt anybody's sentiments. He would be happy to collect and deliver shoes for the visiting masses.

My uncles once disclosed to me that in the old times even the shadow of the Sansis and other low castes was considered to be defiling for the high castes. If the Jats and other higher castes performed an Akhand Paath at their homes, the reciting of Holy Guru Granth Saheb, the Sansis were forbidden to enter that street. They would coerce the untouchables to disappear from the scene and shout at them not to show their face that side until the function was concluded. Even their shadow was considered to be contaminating the environment around their house. Ironically the preachers, who recited the Holy Book, would cover their faces while going in and out from that house to avoid seeing the face of the untouchables.

*　　*　　*

Dai

*W*hen *I was about thirteen or fourteen years old I would sometimes visit my maternal grand-mother during my summer vacations. She was a wonderful woman who loved me very much and I immensely enjoyed spending time in her company. I had noticed that pregnant ladies from the village would often call upon her home and she would examine them before the birth of the child. Moreover they would also appeal to her to visit their homes. Often to gratify her, they would make all efforts to please her and proffer her grains, clothes etc. Later on I comprehended that my grandmother was a self-trained expert Dai, a midwife. She had diverse experience of numerous deliveries in her life. In and around her village, she was a renowned personality in this field. Due to the shortage of medical facilities in the villages at that time, the pregnant ladies were profoundly reliant on her. She was their first and last hope during the critical time of delivery. The ladies had complete trust in her and felt they were in safe hands when she was present with them.*

Even the higher caste people were equally dependent on her and would often request her to perform the delivery of their pregnant ladies. It was ironic that when she performed the deliveries, she had to handle their high caste ladies and newborn babies, not to mention about touching their vessels, clothes and other essentials required at the time of a delivery. But the higher caste women and their babies never became polluted with the touch of an untouchable woman. The men never purified their women and babies with fire like they treated their belongings if she touched them under normal circumstances. She would attend to these ladies for a couple of weeks till they were back on their feet and were capable to tend their children personally. When her work was over, once again she would be treated like another 'untouchable' Sansi woman.

* * *

Worshipping by Sansis

*O**ne day Susan and I were sitting by the canal as my father sought a break for a while. I mentioned to Susan that it was strange that the Sansis were isolated for so long, that they failed to develop any religion of their own or adopt any other religion for several reasons. Always being on the move they remained aloof from the influence of any specific religion, therefore there was never any possibility for them holding any religious gatherings. There was no prominent religious person among them in the past who could sow the seed of any spiritual or religious sentiments among them. The population of the Sansis was sparse and always remained scattered and this hindered their religious growth. While wandering they had no place for religion in their lives, except survival. After the Criminal Act had become effective, their movements had been restricted and they ceased to reach out to each other. Basically in the past, the Sansis had no opportunity to expand any religious growth. To a certain extent they followed the so called Hindu rituals in their own style* *mainly at the time of marriage and death. They would not dream of any high caste Hindu Pundit to perform their rituals.*

I inquired from my father how the Sansis worshipped in the olden times as they had no religious worshipping place like temples of their own. I also asked him how he used to worship during his childhood and youth before he followed The Sant, as previously our family used to worship at the Baba Raul's shrine. Susan was equally inquisitive to seek information of the religious side of the Sansis. My father opened his Pandora's Box to highlight the religious aspect of the Sansis to satisfy our unending curiosity about worshipping.....

"The Sansis had their personal approach for religious reverence because they had neither adopted nor followed any particular religion. They adopted a few Hindu customs temporarily for exclusive occasions like marriage or at the time of death otherwise they seldom practiced any other rituals. They worshipped their own local Deity but had no permanent verbal or written prayers. They would implore verbally according to their desires. When I was young, I would accompany my father, Chhotu, to the nearby village Kalakh where the Sansis from the villages would assemble for their prayers on Diwali festival day. This place was located just outside the village Kalakh which was about five to six miles away from our village. Conceivably this worshipping place was established by our ancestor Bhaga. There was no visible structure at all but only two small mounds of earth and a few bricks were erected there. A common man would not be able to identify this as a worshiping place. On Diwali day, the Sansis would say a prayer to their deity Baba Raul. They would fetch 'Sanni', a mixture of boiled rice, sugar and Desi ghee, as an offering to their deity. They would pour some Desi ghee on the burning fire and pray for their wish to come true and for the well-being of their family and livestock. There was nothing else like meditation, recitation, preaching or chanting of any sort of hymns.

After the demise of our ancestor Bhaga, all his children had established themselves in the nearby villages but unfortunately not even a single family continued living in Kalakh. The next generations carried on worshiping there on rare occasions. But all Sansis preserved their faith in this worshiping place at Kalakh and remained attached.

Once a land survey was in progress in the State and the Patwari, the land revenue accountant, had completed a survey in Kalakh village. Since no Sansi family was residing there hence nobody from the village pointed out to him regarding the Sansi's place of worshipping. One of my other uncles, Nanak, from village Lohgarh, used to chop up dry wood around Kalakh to produce wood charcoal. One day while he was chopping wood near Kalakh he happened to come across the Patwari. The Patwari was accompanied by his staff and other people from the villages to assist him in marking the land. My uncle, Nanak, requested the Patwari, 'Saab, I trust that you must have allotted space for our worship in Kalakh village?'

The Patwari was surprised and replied, 'I have not spotted any outline of any worshipping place in Kalakh.'

'But Saab, we have our worshiping place there in Kalakh. That is our ancestral place for worshiping.' my uncle replied.

The Patwari was astonished and wondered how he had failed to notice a worshipping place and wanted to verify from my uncle, 'Where was your place located?'

My uncle elucidated about that area where we used to go for worshipping. The Patwari was bewildered, 'Well, I had no clue about it. I just observed two small mounds of earth but nothing else. There was no symbol indicating it as a place of worship. As a result I have already accounted for that land in the fields.'

My uncle beseeched the Patwari, 'Saab, we are underprivileged Sansis and nobody would allow us to enter there anymore. If you do not allocate that space to us, we would be uprooted forever from our ancestral devotional place. Where shall we worship then? Please reallocate that space to us.'

The Patwari was puzzled and could not hit upon any instant solution to this problem and indecisively replied, 'I do concur with you and I will certainly endeavour to find some way out.'

My uncle repeatedly appealed and the other people with the Parwari also corroborated to allocate some worshipping place for the Sansis. Ultimately the Patwari contemplated for a while and replied, 'Look, the fact remains that the land survey is finalized in Kalakh but in Majri village it is yet to take off. You know that Kalakh and Majri villages have a common boundary and I could possibly allocate a piece of land there.'

My uncle was extremely pleased and profusely thanked him.

During the land survey of Majri village, the Patwari maintained his word and marked twelve biswas, six hundred square yards, of land to the Sansis for their worshipping place. Later on when my uncle verified from the Patwari, he personally showed that allotted piece of land to my uncle. My uncle in turn informed all the Sansis in our area about the newly allocated space. All the Sansis were contented that at least they acquired some worshipping space of their own.

After this change a fresh opinion was growing among the Sansis. Their belief had been shaken up as their original worshipping place had already been uprooted and there was hardly any sense to establish a new worshipping place which was far off from Narangwal. They thought of searching for a suitable location which should be convenient to all the Sansis of the area. Narangwal was more centrally located than any other village. All the Sansis from our area unanimously formed an opinion that Narangwal was the best location to shift their worshipping place. A majority of the Sansis were living in Narangwal more than any other village. At last they reached a consensus to build their worshiping place permanently in Narangwal. Thus the Sansis of Narangwal had now been entrusted with the tedious responsibility to get space for their worshipping.

The Sansis had no money to buy a piece of land. From the public who would be concerned about the Sansis and donate any space for their religious place? The Sansis had no specific religion and had no Holy book or any other holy scripture belonging to their faith known to public. They only believed in their deity and wished to continue with the similar approach like their ancestors.

The Sansis of Narangwal began their efforts and approached a few big landlords in the village but remained unsuccessful in obtaining any positive response to acquire a piece of land on gratis. Some of the farmers straightway turned down their request but the Sansis continued their efforts. Eventually they succeeded when they approached one farmer named Choudhri Harnam Singh. They briefed him about the whole episode how their worshiping place had been uprooted during the land survey and they now wished to establish their worshiping place in Narangwal. Choudhri was a nice gentleman; he sympathetically considered their request and contemplated in donating a piece of land to the poor Sansis. He owned one field amidst the sand dunes near the village canal where no crops were grown there at that time. He humbly decided to donate two biswas, one hundred square yards, from that field to the Sansis. The Sansis were delighted to acquire this piece of land on which they could finally construct a small structure and liberally worship there.

Now the Sansis decided to build a small shrine there in the name of their deity Sidh Baba Raul. All the Sansis in the area managed to get some donations and contributed some money to buy bricks and cement. They unanimously provided volunteer services during the construction of this small shrine. They visited their old place of worship in Kalakh and to their good luck they managed to collect the few old bricks that they used to worship there. They installed those old bricks in the shrine in Narangwal as a memory of their deity. This new shrine came into existence on March 6, 1938. The Sansis celebrated first worship by dedicating this shrine to their reverential deity Sidh Baba Raul. They engraved His name and the date of construction on the shrine. I was studying in class ten at that time.

Sometimes my uncles and other Sansis would mention about the legendary Sidh Baba Raul when they assembled there on the Diwali festival. As mentioned earlier that in the olden times the Sansis were nomads and wandered from place to place. It was believed that Baba Raul was engaged in meditation from his childhood and wished to be a Yogi. He would meditate rigorously to attain divine powers. Later on his family strongly persuaded him to get married and ultimately he decided to carry on his meditation even after marriage. While wandering around once his family and the family of his bride-to-be happened to meet each other. Both the groups happily spent some days together when his bride-to-be was around. One day while he was meditating, his bride-to-be fetched water in a pitcher. After keeping the pitcher down on the ground, she jerked her hands to shake off the droplets of water to dry them. Unfortunately in this process some drops of water fell on Baba Raul. She inadvertently disturbed his meditation. He perceived these drops of water on him as an awful portent as there is a ritual of sprinkling some water on a dead person only. He seriously considered it and thought that if she was not watchful now then what could he anticipate from her after marriage? He instantly decided to denounce her and thus he broke off the engagement there and then. He firmly made a resolution to renounce this world as well. Later on he took Samadhi, a fast until death. The Sansis strongly believed that he had attained divine powers and thus became an idol for them. They started worshipping him and believed that he fulfilled their wishes and continued doing so until now. The Sansis visit this shrine to pray at their own volition. My family and I prayed there until 1942, after that I came in contact with The Sant.

On Diwali day the Sansis of Narangwal village would make it a point to visit their shrine. They would carry cooked rice and sugar mixture to repay their gratitude towards their deity and perform a ritual by digging out seven lumps of sandy earth behind the shrine. They would then pour some ghee and this mixture on a burning fire and pray in their own simple words like, 'O, Baba Raul khair rakhio', 'O, Baba Raul, bless us.' In the evening one person from each family would light an oil lamp or candles at the shrine. Unmarried girls were prohibited to enter the shrine perhaps because Sidh Baba Raul had renounced his bride-to-be. Now the new generation does not adhere to this restriction.

The Sansis also visit their deity on a very special occasion, like the newly married couple would entreat to gain his blessings. Sometimes the Sansis would pray there to ward off evil spirits from their family member. They would swear in the name of their deity and invoke the curse in his name as well. Furthermore when their wishes are fulfilled then they would also celebrate in thanksgiving at the shrine."

* * *

My second Marriage

*M*arriage gets the top most priority among the Sansis. The parents of a Sansi girl would begin searching for a prospective groom even before she attained puberty. Parents of the children eligible for marriage would scout around for a suitable match during weddings. If there was any possibility for a prospective girl or boy for marriage, then further negotiations would progress either directly or through a common relative. If the families were unknown to each other, then both the sides would explore the family backgrounds through various sources. If both the sides were satisfied then they would proceed for an engagement. Such issues by and large are kept secret until the proposal is formally finalised. At times any enemy of the family may spread malicious rumours about their background so that the proposal does not materialise. Some people adopted such measures to take revenge against the concerned family. Occasionally a family friend from another caste would play a crucial role to search for a suitable match.

There are always a few individuals in every community who are constantly on the lookout to make matches for the young boys and girls. They are called 'bichola', the mediator. In olden times they had great importance because the majority of the people solely relied on them before accepting any proposal. They would personally visit the concerned family and dig out the complete family background before recommending the marriage between a prospective boy and a girl. People would take their word as guaranteed. The bichola was rightfully rewarded at the time of marriage. Quite often they would shoulder a reasonable responsibility to iron out any differences even after marriage, if it cropped up.

Among the Sansi community, out of caste marriages are not acceptable.

I was curious to listen in about how my father got married to my mother. Susan was equally eager to know about his marriage. She was enthusiastic to explore about the various customs at the time of marriage among the Sansi community. She impatiently posed many questions to slake her curiosity. Our tape recorder began rolling when my father commenced narrating the story of his marriage.....

"In 1938 one of our relatives from Burundi village invited us to participate in the wedding of his daughter. My second uncle Gaata, his wife, my father and I got there a day before the nuptials. Relatives from different villages had also reached to grace the auspicious occasion. In the evening we were occupied with the preparations before the marriage and it was quite late by the time we finished all the arrangements. By that time the dinner was ready and they were waiting for us to serve dinner. We settled down in rows on the sheets of cloth and the family distributed Sanaks, before they began serving dinner to the guests. In the first course they served boiled rice topped with ghee and sugar and in the second course we enjoyed a delicious dal and roti. After the men had finished their dinner then the family requested the ladies and children to line up for dinner. As an old tradition, the women folk were always served separately only after the men had finished their dinner. As dinner was finished late, there was hardly any time to wash and clean the Sanaks that night. We all decided to organise the washing up the next morning.

At that time neither metallic nor ceramic plates had entered the market and people made use of Sanaks to serve food during any kind of function. The fashion to serve the guests at tables and chairs did not exist in the village culture.

The next morning we discovered that a heap of Sanaks had been lying for washing near the small well in the yard. Along with the other people, I joined in washing the Sanaks. A middle aged man nonchalantly moved around and I was not aware of his presence. But my aunt was sitting close by and observed that he was looking intently at me. She was acquainted with him personally and perhaps grasped his intentions. Devoid of any formality she surprised the man by asking, 'Maru, what are you searching for over there? By any chance are you exploring the possibility of engagement for your daughter?'

Maru was taken by surprise and laughingly responded, 'Yes, you may be right. I have some intentions like that.'

He was from the village Ramgarh Sardaran.

He approached my aunt and enquired, 'Who is this boy?'

My aunt was amused and replied, 'Maru, he is my nephew Nathu and the only son of my younger brother-in-law, Chhotu. He is educated and has recently passed class ten. He was married earlier when he was very young but his wife had passed away long back.'

Maru advised my aunt that if that was the case, then he would think about marrying his daughter to him. He continued his conversation for a while and finally finished it saying, 'I will discuss it with my family and then arrive at a decision.'

Maru's four sons had accompanied him to attend this wedding. He disclosed this newly found possibility to them. They instantly reached out to meet me and we had a conversation for a while. They returned to their father and instantly approved this proposal. Then Maru contacted my father and uncles for further progress. In principle he agreed to marry his daughter to me but could not finalise such a vital issue without deliberating with his wife, for without her consent he would not be able to conclude it.

His wife had not escorted him to attend this wedding. My father also had no compelling reason to reject this proposal rather he was happily looking forward to get me married. My education was over and my marriage was his next target. He conferred with my uncle and his wife and beyond doubt they considered it to be a gracious proposal.

A few days later Maru conveyed a message to my father saying, 'We are pleased with this proposal and you may visit us to finalise the engagement.' Subsequently my father consulted his brothers and fixed the rendezvous to visit Ramgarh Sardaran.

An interesting incident happened a day before my uncles and father were all set for their visit to village Ramgarh Sardaran to negotiate the finer details of the engagement and wedding. On the previous evening a few guests showed up at my uncle Gaata's house. One of them was named Kasala. After having dinner my uncle placed the charpoys out in the open to sit around and chat while enjoying the hookah. My father also joined them and began chatting. But during the conversation Kasala would vaguely hint about his marriageable daughter. Perhaps he was presently in search of an educated boy for her. My father and uncles desisted to react as he had not specifically mentioned about any particular boy. After a while he mentioned that if he found some suitable boy then he would not delay the marriage of his daughter. My uncle Gaata was a straightforward person and got exasperated with his circuitous talking about the proposal of his daughter and finally remarked, 'Kasala, why are you beating around the bush? If you are interested in your daughter's marriage, you know that there are only two bachelor boys around. One is Nathu and another is Nighahiya. If you have something in mind then why don't you speak out openly?'

Nighahiya was another educated Sansi boy who lived across the road.

Kasala felt a little embarrassed and abruptly reacted, 'Yes, yes, Gaata, we shall discuss it tomorrow.'

After that there was scarcely any further conversation on this issue. They chatted for a little while and then ultimately decided to retire for the night. The next morning Kasala and his friends woke up to discover that my uncles and father were not seen around. Kasala enquired from my aunt, 'Where are Thaman, Gaata and Chhotu?'

She immediately responded, 'Kasala, they have departed early in the morning to Ramgarh Sardaran to settle the engagement of Nathu. You people were sleeping and they did not wish to disturb you.'

Kasala and his friends were now traumatized to learn about this. He was in distress and realised that he had missed the bus. He desperately replied to my aunt, 'In fact I have visited to have a word with Chhotu regarding the marriage of my daughter with Nathu.'

My aunt offered them breakfast but they decided to hurry off without having breakfast."

Marriage in the family provides an excellent opportunity to the Sansis, especially to the boy's side, to pretend as if they belong to a very rich class. They would splurge in every fashion and expend lavishly to portray as if they hardly cared about money. Money is showered over their nearest and dearest relations during a marriage. Costly gifts are purchased way beyond their actual capacity. The drinks and other stuff would flow recklessly during a marriage. There would be an endless list of things to squander money on, to prove their sound financial status.

But soon after the marriage such high profile fake moments would be short-lived and leave its deep imprints with devastating effects on the family. There would be just a few Sansi families who possessed their own money to spend during the marriages of their children. Otherwise the majority of the poor families would generally borrow money either from the farmers or from the money lenders at a very high rate of interest. Suppose a boy was getting married, then his father would approach a farmer to borrow money. The farmer would make a contract with the boy or his father that either one of them or both would work for him until the loan was repaid. The farmer would assign the time period of one year or more which would depend upon how much money was borrowed. The boy or his father had to work at the farmer's place round the clock to finish all and sundry jobs in his home as well as in the fields. He could take a day off for some compelling reason but not without providing his replacement. If he had any emergencies in his own house, again he had to seek more money from the farmer. Under such critical circumstances he would be coerced to borrow more and more money. Consequently his period of contract would be augmented to repay this additional loan. As a result he would become a bonded labourer for an endless period as this loan would hardly ever come to an end within the stipulated time frame.

When money was borrowed from the money lender, he would never provide the loan without any security deposit, guarantor or mortgaging anything. He would highly undervalue the mortgaged items. Under compulsion the family would generally mortgage some ornaments or their house etc. The money lender would fix such a steep rate of interest that besides the principle amount, the family would never be able to return the compounded interest itself. The family would hardly have any steady source of income to pay back the interest on time. The interest plus the basic amount would escalate to such a huge amount which would exceed the value of their security deposit. At this stage the money lender would warn him that he would lose his security deposit but the principle and the interest amount would still remain outstanding.

Generally the Sansis opted to work with the farmers because they would find employment to work in the fields *which would act as a source of income to return the loan. The wife of the contracted person would also find an opportunity to work in the farmer's house and she too would get some money or grains and other produce from there.*

A similar situation could also happen if the family borrowed money for the girl's marriage. The men in the house would work with the farmers after borrowing the money.

When I was studying in high school I used to visit my maternal grandmother's place. There I was friendly with the boys of my age and witnessed that most of the boys were working on contract with the farmers to pay off loans after their marriages. These Sansi boys were illiterate and could only do manual labour. There was hardly any other work available for them to gain any regular income and return the borrowed money.

My father enlightened us about his memoirs as we progressed with his own marriage story. He excitedly recalled those special moments of his life and we continued recording and listening to him about his marriage.....

"After fixing the auspicious date of my wedding, my uncles and father returned in a buoyant mood from Ramgarh Sardaran. My father began preparations for my marriage on top priority; he followed an old tradition to invite our relatives by sending off a messenger with a 'Gath', a piece of cotton yarn. Generally the messenger would convey the invitation verbally, with complete details of the marriage to the relative and hand over the 'Gath' as well. Normally the family would accept this 'Gath' and it was considered that the relative would surely participate in the function. If there was any kind of conflict between the relative and the family, the 'Gath' would not be accepted and a return message would be conveyed through the messenger. Subsequently, if the relative had a genuine reason to repudiate the 'Gath' then the head of the family would personally visit there and iron out the differences. Luckily our messenger had delivered the 'Gath' to all our relations without any resistance.

My father purchased a new set of clothes for me and got a long cotton shirt stitched for him. He engaged his elder sister-in-law to select a few sets of clothes for the girl which was to be presented during a ceremony at the bride's place. He hired an oxen-drawn chariot and one bullock cart to transport the wedding party. In the old times the ladies were forbidden to accompany the wedding party but they would have fun among themselves at home when all the men folk had departed. In the very old times, the wedding party would camp over at the girl's place for seven days. Most of the families would find it unaffordable to serve the guests for seven days. Later on the time was reduced to three days.

This girl was just twelve and I was seventeen years old at the time of our marriage. Luckily, my father had been able to meet the expenditure of my marriage without borrowing money from anybody. He had judiciously put aside some money for this occasion. I had no personal money because I was not yet earning. My father was keen to solemnize the wedding without making a big show. A few guests had arrived a day before to join the wedding party. My father had hired a small band of musicians to accompany the marriage party which was considered a matter of great pride for the boy as well as for the girl's family. According to old traditions a day before my wedding, my father invited the local Sansi community for dinner and the musicians played excellent music at dinner time. In appreciation my father and other relatives offered some money to the musicians. After the dinner was over, my aunts sang old folk songs and danced with the other lady relatives.

The next morning I got dressed up and my aunt performed some traditional customs before we departed from home. I missed my mother at that time because these customs normally were meant to be performed by her. I settled in the chariot with my father and uncles and the other people adjusted themselves in the bullock cart. Our wedding party consisted of about ten to twelve people as well as the musicians. My father and my uncles had exemption certificates but the other people had obtained police permission to travel. The girl's village was more than twenty miles from Narangwal. This long journey had taken hours to reach there. When we arrived at the girl's village, our musicians began playing and the sound of the drums was a signal to the girl's family that the

Baraat, marriage party, had arrived. The people from the girl's neighbourhood emerged from their houses to watch the Baraat. As we were approaching the bride's house, my father and my uncles showered some coins over the chariot. Children and poor people were pouncing to collect the coins. The girl's father along with his relatives and other community members approached to welcome us with great enthusiasm. The tradition of greeting and honouring specific guests in the Baraat is called 'milni'. Selective people like my father, uncles and a few relatives were honoured in this observance. My father was welcomed by the bride's father and presented with a piece of cloth and a silver coin. They cheered and hugged each other tightly. Milni was performed with my uncles and a few other relatives too.

After this ceremony we were led to a nearby house for our stay. The girl's bothers joyfully escorted me to another adjacent house and I comfortably settled in there. We were served tea and light snacks after a while. In a short time my father-in-law, Maru, appeared there and asked me if I wanted anything. Some young Sansi girls came there giggling and made a few jovial remarks about me. I guessed that the bride must have dispatched them to obtain a fresh update about me, what I looked like, what was the colour of my skin, whether I was well-groomed or dumb-looking etc.? The bride always had the curiosity to dig up information about the groom because both of them never had a glimpse of each other before the wedding. The girl's brothers were moving around and they noticed that the girls were troubling me; they immediately shooed them away. I noticed that my uncles and father were merrily enjoying the hookah and engaged in chatting with the other Sansi community members in the local Sansi language.

The sun had set and some members of the Baraat enjoyed drinks before we were invited for dinner. The band started playing and we walked in a merry procession to the bride's house. Before serving dinner, my father and the girl's father performed the tradition of 'Kaulis'. All the people from both the sides were sitting on the ground and an old man lit a fire and poured some ghee on it little by little to keep it aflame. Then he picked up some boiled rice mixed with powdered sugar in both his hands and asked Maru which hand he should proffer to my father. Maru said the 'right hand'. The right hand is seen as a friendly hand. The old man then handed over the contents from his right hand to my father and he ate it. Afterwards he offered the other handful to Maru. This tradition had the significance of sharing food between the two families amicably for the first time. After this ritual was over, we settled down for dinner. The family provided us a good simple meal consisting of black dal, roti and gur. The ladies were teasing the men in the Baraat through traditional folk songs. After dinner we returned to our base.

I had hardly dozed off to sleep when a few girls appeared before midnight to lay henna patterns on my hands. There is a tradition to design intricate henna patterns on the hands of the boy and the girl separately a few hours before the marriage ceremony. The girls were making designs on my palm and joking with me as well. After they finished putting henna patterns on my hands, they instructed me to let it dry properly and only then remove it. They hurriedly vanished as they had to do it for the bride too.

Around midnight, we were informed to be ready and invited for 'phere', the religious ritual for a marriage ceremony. All the members of the wedding party were ready and we followed the band to the girl's house. The girl's family had put up a canopy-like square wooden structure in their yard and decorated it with some banana leaves and floral blossoms. This whole place was reasonably lit with oil lamps. The family had also called a 'Mahant', a priest, who had to solemnise the 'phere' ceremony. He was a Sansi and professionally solemnised Sansi marriages. Below the canopy, he had arranged a small fire on the ground for the bridal couple to perform 'pheres' around it. The family had spread sheets on one side of canopy for the members of the marriage party and we settled there. The rest of the people from the family were sitting opposite to us and everybody was eagerly waiting to witness this ceremony. The Mahant poured a little more ghee on the fire to set it aflame. The family hurriedly spread another sheet of cloth separately on the opposite side of the Mahant and asked me to take a seat on it. When everybody had settled down, the Mahant requested the girl's father to fetch his daughter. A few moments later some ladies appeared with the girl completely bundled with bridal finery from head to toe including covering her face. They were accompanying her while she walked to the canopy and guided her to sit down beside me.

A strange feeling of excitement as well as nervousness prevailed over me for a short moment. I was soon going to wed a pre-teenager. As believed that 'marriages are made in heaven', this was soon going to be true for me now. I was acquainted only with her name, Nihalo, and just blindly going to accept her as my life partner. The Mahant directed us how to perform the 'phere', to circle around the fire seven times. The Mahant directed the girl's father to tie the knot. Like her I carried a long piece of colourful cloth hung over my shoulder. Her father stood up and tied a knot of my piece of cloth with hers. The Mahant signalled us to stand up and we commenced walking in a clockwise direction around the fire. The girl's brothers and other relatives were standing around in a circle to steer her behind me as she was completely rolled up in clothes and possibly could not see properly. While we were slowly moving around the fire, the Mahant was chanting some hymns. I could not make any head or tail of his chanting. Just before the final round was over, the ladies crooned some folk songs indicating the completion of the marriage ceremony. After seven rounds were over, we were asked to be seated again. People from both the sides now happily congratulated each other. My wife's mother brought some gur and put it in our mouths and blessed us. My father and all the other relatives presented some money to us with blessings. He happily showered some coins over the people sitting there. This whole phenomenon necessitated more than three hours. This 'phere' ceremony had to be concluded before sunrise. The custom of 'phere' was adopted from the Hindu marriage rituals. The morning glow of dawn gradually began illuminating the horizon."

Apparently my father, Natha Singh, was fortunate that he escaped from experiencing the needle-pricking during the phere time. At this crucial juncture the girl friends of the bride would fool around with various kinds of tricks to tease the groom. They would ensure sitting right behind the bridal couple to amuse themselves with any tricks. They would indulge in pricking the groom with needles as he would be more vulnerable to any kind of teasing at this particular time. The girls would repeatedly prick the groom from behind with a needle; he would simply hop up each time but would not be able to react. This gesture of the groom would be enough to make them snigger. The phere period is actually merry-making and an enjoyable time for the bride's friends. Sometimes the girls would be so naughty that they would stitch the groom's shirt to the cloth spread under him. Subsequently when he would get up for the phere, then the whole paraphernalia would rise up and get dragged behind him. The girls would make fun of this scene and get immense pleasure from the groom's awkwardness.

The elders would always pick out what mischief was brewing behind the bridal couple but generally would not meddle unless they observed it was crossing a certain limit. Ultimately they would butt in and command the girls to stop. The girls also had another traditional game, to hide the shoes of the groom when he would sit for the phere. They would be enormously delighted when the groom would not be able to discover his shoes after the phere. He would become immobile without his shoes. The girls would bargain with him to return his shoes at a price. Actually at that time a smart thing would be to put on someone else's shoes and walk away to avoid instant embarrassment and settle the issue later on. But mostly, the groom pays the money after bargaining with the young ladies. This kind of fun is common among all castes. In the case of my father it appeared that the girls felt shy probably because he was educated and desisted from playing any serious mischief with him. My father had not mentioned about experiencing the above games during his marriage when he was talking to us.

"After the phere ceremony was over, they served us tea and snacks. We then returned to our camp. Since all the members were awake the whole night, everybody wanted to take a quick nap and I also snoozed for some time. After slumbering for a short time, we felt refreshed. We then received a call for the next ritual. The band led us with every trip to the girl's house. This time my father had to showcase the clothes and gift items, called 'Varee' to the girl's family. These gifts were meant for the bride and her family including their close relatives. When we got there, we settled on the cloth sheets on the ground. The elders and the relatives of the family settled in front of us. The rest of the men and women were eager to see what my father had fetched for the bride. My father opened up an iron trunk and drew out the clothes and small gold ornaments for the bride and her relatives. To honour some specific relatives my father gifted each one with clothes and a coin on it. The gifts and clothes exclusively meant for the bride were received by one lady who took all the items inside the house. All the other women and children followed her to have a glimpse of the gifts. In a short while, the lady brought back the items and displayed it for the men sitting outside. Everybody was pleased and appreciated my father for the nice gifts. The elders shared their hookah, chit-chatted among themselves and exchanged small jokes. After this display was over we returned to our base.

Lunch time was approaching and some members sought to enjoy a few drinks before lunch. This lunch was considered to be the most important meal during the wedding. The family now invited us for lunch. The musicians got ready and they were waiting for us to go to the bride's house. We merrily followed the band and the musicians were doing their best to play excellent music. In appreciation our relatives offered money to the musicians. My father and uncles overwhelmingly threw silver and copper coins on the way and the children pounced to gather the coins. After reaching at the bride's house my father showered more coins and there was utter chaos as the ladies and children had fun scrambling to pick up the coins. The musicians played their best non-stop music for a long time and other people too proffered more money to them. Gradually all the members of the marriage party settled down and waited for lunch to be served."

The Sansis from the bridegroom's clan would often honour earstwhile married girls' in the bride's village. The groom's father would consider it an honour to dispatch the 'pattal' to their homes. The bride's father would place some sweets in the plate which is called a 'pattal'. This tradition was formalised just before the whole marriage party would begin having their lunch. The groom's father would recommend the names of the girls in that village but the bride's father would dispatch the 'pattal' to their homes irrespective whether those girls' were participating in that marriage function or not. This gesture was a great honour to all the Mahla or Beedoo girls married there from the groom's village. If they even honoured their living mother-in-law of that girl, then it was called double 'pattal'. The Sansis would infrequently dispatch double 'pattal'.

My father excitedly continued narrating his story.....

"Before starting our lunch, my father desired to observe a long-standing tradition of dispatching the 'pattal'. He consulted my uncles and they discussed for a while and called my father-in-law, "Maru, we wish to send 'pattals' to some girls from our village."

119

Maru was probably expecting it and replied without any hesitation, "Yes, Chhotu, you name the girls, I will arrange the pattals."

My father and uncles desired to send double 'pattals', so my father responded, "Maru, we also wish to forward double pattals."

Before Maru could answer my father, one of his relatives objected to it and alleged, "Chhotu, we do not have a tradition in our village to send double pattals."

At this point my father and uncles felt irritated with this undue interference of the relative and Maru was trapped between them. Maru replied to my father, "Chhotu, you wait for a little while, I will discuss this with my other relatives."

My father pointed out to his older brother, Thaman, "That relative is unnecessarily meddling in this affair. We are genuinely requesting to honour the girls and their mothers-in-law."

My eldest uncle alleged about the relative and remarked, "It seems to me that he is gratuitously trying to put us down."

Maru was engaged in having a discussion with his other relatives but had not yet reached any conclusion. The other members of the wedding party were waiting for the decision to begin their lunch. I was seated between my father and uncles and curiously listening to their conversation. When I observed that the issue was unreasonably getting delayed, then to finish all this drama I asked to my father, "If that relative is making an undue fuss then we should refuse to have lunch unless they concur to dispatch double 'pattals'."

Incidentally my mother-in-law was around and she overheared this portion of my conversation. She immediately returned to her husband and forewarned him about my decision. There was an instant reaction to my declaration and Maru hurriedly approached my father, "Chhotu, do not worry, we agree to send double pattals. You please enjoy your lunch."

Though there were scarcely one or two double 'pattals' but this case had become a prestige issue for us. When the 'pattal' custom was over we gladly started enjoying our lunch. The family served us delicious food and everybody enjoyed it.

After lunch now the 'khat' ceremony was in the offing where the bride's family would display the gifts for their daughter. We had not demanded any dowry but as a tradition they proffered her some utensils and clothes. But among the community this tradition had a high significance because everybody would be keen to know how many gifts the family had given to their daughter. During this 'khat' ceremony, the family then honoured the members of our wedding party with one coin called 'Sardari'. Sardari is to honour selected relatives from the wedding party. My father proclaimed the names of the guests and the bride's family honoured them with 'Sardari'.

Late in the evening we had a small dinner and after that the elders had ample time to smoke hookah and have long conversations. Some members of the marriage party were feeling tired and decided to sleep early. Some girls appeared at my resting place and they were delighted to chatter more unreservedly with newly found brother-in-law. After a while they left and I cautiously went to sleep as I was aware that these girls could cross any limit and play any mischief in the night while I was asleep but fortunately the night passed by peacefully.

The next day in the morning we began wrapping up and the family invited us for breakfast. After we finished breakfast my father expressed to Maru that we would like to start as early as possible. Maru assured my father that he would not delay us any longer. The girl's family was engaged with all the last minute preparations for sending off their daughter. Her brothers and other people started loading her belongings in the oxen-cart. The Chariot was parked in front of her house. We all were waiting patiently when the ladies escorted the bride to board the chariot. The ladies were singing folk songs intended for such an occasion. One by one the bride bid adieu to her all family members and relatives with tears before stepping into the chariot. Two other ladies escorted her to my village.

Finally the chariot surged forward and my father and uncles showered coins over the chariot. Then the elders from the community requested them to stop showering any more coins. The men followed the chariot to a short distance and stopped to perform a small ceremony of 'piale'. My father and Maru sat down on the ground and a man placed two small earthen pots filled with water between them. Both of them picked up the pots simultaneously and touched it to their lips and dropped the pots there instantly. They repeated this ritual twice and then stood up. At the last minute just before departure my father and my father-in-law shared cardamom with the all the other members. This meant that both the families have departed on a pleasant note.

After an exhausting journey, we finally reached home in the evening and my aunt along with the other ladies was waiting for us. All the traditional welcoming customs for the bride were performed by my aunt. The musicians played homecoming music while my aunt was welcoming my wife. My wife along with the other ladies settled in one room. The ladies at home had arranged dinner for us. We finished our dinner and gradually everybody settled down for the night."

My father desired to take a break for a while before he could restart telling his story.

In fact, in old times there was a playful event after the wedding called 'Kangna', which was developed to introduce the bride and groom for the first time in a playful manner. Both of them were strangers as they had never seen or met one another before marriage. The Ladies from the house would put water in a big vessel and add some colour to make it look colourful as well as opaque. The bride and groom would sit opposite each other on either side of the vessel. Only the ladies and the young folk were permitted to watch this playful fun. The male elders would intentionally stay away from the event. One of the ladies would toss a coin in the coloured water and both the bride and the groom would search for the coin in the water with both hands. Since no one could see the coin in the water they would attempt to search for it and snatch it from each other's hand underwater. The water would splash on both of them in the snatching process. Also informally they would have an opportunity to touch each other for the first time. Whosoever managed to snatch the coin, would be the winner. The ladies would support the bride and the boys would encourage the groom to grab the coin in the water first. This coin is tossed thrice into the vessel. If the bride grabs the coin more times than the groom, then the ladies would assume that the bride would be bossing the groom in life or vice versa.

As my father had rested for some time he was now ready to elucidate further.....

"The next day some of our relatives had departed early in the morning. My aunt with the help of the other ladies prepared breakfast and served it to everybody. After this my aunt had set the stage for us to play 'kangna'. My wife and I played 'Kangna' while the onlookers enjoyed this fun. After marriage every newly married couple would usually visit a religious place to receive the blessings from God or their deity. Since the Sansis now had their own shrine of Sidh Baba Raul, we had to go there for his blessings. After playing 'Kangna', we intended to visit our shrine. This time also only the ladies and young boys and girls from our community accompanied us. Those ladies who had accompanied the bride from her village escorted the bride everywhere. We all walked through the barren fields to reach Sidh Baba Raul's shrine. Since there was no priest, we prayed on our own. After a short prayer, we played 'Chhittiyan', a ritual of gently smacking each other. A young boy had procured two strong but flexible branches from a tree. One branch was provided to the bride and the other one to me. We had to spank each other ten times. We began spanking each other gently, and our supporters from either side were pressurising us to strike harder the next time. But we honoured each other and smacked lightly. The onlookers enjoyed this workout and after this ritual we returned home. We were the first couple to play Chhittiyan at our newly built Baba Raul's shrine.

*   *   *

Early days of Marriage

*M*y father had reached a crucial juncture in his life. He had finished his High School education which was considered to be a respectable standard at that time, particularly for a Sansi. To think of joining college was beyond his dreams as the colleges were located in big cities only. First of all, the economic condition of his father was too impecunious to afford the expenses of the college. Only affluent parents could afford to send their children to college at that time. Secondly he was married now and had incurred the additional responsibility to support the family. Probably he and his wife had expected that he would soon get a job and earn some regular income. He could not get any opening for a job for a long time. When all odds were against him he decided to take up any profession like the other poor people. He recognised and accepted the fact of life that somehow he had to earn money and did not feel embarrassed doing any kind of work like the other illiterate Sansis. He ignored the fact *that he had passed Matriculation but aimed at the prime and practical aspect of life, survival.*

My father added to the story of his struggle in life.......

"After marriage my mother-in-law initially declined to allow my wife to live with us as she was underage. But her family could not withstand the pressure from my father to send her because he was unable to handle the domestic work any longer. I would help him in doing the domestic chores as much as I could. After six months or so my wife finally came to live with us. Life was tough for all of us in its own way. Being married now and with no source of income, we were in an arduous financial situation to run the house. My idle presence at home began irking my father. I was equally concerned and made serious efforts to search for work. To look for job advertisements in the newspaper was nearly impossible. Even to obtain a copy of a newspaper on a regular basis was beyond my reach. I would request some people from the village to procure a copy of the newspaper from Ludhiana city for me. Being in the village, it was even more complicated to find a source of information to search for a job. I optimistically maintained silence to get some work but my father repeatedly demanded to start any kind of work. I was equally worried as my wife too had no money for her needs. I felt trapped at one stage and I realistically comprehended that there was hardly any scope to expect a job immediately. At present I had only one solution to earn some money like other illiterate Sansis. As an only alternative I opted to graze buffaloes belonging to various families.

My wife being a teenage girl had her own predicaments. She suddenly had been set apart from her big family and would find it uncomfortable to remain alone in the house when we moved out to graze buffaloes. Unfortunately she had no mother-in-law, my uncles had no daughters-in-law and there were no other Sansi girls in the neighbourhood to give her company. She began feeling desperately lonely and conveyed it to her mother. Her mother would often visit and stay with us for some days. After her departure the same situation would crop up again. Finally my wife bluntly cautioned her mother that she would not stay alone anymore. Ultimately her family became apprehensive and decided to send her second brother to stay with us to give her company. He was also a young child and quite often he would squabble with her and run away back to his village. Later on his parents would pacify him and send him back. This drama would repeatedly recur. Her bother resided with us for more than three years. Our main concern was that she should cook food and handle all the household chores. But she was too young to bear this load at her tender age. Gradually but with immense difficulty she got acclimatised to manage this burden.

At last I was determined to graze buffaloes just to raise some money to run the house. I approached the Jat families in the village who were willing to send their buffaloes for grazing on a contract basis. Some Sansi families from our village were already grazing buffaloes; the situation was more cumbersome for me to persuade the people to send their buffaloes with me. I managed to gather eight to ten buffaloes in the beginning and steadily augmented it up to twenty. The rate of the contract was one rupee per buffalo per month or ten seers of wheat or cooked food in the evening. I would decide the mode of payment depending on our requirement at home. But some Jat families could afford to provide cooked food only. They had limitations to make payment in cash. My father and my wife would assist me in the morning to gather the buffaloes in front of our house. The three of us would then drive the buffaloes to the fields. Once the buffaloes were out in the open fields then my wife would return home to complete her domestic chores. My father would organize fodder for our own buffalo and remain busy with other errands.

The condition of the Sansis in the village was so miserable that nobody paid attention if their newlywed bride was wandering in the fields, accumulating grass for their own buffalo or gathering dry dung cakes etc. My wife had started working to assist the family in every respect shortly after she joined us after marriage. We were very poor; hence hardly cared about the dignity or status in the village. My wife would cook rotis for lunch and fetch it to the fields for me. On her return she would then gather dry twigs and dry dung cakes for cooking at home. During the wheat harvesting time she would segregate the left over grains from the fields after the farmers had finished winnowing. Then she would grind the grains at home to produce flour from it for cooking rotis. There were hardly any grinding mills at that time and secondly we could not spare money to expend for grinding grains from the flour mill. She had an appallingly tiresome life in those days. Sometimes she would not withstand this house hold pressure and get irritated. My father expected her to accomplish all the domestic chores. As a result both of them would nit-pick with each other and I could not judiciously side anyone.

I would drive the buffaloes to the canal side and let them graze there for the entire day. During the summers I would rest under the shady trees along with buffaloes. Grazing buffaloes was not an effortless occupation as I had to be watchful of the crops or the buffaloes wandering into the plantations by the canal side. I had to walk more than the buffaloes every day as some buffaloes would drift away from the rest of the herd and I had to run behind them to keep them under control. Other Sansis would graze their lot of buffaloes in the near vicinity. Some individuals would also join us with their own buffaloes. We had each other's company during the day.

The buffaloes had to drink clean water during the day and the only available source was the canal. The water in the ponds was dirty and basically unfit for drinking. But to water the buffaloes in the canal was always dicey. Officially it was forbidden as buffaloes would erode the banks of the canal. We would sneak the buffaloes into the canal when nobody was around for checking. Buffaloes would drink water and plunge into it as well for some time. But occasionally when a buffalo would swim across the canal, to bring her back was really a tedious task. I did not know how to swim so I had to hang around till I found someone on the other side of canal to fetch the buffalo and push her back. If this method did not work then I had to go over the bridge and search for the buffalo. In the mean time I would request to my other buffalo-grazing companions to handle my buffaloes until my return. To get hold of my buffalo and bring her back would add a few extra miles to my daily walking. I would also reciprocate if their buffalo passed over to the other side of the canal. In the evening my wife and father would once again join me to return the buffaloes back to the village and hand over each buffalo to its respective owner.

Some people in the village would often ask me why I was grazing buffaloes. Instead they would suggest that I should move out and explore the possibility of some job. They could easily provide such free advice but the reality of life was completely different.

My father collected the money which we earned from grazing the buffaloes. We meagrely utilised the money to run the house. When we required anything, only then would I ask him for some money. Otherwise he would gather the silver rupee coins in an earthen pot and then seal it with mud. He would then dig a pit and mark its location in his mind e.g. like near the hearth, near the trough or in a certain corner of the house to conceal the money pot therein and mud wash the place to level the surface. He would solely deal with the sale and purchase of the buffalo. There were hardly any banks in the countryside at that time. People had created their own banks at their homes by burying the money which was safe and handy for them at any time."

My grandfather was an illiterate man but he had acquired the ability to count the silver rupee coins in his own way like the other illiterate people. At that time people counted money in 'veehan', in twenties. For example to count thirty two, they would count as eight less than two 'veehan', and to count forty two, would be two veehan plus two. Probably he sought help from my father to count the small change as he could not keep track of other numbers.

My grandfather and I shared quite a warm relationship with each other when I was young. Before I joined primary school, I would accompany him holding his long stick to graze goats as his eyesight had become very weak. Being quite old, his mobility had decreased. Sometimes he would feel the urge to munch some biscuits etc. Such things were a delicacy at that time. If he wished to buy something exclusively, he would then only call me. He trusted me enough to share the location of his hidden treasure. We would shut the main door and then in one corner of the house he would measure the distance from the wall with his hands. He would direct me to excavate carefully to avoid damaging his money pot. I would dig almost a foot deep and finally sense a pot appearing there. Gradually I would remove all the soil and unearth the pot. At that point he would ask me to stop and insert his hand to get hold of some coins. There used to be silver rupee coins along with small change of half a rupee, quarter rupee and an Anna, one sixteenth of a rupee etc. He would direct me to count the change and then retain the small change coins to spend. He would re-seal the pot with wet mud once again and I would place the pot back in the ground, refill the dug up place and he would level it up with some more wet mud. He would hand over some money and ask me to buy whatever he desired to eat. He would save the remainder of the coins for future use. I experienced pleasure in his companionship as well as doing this petite task for him. I infer that my father and mother were acquainted with the hidden treasure of my grandfather but they never dug it out. They never asked me anything regarding this money.

"Like other people, my father would desist from expending money to buy unnecessary things. My father had a genuine motive to save money as nobody would lend him any during an emergency or for any special event. He had no inclination or thought to elevate our standard of living because there was no dependable source of regular income. His main objective was to live with the least. Our life was supported by the buffalo which provided plenty of milk, and we prepared yoghurt and ghee at home almost throughout the year. As a result we would eat staple but nutritious food.

My wife was over burdened with duties of a housewife when under normal circumstances she should have been enjoying the zenith of the adolescent period of her life.

Once my mother-in-law visited us and my wife cried and complained to her about the unbearable work load. My wife narrated the whole situation about how she had to work from dawn till late evening. My mother-in-law got fed up with her regular complaints each time she visited her daughter. The next day she decided to take her daughter back to her village without informing us. We only came to know of this after we returned home in the evening. We felt gravely offended with her gesture. My in-laws contemplated that we would approach and request them to send my wife back to our village. We also became obstinate and were determined not to ask them to send her back. Neither of us approached each other for a long time and ultimately there was a deadlock.

One day I was grazing buffaloes by the side of the canal. I casually embarked on the bank of the canal. A man passed by but unexpectedly he stopped. He asked me, "Are you Nathu?"

I was astonished when he unpredictably tried to identify me. I got alert and replied, "Yes."

He posed another question and inquired, "Do you recognize me?"

I tried refreshing my memory and looked intently at him. I recognised him as the brother of my mother-in-law. I answered quickly, "Yes."

He straightway asked me, "Nathu, why don't you go to your in-laws and fetch your wife?"

I recounted the whole episode to him, "Uncle, first and foremost my mother-in-law had complained that her daughter had to run our entire household single-handedly. But we have our own limitations. Secondly, she had taken her back without our consent as well as without informing us which is objectionable."

He attempted to placate me, "Nathu, I have already condemned them for that mistake. They are feeling embarrassed now and dare not approach you directly. I suggest you bring your wife back home and they will not object to it."

I discreetly replied, "Uncle, I will discuss this with my father and then decide."

After this short discussion he went his way.

My father and I decided to bring my wife back as my in-laws had realised their fault. There was no point in stretching this issue any longer. Finally after more than six months I brought my wife back home."

Such incidents would often happen in society especially when the parents marry their daughters at an immature age. The situation takes a dangerous turn when the parents take their daughter back without the consent from her in-laws which ultimately leads to an impasse. The parents would justify because their daughter was in an awful situation. But the in-laws would make it their prestige issue and would not fetch her for a long time. The girl's parents would not be able to keep her with them for long because of the social stigma. The people in the community would begin blaming the parents and conclude that the girl would be at fault and that is why she is not going back to her in-laws. The parents would then request the close relatives to intervene and negotiate to sort out the matter. Sometimes the girl would be forced to return unwillingly. Such gaffes are common among the Sansis.

*   *   *

Merciless Thrashing

66 **A** s every profession has its hazards, I also encountered the peril of grazing buffaloes especially from the irrigation and the forest departments. The forest officer had his duty to preserve the plantation alongside the canal and the irrigation officer was supposed to oversee the embankments or any other danger to the canal. They would make rounds on the bicycle off and on and caution the buffalo grazing people to protect the plantation and the erosion of the edges of the canal. We also had our limitations which coerced us to move our buffaloes near the canal at times.

One day my father appeared unexpectedly when I was grazing buffaloes near the canal as one of our relatives had visited us to see me. My father came to relieve me for a while. My other companions were grazing buffaloes nearby. I returned home and my father tried to drive his herd of buffaloes away from the others to avoid the collision between the animals. He thought of manoeuvring the buffaloes across the canal as it was nearly dry. As ill luck would have it, when he was herding the buffaloes across the canal, suddenly the nehri Babu, the irrigation officer, appeared on his bicycle. He yelled at my father and demanded him to return instantly. My father realised that he was in serious trouble. He was terrified but returned to face the irrigation officer.

When my father neared him, the nehri Babu was furious and thundered, 'Who authorized you to drive the buffaloes through the canal?'

My father was shivering with fear and apologetically pleaded to him, 'Saab, please pardon me and I will not repeat it.'

As a gesture to bestow an apology my father bowed down to touch the feet of the nehri Babu. The moment my father bent down, he held my father by his head and began repeatedly kicking him in the chest with his knee. The impact was so severe that my father was crying with pain but requesting him for pardon. The nehri Babu continued yelling and simultaneously continued hitting my father. He was not prepared to listen to my father at all. The other people rushed to see what was happening. They continued watching this brutal scene but no one dared to utter a word to the nehri Babu to stop. His ferocity calmed down only when my father became unconscious. He left my father there crying with pain, got on his bicycle and rode away.

My companions sent a message to me about my father. My wife and I swiftly rushed there. My father was lying there in an unconscious state. People were just waiting for me to come and I observed that my father would not be able to walk. I rushed back home to fetch a cot and asked my wife to manage the buffaloes. I laid my father on the cot with the help of the other people and carried him home. My uncles and neighbours gathered to see him. My father slowly regained consciousness but he still had the unbearable pain in his chest. I asked my father to see the doctor as his condition was not stable. My father refused to go to the doctor and suggested to try some home remedies to nurse his internal injury. In the first place there was no qualified doctor in the village. Secondly it was also very expensive to go to the city and get medical aid. We nursed him with home treatment for a few days but there was no sign of any improvement, instead his condition was deteriorating day by day. Ultimately he got a chest infection. Now we had no other choice except to hospitalize him under compelling circumstances.

The people in the village were sympathetic with my father and suggested to lodge a case against nehri Babu. My father lodged a complaint with the police against the nehri Babu and a case was registered. The people who were present on the scene assured my father that they would vouch for him as witnesses in the court. Now the nehri Babu was in serious trouble and his job was at stake. He began contacting the influential people in our village and requested them to protect him as he belonged to the higher caste like them. He also began showering favours to the witnesses as well. Then higher caste people contacted my father and told him to drop the case but my father declined it straightway. With the passage of time the nehri Babu pressurised the witnesses through various channels and they began changing their colours. We had our doubts now that the witnesses would not stand with us in the courtroom anymore. Ultimately they reluctantly informed us that they would not testify in our favour. The nehri Babu continued mounting pressure on us through the prominent people in the village. They tried to persuade my father by luring him with a meagre amount of money as compensation. When the Jats concluded that my father was not yielding, they even threatened him that they would not permit him to pass through their fields. But my father still remained unyielding and was determined not to withdraw the suit. On the other hand the nehri Babu was successful in winning over most of the Jats in his favour who further influenced all the eyewitnesses.

Who really cared about the cruelty towards an underprivileged, poverty-stricken Sansi, who had been mercilessly hammered, nearly to death in front of the mute bystanders?

Now the Jats took up this case as their personal prestige issue against my father. How could a Sansi dare say 'no' when he was supposed to blindly abide by their diktats? On the other hand unless the case was withdrawn nothing would have changed practically. The case could prolong for years and perhaps the nehri Babu's further promotions could have been jeopardised or he could have even faced suspension. Later on even the police began favouring the nehri Babu and diluted the case to a great extent. At one point we found ourselves absolutely isolated and helpless. We were poor and one way or the other we were dependent on the Jats. They were threatening us day in day out by not allowing us to graze the buffaloes in their fields. Under discriminating circumstances we sensed that we could not expect any justice in the court. The witnesses had turned hostile and the court would not be able to take any action. Above all we had no money to fight the case in the court for long time. All the odds were against us and there was absolutely no ray of hope for justice. In the end my father was compelled to drop the case under duress."

My father appeared defenceless while telling us the tale of his father who was brutally trampled by an irrigation officer. Though my grandfather had trespassed by crossing with the buffaloes thru the canal, the irrigation officer could have taken sterner official action according to the guidelines of the department. He had absolutely no right to mercilessly beat up my grandfather. As Susan and I listened to my father, we could glaringly sense the high handedness of this government official and the Jats. The Sansis were vulnerable to succumb to the pressure from the Jats. We could feel a deep ache in his voice but he continued narrating his story further.....

"During those days the farmers had a single crop in a year and most of the farming was dependant on the rains. The farmers were unable to irrigate all their fields with the oxen-driven wells, otherwise the rest of the fields were open for grazing animals throughout the year. With great caution we would drive the buffaloes across the canal and graze them freely. We had identified some enraged animals among our herd and would try to isolate them from each other as far as possible. But sporadically the buffaloes would swiftly attack one another and we had a tough time when they went head on with each other. It was a Herculean task to disengage them. In the duel they would lock their horns and if they did not disengage automatically, it would even rupture their horns. The farmers would get annoyed when they found that their buffalo had wrecked her horn. We were completely helpless in this regard.

The Irrigation department had planted new trees on both the sides of the canal. Wild grass would often grow amongst the trees after the rainy season. A forest Overseer, who had been deputed to patrol the plantations, would often come on his bicycle to monitor if any damage had occurred to the trees. He would also keep an eye if anybody was chopping off the old trees. He had engraved the numbers on all the old trees. If any tree was missing, he was supposed to probe and report it to his department. If somebody was trapped on the spot then he was punished under the law. This Overseer seemed to be a gentleman and he would seldom bother us gratuitously but we were always scared of him. We would control the buffaloes in such a manner that they would not enter the forest territory along the canal. One day while I was grazing buffaloes with my other companions, the Overseer arrived there and instructed me to keep the buffaloes away from the forest zone to avoid any damage to the plantation. I managed to contain the rest of the buffaloes but one buffalo kept on straying towards the plantation over and over again. I dashed to drive her away from the trees. Then one of my companions observed this and commented from a distance, "Nathu, you have wasted your time in passing Matriculation. You cannot even control a buffalo!"

The Overseer overheard him and out of curiosity enquired from my companions, 'Is it true that he is really a Matriculation, Class ten, pass or are you just making fun of him?'

'Saab, sir, he is really a Matriculation pass.' my companion confidently answered.

Perhaps the Overseer still did not believe this and in the meanwhile I reached there. He then directly questioned me, "Are you really a Matriculation pass or are they making a fun of you?"

I replied, "Saab, I have passed Matriculation."

He was bewildered at first but then he asked about my grades and other relevant information. Finally he asked me, "Why don't you apply for a job?"

"Saab, I have applied at a few places but nothing has materialised so far." I answered unenthusiastically.

"Look, there is one vacancy as a telegraph operator using the Morse code system in our forest office in Kaind village.

You are qualified for it. I advise you to put forward your application." He informed me excitedly.

He further added, "You meet me in my office and I will recommend your name to our SDO, Sub-Divisional Officer.

I was delighted to obtain this information and applied for the post. One day I ventured into the office of the Overseer. He was there and introduced me to the head clerk in the office and advised my background to him. He then confidentially informed me that if the head clerk asked for a gift, he would proffer it to him.

An interview letter came by post. I thought it would be sagacious to meet the head clerk a day before the interview. He was alone in his office and I requested him, "Saab, you know that tomorrow is my interview for the post of a telegraph operator. If you help me to get this job then I shall offer you something."

The head clerk frowned at me and retorted, "What do you mean by it? Do you think I accept bribes? How dared you say this to me?"

I felt humiliated and speechless. At that time I was ignorant how to speak to ask for a favour. Somehow I managed to reply, "Saab, I was guided by the Overseer like this." I had no other choice except to give the reference of the Overseer.

The head clerk now had cooled down a bit and advised me, "Never mention anything like this to anyone. As you are a poor man, this time I will ignore it. As far as your job is concerned, there are two candidates for this post. You have the recommendation of the SDO of Kaind; the other candidate has the recommendation of the X-EN, the Executive Engineer, of Patiala. I don't know what our X-EN would decide. I will try to be in your favour." After this I hurriedly escaped from there.

The next day I appeared for the interview and they asked me a few general questions. Unfortunately I never met the Overseer again but waited for the interview result. One day while I was discussing my interview with an old man in our village, he straightaway posed me a simple question, "Nathu, who was the head clerk there?"

I mentioned the name of the head clerk. He was a pundit, a Brahmin. The old man bluntly declared, "Then you will not be selected. A pundit would never recommend you for this post."

What he meant to say was that since I belonged to the lowest caste, an untouchable, the head clerk, a pundit, would never turn in my favour. If selected, I would be working in his office and he would not stomach the shadow of a Sansi around him. It turned out to be true. The other candidate was selected".

*   *   *

The Sant

I had heard as well as observed that the Sansis believed in superstitions, ghosts, evil spirits etc. Generally among the Sansis if someone fell ill, they would not seek medical assistance in the beginning, they would make efforts to cure the person with home remedies or approach the quacks. After exercising futile antidotes, they would conclude that the person is under the ill effect of some evil spirit. Even a minor illness would be deliberated as the consequence of some detrimental spirit. To heal their sick, the Sansis would rush to the faith healers, pray to their deity or consult a 'Tantric', a black magic practitioner. The faith healer may propose to sacrifice a fowl or a goat to appease their ancestors or deity for the speedy recovery of their ailing person. The Sansis would linger on with such remedies and as a last resort they would opt for proper medical assistance. Sometimes it would be too late to the save the life of the person. Superstitions prevailed heavily especially among the illiterate Sansis.

Generally the evil spirit is thought to be unleashed by practitioners of 'black magic' or Tantrics. People, who sought to harm their enemies physically or financially, would often approach the 'black magic' practitioners. The Tantrics would direct the person to conceal a pig or a goat's head in the doorway or in the wall of the house of their enemy. They would recommend various ways and means to the people to avenge their enemies. Occasionally things like lemons, chillies, a bottle of country liquor, a fowl or a pair of iron locks is placed in the night on the cross roads of the village. They would believe that whoever would step over it, would be possessed by the effect of the evil spirit.

People under the influence of the evil spell would then seek assistance from other Tantrics or faith healers to dispel the effect of the evil spirit. The Tantrics would confer amulets or holy water to drink and sprinkle around the house. They would give some ash from their holy fire to sprinkle in the house. Then the ill effects from the concerned person would be eradicated. There was a strong belief among the Sansis that no medicine would have any effect once a person was under the spell of an evil spirit.

If a buffalo skipped giving milk at one time, the Sansis would imagine that she was under the effect of some evil shadow. If a crow flew over their house and threw a piece of bone there, they would consider that their deity wished *them to cook meat in the house. If a baby cried most of the time, they would deduce that the child was under the spell of some evil spirit. If somebody sneezed just before the exit from their house, they would construe it as a bad omen and believed that their job would be abortive. The shuddering of the dog's ears just before they initiated any job would be deemed as a bad omen. Interestingly they had marked particular individuals from the village and evaded seeing their faces before leaving on a journey or any other significant mission. Similarly some persons were also labelled as a good omen if they met them just before they commenced their journey or any other auspicious assignment. Other higher castes always considered it as an awful omen if they faced an untouchable before setting out for an important mission. If their mission remained unsuccessful, they would undoubtedly curse the lower caste person.*

The ingress of The Sant in the life of my father was most enduring and significant. My grandfather undeniably believed that my father was under the spell of an evil shadow as he felt lifeless most of the time. Despite their best efforts, he remained in the same condition for a long time. This illness led him to come in contact with The Sant. Once he bestowed his faith in The Sant, there was an absolute transformation in his unguided life. A true turning point in his life had taken place thus shedding the clouds of superstitions forever. Had he not come in contact with The Sant, he would have remained Nathu throughout his lifetime. Nobody would have respectfully addressed him as Natha Singh. Probably his children too would have had half names like him. He had established a religious base in the presence of The Sant which provided both moral and spiritual support in his life. Otherwise our family would still have been praying at Sidh Baba Raul's shrine like the other Sansis of our village. The Sant had enhanced his morale by enfolding him in his inner circle. My father gained The Sant's admiration there even though he belonged to the untouchables. To a great extent it facilitated him to get rid of his inferiority complex of being an untouchable when he served the high caste people at The Sant's gathering,. A new era had dawned upon his life after The Sant gathered him in his fold. I was fortunate right from my childhood to have an opportunity to go with my father while he attended the monthly gathering at The Sant's place. I realised that my father was in a different world in the presence of The Sant. I had observed that he felt elated when The Sant deputed him to execute any important work. He had an absolute conviction towards The Sant and he was one among his few ardent followers.

During our recording, the entire curtain had unfolded as to how he had commenced the journey of his life with The Sant. Susan and I were astounded when he channelled his thoughts to describe his extensive association with The Sant.....

"A few years after my marriage, we still continued facing the hardships of life. This was the fifth year of my grazing the buffaloes. In the beginning of 1943 I began feeling a strange drowsiness most of the time. Though I was not terribly sick but still continued feeling totally listless. I had no energy to opt for any work. I would remain lethargic and in a depressing disposition most of the time. I would coerce myself to go for grazing buffaloes but sometimes my father had to replace me because of my mysterious illness. My father and wife were solemnly concerned about my dubious state of health and endeavoured various ways and means to perk up my condition. They consulted many people and applied numerous home remedies but nothing was working successfully and I continued dwelling in the state of melancholy for a long time. My father and wife now had diversified apprehensions that my illness had some other reason. Like other Sansis their prime focus concluded that I was under the shadow of some evil spirit which was hampering the improvement in my condition. My father prayed at Baba Raul's shrine for me to get better. He discussed with our relatives to discover some way out for my well being. My in-laws were equally troubled about my health. My uncles alleged that I was under the shadow of a strong evil spirit. My father got in touch with some renowned faith-healers and they applied their means to dispel the ill effects of the evil shadow. They even told my father to sacrifice a goat to chase away the evil spirit. Any evil spirit remained there but one of our goats had vanished forever.

My eldest uncle Thaman had three sons but unfortunately none of them survived. Uncle Thaman had one surviving daughter, Kirpi and she was almost of the same age as my father. She was married to Kehru in the village Pakhowal. My father was a lot younger than his brothers.

Most of our relatives were aware of my condition as I constantly lingered on in a state of stupor. My father had informed each of our relatives to look out for any solution as my condition was not improving. My uncle Thaman's daughter Kirpi and her husband were frequent visitors to one Sant in the village Burj Lattan. His name was Bhagwan Singh. They thought of introducing me to The Sant but sought to obtain consent from my father. There were some stipulations attached before taking me there. They discussed about The Sant with my father and informed him that The Sant strictly adheres to the Sikh religion. He has certain pre-conditions before he acquiesced to anybody becoming his follower. One of his preconditions was that the whole family should strictly abstain from smoking, drinking of alcohol and eating of non vegetarian food. Nobody should even enter the house with such banned items. Otherwise The Sant had no restrictions for any caste or creed. Kirpi advised my father that if he wished to send Nathu to The Sant, he would have to strictly comply with such pre conditions accordingly. She asked him to think about it and let her know, only then she would have a word with The Sant.

Now my father was in a perplexed state of mind whether to accept the pre-conditions or not. He was unwilling to renounce the hookah as he had become addicted to it. He had relished smoking for a long time. Secondly it was a ritual to share the hookah in the community; consequently he would be deprived of this diminutive luxury while being in his social circle. Thirdly the hookah was essential to welcome a guest at home if somebody smoked; he would not be able to offer it anymore. He had his own logic not to quit smoking and dreaded to give his consent if he thought of sending me to The Sant. For quite some time he was in a quandary to come to any decision. On the other hand he was also gravely apprehensive about my prolonged illness. My father had already lost two sons and one daughter before I was born. Being his only living son, he could not afford to miss this opportunity to bring me back to a normal condition.

After a tremendous struggle, my father finally got mentally prepared to accept the stipulations of The Sant. At last with heavy heart one day he said to me, "Look Nathu, it would be extremely problematic for me to give up smoking but I can survive without occasional drinking and the eating of non-vegetarian food. On the other hand you are most precious to me; hence for your well being I have decided my priority now."

I could sense critical anguish in his decision and had great commiseration for him. I impelled him, "Father, once you are determined to relinquish smoking then gradually you would be able to overcome your addiction. Drinking and the eating meat are not necessary, and I have to forsake it forever as well."

Actually I had pity on my father as I looked at his gloomy face when he dejectedly said, "Nathu, I am at the crossroads of my life today. If something unfortunate happens to you, the people would indict me forever that he lost his son because he declined to give up smoking. You are beloved to me, therefore for your sake I have decided to renounce smoking and the other things forever."

I appreciated his great sacrifice for me and could not utter a word to him. He quietly walked away and the same day he removed the hookah from our house forever. I could not imagine how he managed to overcome his addiction to smoking but he never complained nor uttered a word to anybody after this. Afterwards his elder brothers refrained from smoking in front of him or my father would avoid being with them when he found them enjoying the hookah together. After some time he became stable and only then he sent a communication to our relatives Kirpi and Kehru that we were ultimately prepared to obey the pre-conditions of The Sant."

*   *   *

Renaissance with The Sant

"My cousin Kirpi visited our village after my father conveyed a message to her to seek assistance from The Sant regarding my illness. She was confident that The Sant would certainly get me back to normal. We planned to meet The Sant on 'Dasmi', the tenth day of the moon at his residence. At that time he used to attend the gathering at his house on that particular day only. I walked alone to his home which was approximately ten miles away from our village. On arrival I discovered that an old man was sitting there and I mistook him for The Sant. Other people like me were indolently sitting around devoid of much activity. I decided to wait for my relatives who had not yet arrived. After a while my relatives also joined me. I was about to inquire about that old man, but in meantime a young man in white accompanied by a few followers entered the house and my cousin signalled to me that he was The Sant. Other people who were waiting for The Sant stood up to greet him. I was quite stunned to see that The Sant was a young man. Actually The Sant had returned after attending a religious ceremony in the village. After sometime his followers set the stage and The

Sant initiated his 'Dasmi' rituals in the presence of Sikh's Holy Book, Sri Guru Granth Saheb. When the ceremony was over, Prasad was served to all. After a short beak, The Sant began listening to the problems of the people one by one. We patiently awaited for our turn and I was curiously listening to the numerous sufferings of different people. When our turn came, then Kirpi and Kehru introduced me to The Sant. They described the whole story about my illness and informed him that my father had already renounced all the forbidden things. The whole family would follow his instructions. They fervently appealed to him to bless me, to get rid of my prolonged illness. He closed his eyes for a few moments and assured us that I would soon be normal. He advised us to be present on the next 'Dasmi'. My cousin was relieved that The Sant had promised to safeguard me. By evening, I returned home and informed my wife and father regarding the assurance promised by The Sant. They heaved a sigh of relief to a great extent.

We impatiently waited for the next 'Dasmi' and I chalked out a programme with my cousin to visit The Sant together. On the designated day we arrived early at The Sant's place. There was the usual crowd to take part in the 'Dasmi' gathering. After the standard ceremony was over, he especially signalled us to come forward. We proceeded ahead and I sat down in front of him. He closed his eyes and recited some inaudible mantras and then blew on my face. He repeated this gesture five times. He sprinkled a handful of Holy Water on my face twice. He instructed me to sip some holy water every day and sprinkle some in the home. He advised me to add more water in the bottle before it was over. He also provided me with some 'guggal', a resin of a tree, to consecrate our house with its smoke every morning and evening. He asked one of his followers to pour some Holy water in another bottle and handed it over to me. He strictly instructed me that nobody should enter our house with tobacco, alcohol and non-vegetarian stuff. No person in the family should worship any deity anymore except God. He directed me to stop shaving and trimming my hair. He then asked me to establish my faith in Sikhism and follow its principles. We bestowed our thanks and promised to strictly adhere to his instructions. We returned home before sun set. My wife and father were excited and I conveyed the instructions stipulated by The Sant.

We adhered to the instructions at home and followed the procedure guided by The Sant. There was a significant improvement in my condition day by day. My family and my in-laws were alleviated at my recovery. I began visiting The Sant every 'Dasmi' and he would repeat the same procedure. After a few months I came back to my normal self. My father and my wife were very cheerful and they would alert every visitor to offload any tobacco items outside before they entered our house. My wife had told her mother also about the new restrictions in our household. My father-in-law and my brothers-in-law used to smoke and savour drinks and meat. Now whenever I visited my in-laws, they would abstain from smoking and drinking in my presence. My mother-in-law would cook food for me on a separate Chula. She wouldn't let anybody take fire from that Chula to kindle the hookah or light a cigarette. They avoided cooking meat in the house as long as I stayed there and religiously implemented all the 'Don'ts' advised and imposed by The Sant. Indeed she was really very happy about my well being.

A slow but steady transformation was taking place in my life but I was not conscious of it.

On every 'Dasmi', I visited The Sant and began actively participating in providing my services there. I was becoming familiar with him now like his other regular followers. I would often go alone but later on my wife also expressed her desire to join me. We would stay there for few days to render our services even after the religious ceremony was over.

With the passage of time The Sant began trusting me more and I was gradually gaining access to the inner circle of his followers. Now he deputed me and another close follower Gurdial Singh, to write paper amulets. Gurdial Singh and I were now staunch disciples of The Sant. Gurdial Singh belonged to the same village as of The Sant. The Sant found us most dependable to accomplish this specialized task. He would guide us how and what to write for different categories of amulets. Every year a month before Diwali festival he would hint to begin preparations for writing the paper amulets. We would write the matter with full sanctity and devotion and hand over this material to The Sant on Diwali day. On the 'Dasmi' gathering, I would also chalk out the list of programmes for The Sant. He would recommend the people to convene a religious ceremony at their homes after their wish was fulfilled. His schedule used to be a busy one and it was my duty to remind him regarding the upcoming engagements during the month before the next 'Dasmi'."

<u>Sample of Paper Amulets</u>

These are two samples of Paper Amulets. One amulet adds up to the total of the number 15 and the second one to a total of 34. The first one was used to put in the water bottle and drink that water.

The second with the number 34 has one in-built paper amulet totalling number 15. This paper amulet was to be put on the person by enclosing it in a metal cover.

*   *   *

My father considered it essential for his children to be religious like him. He wanted to sow this seed in us when we were very young. I began accompanying my father when I was about six or seven years old to attended the monthly gathering of The Sant. I would participate in rendering my services in the Gurudwara. As I grew up I became almost as regular as my father to attend this monthly gathering. I remember those days when my father used to gear up to prepare paper amulets before Diwali. He would organize a fresh black ink pot, a special writing nib and purchase sheets of white paper to sketch the amulets by free hand. He would sit for hours and draw these amulets in hundreds on white paper sheets in a systematic manner. He would uphold the sanctity while writing the amulets. On Diwali day, The Sant would convene a special recitation with his selective followers for the whole night. There was no public gathering ever on Diwali day. I had never joined my father to attend Diwali day recitation at The Sant's place.

During the monthly gathering I would often observe some people who appeared to be under a bizarre effect and they would continue murmuring something or would act in a very odd, weird way. The Sant would attend to these people individually after the religious ceremony was over. Hours would pass by before The Sant finished attending to so many people. A majority of the people would return to their homes the same evening. Sometimes he would give priority to attend to those people who had arrived from far off places otherwise they had to stay there overnight. There was a proper arrangement for such people for food and accommodation. My father and I would generally return home the same evening as both of us had to attend school the next day. Sometimes my mother would also manage take some time off from her busy schedule at home to attend the monthly ceremony. There were a few other families from our village who would occasionally visit The Sant for help.

My father conscientiously obeyed every word of The Sant. The Sant also had a high regard for my father. He behaved with my father with the same deference like his other followers. My father cherished to be in the company of The Sant in this secure ambience. He served there with full dedication and devotion. My father and mother regularly *recited holy hymns at home as directed by The Sant. The image of my father enhanced in the eyes of the Jats' and other higher castes. The Sant never expected or demanded anything from anybody.*

*　　*　　*

A Breakthrough

"There was a blind Jat preacher in our village, Raagi Harnam Singh. He would sing in the Gurudwara and at other religious functions in the village. I would take a buffalo for grazing from his house also. He and his wife appreciated that I visited The Sant every month and recited the Holy Book there. One day when I went to deliver their buffalo, his wife asked me, "Nathu, if you can arrange a steek, a holy book with extended meanings, of 'Japji Saheb', religious couplets, then Raagi would give you lessons how to read it correctly and I will listen to it as well."

I appreciated her idea and replied, "Auntie, I would look for it and let you know."

As I would run from house to house to gather buffaloes, I inquired from a few houses but I could not procure it. I also asked for it from Gurbachan Singh's sister in our neighbourhood. She asked me to wait as she went to search for it immediately. Her grandfather had a collection of some holy books in his house. After a few minutes she returned with another steek but not the same one which I needed. I picked it up and advised Raagi and his wife about it. They were contented that I got at least one steek.

In the evening after delivering the buffaloes in the village, I would visit Raagi's house to read the steek aloud to them and they would listen to it. Raagi was a learned person in religious preaching; he would rectify any mistake in my pronunciation and elaborate the meanings more extensively. Daily I would spend almost more than an hour with them. I continued this routine for a few months till the reading of the steek was over.

During that period one evening when I went to Raagi's house, he was not at home. I enquired from his wife, "Auntie, where is Raagi ji?"

We add the word 'ji' to the name as a mark of respect.

She replied, "Today, he is engaged with his brother."

I wanted to clarify and asked, "Is he with his brother Ram Singh?"

She quickly replied, "No, he is with the Secretary Gopal Singh."

Gopal Singh was the Secretary in the District Education Board in Ludhiana. He had settled in Ludhiana but would occasionally visit our village to collect the revenue of his land. Without wasting any time I headed to meet Raagi ji there. When I called for him, Raagi ji heard my voice and emerged from his brother's room.

He asked me, "Nathu, how come you are here?"

Light-heartedly I asked him, "Raagi ji, you would often boast that your brother is a secretary in the Education Department. Then why don't you recommend me for a placement as a temporary teacher?"

Raagi was amazed by my unpredicted request. He thought for a while and replied, "Nathu, actually it never occurred to me but you come with me right now. I will recommend it to the Secretary to help you."

He immediately returned to the room and enthusiastically asked his brother, "Gopal Singh, here we have a Sansi boy who has passed Matriculation but he is unemployed. I wish you to help him to get a teacher's job."

The Secretary abruptly questioned, "Is he Nigahia?"

"No, No, he is Nathu." Raagi ji promptly replied.

Raagi ji summoned me in the room and I greeted the Secretary, "Sat Sri Akal."

He acknowledged my greeting and asked me, "Nathu, do you want to become a teacher?"

"Yes."

He raised no further queries and advised me, "Fine, you write an application and see me in my office tomorrow."

I asked him, "Saab, What shall I write in the application?"

He advised me, "Just mention your bio-data and a simple request for a job as a temporary teacher."

Then I suddenly realised that I had no clean clothes ready to use. I decided it was better to inform him straightway, "Saab, I don't have any clean clothes. I will not be able to come tomorrow."

He looked at me and smiled, "Never mind, then come after two days."

Raagi ji was glad that his brother had honoured his request. I thanked both of them. I was aware of the incident that the Secretary had an awful experience with Nigahia, another Sansi boy. Some time back Nigahia had approached him for a job. There was only one regular vacancy but another candidate from a nearby village was more qualified to get that job on merit basis. But Nighahia wanted the job with the seniority from the beginning. The Secretary promised Nigahia, 'Look Nighahia, I can proffer you a job but you would be junior to the other candidate for the time being. Don't worry; I will raise your seniority with the passage of time.'

But Nigahia resented at this and declined to accept the offer. He felt bitter about it and said, 'Saab, if you cannot help me now, then what can I anticipate from you in the future?' As Nighaia turned down his offer, the secretary got annoyed with him and felt insulted.

I arrived home and informed my wife and father about this opportunity. I asked my wife to wash my clothes. After two days I visited the Secretary in his office and handed over my application to him.

He looked at it and said, "Nathu, this is all right. You don't worry; I shall work out something for you."

He marked some recommendation on my application and summoned the clerk to forward my application to the Establishment Department.

The Establishment clerk wanted to enquire from me, "Nathu, where do you prefer to join your duty?"

I offhandedly answered, "Anywhere."

He then advised me, "You may check with me after fifteen, twenty days. I will get it processed."

I continued waiting for almost two weeks and there was no response from the Secretary's office. I contemplated visiting there to ask about the status of my application. A few days later I landed in the Secretary's office in Ludhiana. I was desperately searching for the establishment clerk but unfortunately couldn't trace him. Actually in the meanwhile the establishment clerk had been transferred to another section. Incidentally a man from my village, who also worked there, noticed me and reported to the Secretary that I was there. The man came back and asked me to meet the Secretary.

I entered the Secretary's room and greeted him, "Sat Sri Akal."

He looked at me scornfully and asked me, "Nathu, why did you come to this office?"

I hesitantly replied, "Saab, I just came to enquire about my request for a job."

He retorted, "Why? Then what am I sitting here for?"

He admonished me, "There is no need for you to pursue your request in my office. This is my responsibility to follow it up. You can visit the city whenever you wish but not for this purpose."

I had no words to answer and returned home in a dismal mood. But within the next ten days I received an appointment letter for a temporary teacher. I had been asked to report to the primary school in the village Katani Kalan. We were very delighted and I went to Raagi's house to thank him. Though the place was quite far off from my village I could not afford to decline this glorious opportunity.

I had been grazing buffaloes for the last eight years before I got this temporary teacher's job."

Basically the Jats' and the other higher castes had a natural but inherent hate towards the lower castes. There were some exceptional Jat families who had a slightly soft corner for my father because he was educated and had adopted Sikhism. Raagi Harnam Singh's wife would not have normally tolerated a Sansi entering her house. The couple must have observed the religious dedication in my father. They were aware that he went to attend the religious ceremony every month with The Sant and hence provided him a chance to read the steek, which in turn had helped him to raise his knowledge how to accurately recite the Holy Book. They had recognized the religious character in him; otherwise they would not have offered him the liberty to sit near them. Under normal circumstances they would not have given this small opportunity to any other Sansi. It is most important for anyone to grasp the grammatical part and proper pronunciation of the words in the Sikhs' Holy Book to understand the true meanings of the verses written therein. Otherwise it would become tricky to grasp the genuine meaning of what was quoted there. My father had been able to create a small space in the heart of the Raagi's family which paved the way for him to acquire his first job. Raagi gladly recommended my father to his brother only because he had indisputably trusted my father.

*　*　*

Days in Katani

My father was thrilled to share the story when he joined the school as a temporary school teacher. We listened to him intently as he was now exposing the dormant part of his life which was unknown to us......

"Actually the news about my posting to the Primary School in Katani village was already out. It had been proclaimed that a Sansi teacher was joining the school. On my maiden visit I carried only my most essential clothes but no other luggage. In those days for an outsider, accommodation was unavailable in the villages for a short stay. The best option for a lower caste person was to search for a place among his own community people. In the old times the people from the same community would come forward to help a visitor. At that time people trusted an outsider without any misgivings. I also had no other alternative except to look for a Sansi family there. When I reached there I inquired if any Sansi family was living in that village. Luckily there was one Sansi family and I headed to their house. I introduced myself and they were overwhelmed to know that a Sansi had come to their village school. I requested them that I would like to stay with them for a short time until I made a permanent arrangement for my accommodation. They happily allowed me to stay in their home. Fortunately their house was just beside the school.

The next day I contacted the headmaster at the school and handed over my appointment letter to him. He welcomed me, accepted my letter and requested me to submit the joining report. I joined my duty on 15th July, 1946. My salary including all allowances was forty five rupees a month. The name of the headmaster was Mohammed Husain and he had prior information that the Education Secretary had posted me there. The headmaster assigned the charge of the second grade students to me. Being my first job, in the beginning it was slightly strange for me. However in a few days I quickly mingled with the children as we became acquainted with each other. There was no difficulty while teaching the children.

The headmaster was kind and he came to know that I was temporarily putting up with a Sansi family. Perhaps he envisaged my accommodation problem and tried to facilitate me. At that time it was rare to find such a beautiful set up in the village primary school like in Katani. Besides the classrooms, there were two nice medium sized rooms with a porch in the front. In one corner there was a small well and a hand pump in the courtyard. This set up was lying unoccupied and the Headmaster authorized me to stay there on gratis. I was extremely fortunate to avail such an accommodation in the school premises. The headmaster and one more teacher would return to their homes every day in the nearby villages.

The headmaster believed in strict discipline in the school. He had a unique principle that he would not usually permit any ladies to enter the school. If he noticed that a lady was visiting the school he would immediately send a child as soon as she entered the school premises to inquire as to why she had come. The child would ask the lady to wait and find out the reason of her visit. The child would report back to him. If the issue was minor, then he would direct the child what to answer and send her back from there. Otherwise he would permit her to come in and solve the problem.

Our headmaster had a distinctive personality. From the appearance of his attire, anybody would categorically assume that either he was a policeman or a scoundrel. He used to wear a long shirt and chaadra, a piece of cloth trussed around the waist with a typical style of tying. He would proudly display the widely fanned-out end piece of his starched turban. He would dress like this before and after the school hours. As soon as he would reach the school, first he would change his clothes and dress in a normal shirt and shorts or pyjama. He smoked heavily but always avoided it when he was in his classroom. When he smoked in our presence, he would request us to be away from the smoke.

In this school there were almost one hundred pupils and three teachers including the headmaster. Before I joined, there were two vacant posts in this primary school. Both the vacancies were filled up at the same time. Another teacher like me had just joined there prior to me. Gardening was the favourite hobby of this new teacher and he would decorate the school with different types of flowering plants. He would water the garden with the help of the students from the well water.

One day the headmaster came to my classroom and suggested, "Nathu, Why don't you also take interest in gardening like other teacher?"

"Sir, I manage the classes while other teacher is engaged in gardening", I replied

He suggested, "You should also develop your interest in gardening, it inculcates a tendency of working manually. Mere teaching is not enough in life."

I solemnly agreed to it and then began participating in the gardening activities from time to time along with the other teacher.

Some children from the nearby villages also studied in this school. One day some of the pupils of fourth standard landed early in the school and unexpectedly turned up in my room. I was a bit surprised to see them so early and they seemed to be very apprehensive. One of them was named Major and I asked him, "Major, why have you come so early to school today?"

He anxiously replied, "Masterji, today we will be punished in class."

I got slightly concerned about their uneasiness reflecting on their faces and curiously asked, "Why? What happened?"

He bluntly remarked, "Masterji, we have been unable to complete our maths assignment today."

I simply advised, "If you could not find time at home, you can attempt it now".

Major was in distress and answered back, "But Masterji we do not know how to solve it?"

I said, "You could have taken help from some other students."

He was nervous and piteously answered, "None of us have been able to work out the exercise. Basically yesterday we could not grasp it in the class itself."

I light-heartedly said, "Why are you worried then? You are with the majority and you all may be spared."

He could not utter a word further and I had understood their dilemma. In the beginning itself I had sensed their purpose when they approached me. I encouraged them, "Don't you worry, let me cook my food and get ready and then I will assist you to finish your homework."

They were so excited now and wanted me to get ready quickly. They got the water from the well for my bath while I prepared my food. I hurriedly finished my breakfast and got dressed. In the meanwhile some other students of the same class had also arrived early. I asked Major to call the other students also to the classroom. I assisted them in solving their maths problems and they paid full attention to learn it very well. During this time, our Headmaster passed by the classroom and he observed that I was coaching an extra class to his students. I simply nodded to greet him and he responded quietly. The students were unaware of his arrival.

Our headmaster was in-charge of class four students and taught mathematics as well as other subjects. This primary school was up to class four only. The next day we were chatting together during the break time. Without any formality and hesitation the headmaster proclaimed, "Nathu, now onwards you should teach maths to class four students." He assigned the other teacher to give Urdu dictation to his class. Both of us were stunned by his sudden decision.

I had no prior experience in teaching mathematics to a higher class as I was the junior most untrained teacher. I thought that the headmaster may also feel hurt too. I undecidedly replied, "Sir, we are untrained teachers, how could we give lessons to a higher class and besides you are much more experienced than us."

The headmaster was rather impressed when he had discovered that his students were deeply involved in learning when I was teaching them. He appreciated this and remarked, "Yesterday morning when I arrived, you were teaching them maths. There were hardly any students who were even aware that I had come as they were so deeply absorbed in learning. There are some students who do not pay attention at all when I teach them. This means your method of teaching is superior to mine."

I then began taking mathematics classes of the fourth grade students.

Another day when the headmaster was examining the Urdu hand writing of fourth grade students, he noticed that one student had magnificently written that Urdu word. It was absolutely in a different style from the others. The headmaster was impressed and asked that student, 'How did you learn to write this Urdu word?'

The student replied, 'The new teacher taught me how to write it'.

The headmaster appreciated the other new teacher and remarked to him, 'Your Urdu handwriting is stunning. I have noticed it from one particular student whom you have beautifully guided how to write Urdu words and there is a vast improvement in his handwriting. You take charge for giving Urdu dictation to my class'.

The headmaster would not sit idle in his office or observe us when we taught Mathematics or Urdu to his class. During that time he would take over our classes respectively and teach the young children with lots of love and affection. He did not mind sitting on the ground alongside the little children and assist them to read and write. The headmaster had assigned me an additional job to observe the periods in our school. We did not have a clock or a watch in our school. Nearby there was another middle school up to grade eight only. We were indirectly dependant on them in sounding the gong when a period was over. When their period was over, I would immediately ask one of our students to sound the bell in our school too".

My father had experienced the turmoil during the Independence of India when he was teaching in Katani. He described his observations of that gory era. He would sometimes mention about those days in general, but not with extended details of his personal experience and observations. The Independence of India brought turbulence in his life as well. Susan pushed the button on for recording when my father began speaking again after a brief interval.....

"The Independence movement in India was in full swing during that period when we were still in Katani. We would hear diversified stories that the British were on the verge to quit India. Rumours were spreading among the people about the partition of our country. We had no radio, newspaper or any other media of communication available to us in the school. There was no authentic source which would provide current information on a regular basis. Mostly we relied on the verbal information without any authenticity. A strange feeling of uncertainty had engulfed the masses and everybody had some suspicion in his mind. At last there was confirmation that India had become an independent nation and in reality Pakistan had come into existence. The line of division between the two nations had deeply left its imprints in the hearts of the various communities too. The partition between India and Pakistan led to a mass exodus from both nations. Suddenly the hate against a particular community plagued the masses. In no time friends had turned into foes. All of a sudden rumours impregnated the minds of the people with abhorrence against Muslims in the whole country and Punjab was no exception.

One day a doctor from the village turned up at the school and asked me, "Masterji, What would you do now? Circumstances are too volatile and I understand that you and your wife are not protected here as this school is outside the village."

I had my apprehensions as the situation seemed to be beyond control. I knew that my wife and I were vulnerable to any sort of peril but my job was important for our survival. I replied with trepidation, "Doctor, we will stay here only as I cannot afford to quit my job."

The doctor was really concerned about our security. He suggested, "Masterji, in that case, I suggest you better shift to my house to avoid any unwarranted danger. You would be safer in the village than in the school."

We willingly decided and quickly moved out to stay with the doctor.

The situation was dangerous and we often heard that people slaughtered the Muslims, burnt their houses and looted their properties in the night. There was panic in the consciousness of the masses and they had lost faith in each other. Sometimes we would watch soaring spirals of the smoke rising from a few houses in the close by villages. So far nothing had occurred in this village. The rumours in the air added more fuel to spread panic among the people. The government had swung into action and undertook serious steps to rein in the situation. The armed forces had moved in to restrain the state of affairs. They would patrol the villages to maintain intense vigil round the clock to avoid any further damage. People from each village had voluntarily organised night patrolling for the safeguard of their village. One person from each family was put on rotation for perambulation during the night.

Later on when the overall situation had gradually returned to normal, we decided to rent a home in the village. We could have returned to the school premises, but my wife had formed her own circle of friends when we were staying with the doctor.

My wife was pregnant at that time and we expected the child soon. Practically it was better to be in the village to have an easy access to obtain any assistance at the time of delivery. My mother-in-law had joined us after the riots were over. She was an expert domestic Dai. She stayed with us for more than two months. Our first son Bhajan Singh, was born in June, 1948.

After Independence a lot of people were displaced from their dwelling places in both the countries. On a war footing our administration was engaged in planning to rehabilitate those people who had migrated from Pakistan. The government authorities had given top most priority to these refugees. They were assisting them to re-establish themselves by providing shelter and offering jobs in various departments. To create more jobs for them, the government had issued an order to terminate the services of all temporary teachers and the vacant posts were being filled on priority with refugee trained teachers. The same genus of instructions was released in other government departments also. As a consequence I also received a termination letter from the education department. That was the end of my temporary teaching job. I was discharged from the school on 9th October, 1948. My wife and I along with our son returned to our village from there. My total service in Katani was two years and three months."

*   *   *

Modification in Name

66 **I** n December, 1946, The Sant specially announced during the gathering that at the next gathering, he would baptise his followers with 'Amrit', Holy Water. Those people, who were keen, should come prepared. He categorically specified what was required during the ceremony. The Sant recommended my wife and me to receive 'Amrit' and be true Sikhs. There were other people too who were also enthusiastic in following Sikhism. He elaborated in details how to abide by the principles of Sikhism after receiving the 'Amrit'. My wife and I discussed and decided to participate in the baptism. We began our full-fledged preparations for the baptism.

At the next gathering, people who intended to receive 'Amrit' had come prepared with the necessary items. On the day of the baptism, The Sant prepared the 'Amrit', according to the guidelines of Sikhism, with the help of five followers. After the Holy Water was ready he started baptising. We were observing the others when The Sant followed a set procedure to baptise each one. My wife and I were eagerly watching the whole process and awaiting our turn. Finally The Sant executed the rituals and baptised us with 'Amrit' just like the others. When he had almost finished with us, he called for a special attention from the whole gathering. Everybody became attentive. We were astonished because he had not done such a thing for anybody else.

The Sant proclaimed with full ardour, "Please listen carefully; from now onwards everybody should address Nathu as Natha Singh and his wife Nihalo as Nihal Kaur. Nobody should call them by their half names anymore."

Perhaps he wished his followers to be addressed respectfully with their complete names. Half names or nick names gave the impression of some inferiority complex, especially at any congregation.

With this announcement, the whole gathering roared five times with the Sikh slogan, "BOLE SO NIHAL, SAT SRI AKAL."

(With contentment proclaime, TRUTH IS SUPREME AND IMMORTAL).

This slogan is used quite often among the Sikhs for any kind of appreciation or at the end of any function or even during an assault in war fields.

I could hardly believe what we had just heard and I was almost in tears. From Nathu, I have now been labelled as Natha Singh. This gesture had enhanced immense regard in my heart for The Sant. I felt liberated from the tag of my half name. My wife too was glad with this declaration. Everybody there congratulated us with full fervour. That was truly the happiest day of my life.

I now decided to change my name officially as well. I sent out a press release in the newspapers and informed all the concerned departments to amend their records accordingly."

*   *   *

My father, Nathu had now become Natha Singh. The Sant had unleashed a new epoch in his life. He had vanquished a psychological siege from his mind which brought him at par with the other people. His half name had always shadowed a big inferiority complex on his personality. He could have altered his name officially without any restriction but being socially elevated by The Sant, made an authentic difference in his life. It immediately reflected an impression that the person belonged to a low caste. His half name had become his identity as a low caste sans any introduction. He wasn't ashamed of his caste but being recognized by his name as a low caste really made him cantankerous. For a stranger his half name would become a basis to hate him, when practically that stranger had nothing to do with him. In the past he felt the sting in his heart whenever his half name exposed him to be a low caste. Nobody displays a tag around his neck to declare his low caste, but being branded in a particular situation where it had no relevance at all, made it even more agonizing. He was educated and deserved to be addressed with some respect like all the other educated people. But now The Sant had religiously stamped his full name and my father had become a true Sikh. The word 'Singh' was included with his name which not only completed his name but added some respect also. This modification had infused a tremendous relief and began to foster a new confidence in him.

Sansis and other low caste people including ladies generally had half names, such as Baggoo, Chhotu, Massa, Biroo, Gaata, Thaman etc. Nobody made any attempt to look for a respectable name after the child was born. Different trends were followed while assigning names in the family. Sometimes a really simple method was adopted to name a child. If the child was born on a Monday (Somvar), his name could be Somu, or if on Tuesday (Mangalvar), then the name could be Mangal or Manglu, if on a Wednesday (Budhwar) it could be Budhu etc. Sometimes they would name a child from his appearance, e.g. if the child appeared innocent, would be named as Bhola. If the child looked stout, would be named, Thaman. The youngest child could be named, Chhotu. If the child appeared weak then he was named Chuha, meaning rat. There was no specific propensity to pick a name for a baby. Sometimes names were even based on the Hindu gods and goddesses. Some names originated from the Indian names of the months. If the child was born in a month name 'Vaisakh', the child's name could be Visakha, for 'Sawan' would be named as 'Saun' or 'Sawan', for the month 'Maghar' the name could be 'Maghar', and for 'Phagan' would be named as 'Phagan' or "Phagu" etc.

The Jats always practiced to name their children properly. They would assign the name in a religious manner. They would generally go to the Gurudwara and ask the preacher to read a verse from the Holy Book. The first letter of the verse would be used to keep the name of the child and add 'Singh' or 'Kaur' along with it for the male and female child respectively. Later on names were then followed by their surname. The Jats children also had nicknames, such as Mahi, Ghulla, Saun, Ghaoo etc. but these names were generally used in the village. But outside the village and for any other official purpose, they would use their full names. Unfortunately the low caste people had to use their half names everywhere.

My father ensured to assign proper names to his children in a religious manner as followed by the Jats. He always requested The Sant to do the honour of naming his children. He rarely allowed anyone to address us by any nickname. If anyone attempted to give a nickname, he felt offended and straightway forbade that person from doing so. On a few occasions I observed my father striving to complete the name of other people too if someone just had half a name. He would add the second part of the name himself thus making it sound respectful. When he talked to other persons in the Sansi community, at his discretion he would address them by completing their names like, Tulsi Ram, though he was only called Tulsi, Sadhu Singh, was called just Sadhu by everyone else. However the elders from the Sansi community from his generation always addressed him as 'Nathu'.

*　　*　　*

Sansis Courts

*M*y uncles also updated me that in the ancient times the Sansis had hardly ever approached regular government courts to resolve their disputes which occurred within their own community. They remained subdued when they had dispute outside the community. The Sansis were so poor that it was tough for them to stomach the expenses in the government courts for the fees and for hiring of lawyers. Nobody was certain when any decision would be reached. The law had also restricted their mobility. Since the courts were in the cities, each time to be present there, they had to seek police permission. If their opponent was powerful then he could manipulate to prolong the case for years. Government courts always based their decision on proofs and witnesses. Possibly the Sansis could provide proof but it was nearly impossible to produce a witness who would come forward in their favour. The rival would play all pressure tactics either to compel the witness to deny the facts or coerce him to turn hostile. So there was hardly any likelihood for them to *seek true justice from the government courts. Usually they preferred to lie low and bear the injustice.*

To avoid the cumbersome process of the government courts, the Sansi community contemplated to settle atleast their own disputes within the community rather than approaching government courts. They worked out their own viable virtual judicial system incurring hardly any expenses at that time. I had personally heard some stories that when one Sansi had a problem with another Sansi in the community, he would raise the issue in the community for its settlement. No other caste person could meddle in their decision making procedure nor would they entertain the disputes of other communities.

There was a proper virtually assigned judge from the community and both the sides would pursue the case through their advocate, i.e. any person who could represent the side effectively. Most of them were illiterate people. But the judge had the authority and his decision was binding on both sides. There was a provision to appeal at a third place in case one side was not satisfied with the decision.

My father carried on in defining the justice system further.....

"As the population of the Sansis had considerably augmented, they widened the set up of their judicial system. They divided different large areas into separate zones and then further into sub-zones. For each sub-zone they designated a Lumberdar as a Sansi headman. There was no election procedure for the selection of these Lumberdars. The Sansis from that sub-zone would opt to nominate a responsible person as their head. These Lumberdars had the authority of 'Mohar', stamp. The mohar didn't exist physically but his word was a stamp itself. This headman had the respect of the whole community. The issues concerned with the entire community of each area was deliberated and determined at the sub-zonal level.

There was a set procedure to submit any case in the Sansi community. In old times if a Sansi who had a dispute with another Sansi, would present his case in the community and tender 'gur' along with one rupee twenty five paisa to register his case. The community would nominate a judge and he would summon both the parties. He would decide and demand jewellery or cash as a security deposit. This deposit was collected as a binding of decisions on both sides. If one party absconded in the middle of the hearings, his deposit was forfeited. The other party was declared the winner of the case and received that deposit as compensation. The second motive of the security deposit was that both parties would maintain proper discipline during the proceedings. If anybody misbehaved or acted unruly at any point, the judge would impose a penalty on him.

Anybody could observe and listen to the proceedings of the Sansi court but not utter a word without the permission from the judge. The Sansis would gather in the open designated space and while listening to the case, they would enjoy sharing hookah with each other. Both the sides would present their case through their advocates, called 'bhorwal'. The advocates would formulate their strategy to convince the judge with their point of view. If need be then they would provide an evidence to substantiate their view. They would often enlighten their point in a very captivating manner. It could be through a long narrative about a king, animals or folk tales etc. this would expend considerable time. At the conclusion of the whole story they would co-relate the moral of that story with their point of view. The judge would continue listening to both the sides one by one. There was nothing in writing and the judge would just register all the points in his head. He could also cross-question both the concerned parties. If necessary the judge would discuss the point with other community members before reaching any conclusion. He would then proclaim his verdict on the basis of his judgement. If the decision was acceptable to both parties then the looser would disburse all the expenses incurred during the proceedings. When the case was closed then the judge would return their security deposits to each of the concerned parties.

If the looser requested for a 'parakh', appeal, then the judge would forward their case to the next agreeable place to both sides. The judge would accompany both parties to that place with 'gur' and introduce them to the community there. He would also brief them about the dispute and his decision. The whole process would restart there.

During the British times the district courts honoured the Sansi courts. One could not file a suit in the government court if his case was in progress in the Sansi court. Even if one of the parties endeavoured for it then the opposite party would inform the government court that their case was pending in the Sansi court. The government court judge would refuse to listen to them till their case was adjudicated in their community.

'Parakh' would no longer stretch the case forever. Finally a decision had to be acknowledged one way or the other by both the parties. If either or both the parties still would not abide by the judgment then the judge would demand to conclude it on the basis of 'Varana' or 'naim'. Under critical circumstances one of the parties may openly challenge their opponent to accept the decision or come forward for Varana. If one of them repudiated to accept this challenge, he was believed to be guilty.

Varana

Varana was a process implemented in extreme cases to ascertain the guilty person. This method was devised in old times and I had witnessed it once in my life. This procedure was entirely based on faith and myth. The secret behind this progression is very simple and effective. People always believed that an innocent person does not have a guilty conscience. He is intrepid in his head and being truthful, he is prepared to undergo any sort of trial.

The Sansis firmly believed that the water is a 'devta', an angel. The devta won't tolerate the guilty person to stay in his embrace. If the person is innocent then he can be underneath the water as he has no guilt in his mind. The guilty person will always carry panic in his conscience and bubble up in no time. Hence truth will always prevail.

When the concerned persons did not abide by the decision, then Varana was the last resort. This happened in rare cases but it had a significant occurrence in the Sansi community. The whole community in that area, including the general public would take a deep interest to witness this soul searching event.

There was a proper course of action before the individuals were primed for Varana. The judge would announce the date for Varana and firmly fix the terms and conditions of this gruelling exercise. He may demand an additional security deposit from both the persons. Once the concerned individuals were determined to undergo Varana then both of them were kept in isolation for a certain number of days and observe celibacy. This was a sort of purification process and time to probe their conscience and admit the guilt if any one of them was at fault. They were repeatedly asked by the judge during this period if any one of them had altered his mind to withdraw.

To initiate the process of Varana the judge would select a pond about six to eight feet deep water. In the deepest part of the pond, two platforms were constructed above the waterline. A long bamboo pole was erected beside the each platform. There would be an attendant on each platform. The judge would ensure this arrangement personally and he would be solely responsible for any deficiency in the foundation. Everything was properly marked and set up well in advance.

On the designated day, both the individuals contesting Varana were fetched from the isolation. The judge would elucidate the rules once again to them. He would repeatedly enquire from them if they had second opinion in their mind. If both persons were still obstinate, then he would allow them to proceed. The attendants would guide them to the platform in the pond. The attendants would stand on each platform and each contestant would stand in the water by holding the bamboo pole. The judge would verbalise a short prayer to the water 'devta' to bestow justice to the innocent person.

There were two methods adopted while going for Varana and choice was open for the contestants. One was based 'on breath' and the other was on 'khundi', a stick with a bent head. The contestants would watch for the signal from the judge when the Varana was 'on breath'. Both men would leave the poles and plunge into the water by holding their breath after the signal was flaunted by the judge. They would endeavour to stay underneath water as long as they could hold their breath. The one who came out from the water first was considered to be guilty.

The Sansis strongly believed that the guilty person would hardly be able to immerse his head under water. During this time if the other person was still under water then the attendant on the platform would plunge into the water and bring him up.

If the Varana was contested on 'khundi', then the modus operandi was different. In this process, a 'khundi' was erected at a distance of 100 yards away from the pond. A fast runner was kept standby to sprint from the pond to fetch the 'khundi' and return to the pond with it. The distance to the 'khundi' was pre announced to both persons. When the judge flaged the signal, both the contenders would leap into the water and the runner would dash from the pond to fetch the 'khundi'. Anyone who surfaced first from the water before the runner returned with the 'khundi', would be adjudged guilty. If none of them poped up then both were believed to be innocent but this situation had never occurred.

In the old days, sometimes the opponents' were permitted to use expert divers as their substitutes. Since the expert divers had no guilt in their minds they could effortlessly stay under water. In certain cases they held their breath for so long that they ultimately expired under water. Consequently the substitutes were banned and only the persons involved in the dispute had to participate in the Varana.

The guilty person would find no place to hide his face to avoid public embarrassment and he would be severely and candidly condemned among the community. Everybody would censure him and he was damned for not voluntarily accepting the verdict.

Naim

"If the Sansis were involved in a petty dispute, rather than calling a Sansi court, they would often decide the issue by insisting on taking the naim from the accused. To invoke the naim means to take an oath in the name of their deity or some religious place or on their own child etc. Generally this method was applied for resolving small family disputes among the Sansis. For example, if a person accused the other person for a small theft or over a petty problem, the accuser would insist from the accused to bestow the naim to confirm that he was not culpable. After the accused called upon the naim, a period of ten to fifteen days was fixed to observe the ill effect. During that period if the accused or anyone in his family fell sick, then he was automatically considered guilty. The accuser would believe that their deity had chastised him by making him sick. In every area, the Sansis have their own 'jathera', a local deity, like Baba Raul in our village.

Binda

There was another method called Binda to dig out the truth from the guilty person. This method was an extreme measure. Binda is an iron plough, about two feet in length and one foot wide generally used by the farmers in the old days to plough the fields. They would heat up two iron ploughs to glowing red. Then they would place seven Peepul tree leaves on the hand of each concerned person who were involved in the dispute. On the top of these Peepul leaves they would place the hot plough. They would be asked to take seven steps with the hot plough on their hand. The Sansis believed that the hand of the true person would not get burnt. The person who dropped the plough first was considered to be the guilty. This system was also based on the belief that the true person had the nerve to carry the hot plough on his hand and the guilty person had the fright in his mind that his hand would get burnt. Binda was said to be in practice in very old times".

* * *

Reincarnation

We were untiringly listening to the happenings in the life of my father. He had great vigour and enthusiasm to ceaselessly speak for a long period. After a long spell of talking, I would ask my father if he required a break for some time. Instead he would ask us if we were tired and wanted to take rest. Otherwise he was ever geared up to talk nonstop about his memoirs. We replaced the batteries in our tape recorder and switched it on once again to record another episode of my father's life story.....

"My presence at the monthly function of The Sant was always essential because I was now one among the few ardent followers who would co-ordinate the monthly programs before the full moon day. Irrespective of time and situation I would make it a point to arrange my leave in advance to participate on a regular basis. One follower of The Sant was serving in the Indian army and he wished to present a copy of the Sikhs' Holy book, to The Sant. During his long annual leave he fetched a copy of the

Holy Book without notifying The Sant in advance. The Sant did not have a proper Gurudwara at that time and he already had a copy of the Holy Book at his home. Since his disciple had fetched another copy of the Holy Book, now The Sant considered it absolutely necessary to build a Gurudwara. At one monthly gathering, he proclaimed his wish for constructing a Gurudwara. For this holy cause, a man from his village enthusiastically donated a piece of his land for the site of Gurudwara. This land was at the most ideal location and convenient for the people to comfortably visit. After all the government formalities were completed to transfer this land, The Sant then organised a ceremony to lay the foundation stone of the Gurudwara.

Many people donated building material while the construction was in progress. The followers of The Sant willingly contributed financially and involved themselves manually for labour during the construction. I along with my wife camped there for some days to bestow our services along with the other followers. Day by day the Gurudwara building was gradually coming into existance. The Sant had designed the Gurudwara in two parts. The main building had three adjacent rooms, one for the Holy Book, the second for the serving disciples during the function and the third room was for The Sant to attend to the visitors after the monthly function. In the central room there was one underground bunker exclusively meant for The Sant to recite peacefully.

Three rooms of the main building were complete and now we were engaged in the construction of two other rooms meant for the visitors. There was another follower of The Sant named Sarmakh. He was a bachelor and used to practice black magic in the past. He once visited there and attempted to gauge the spiritual powers of The Sant with his black magical powers. The spiritual powers of The Sant turned out to be too potent for him and ultimately he admitted his defeat and surrendered. He divulged to The Sant that he would dispense with his black magic and remain in his service until death.

Our first son was very frail after birth and he would often cry a lot. My wife would carry him around and continue extending her services in the construction work. Sarmakh would often comment about my wife that a mother should ideally be like her. She is concerned about her crying son and yet at the same time voluntarily dedicated herself to the construction work. Time and again The Sant would spend time with his followers to monitor the construction. One day when The Sant was supervising the construction work, Sarmakh repeated the same comment about my wife. The Sant also heard his remarks and casually asked him, "Sarmakh, do you wish to accept Nihalo as your mother in your next birth?"

Sarmakh did not answer but rather appeared to be lost in some dream world for a moment. When there was no response from Sarmakh, The Sant repeated his question, "Sarmakh you have not riposted to my question. Would you prefer her to be your mother in your next birth?"

In fact we were all stunned when The Sant again asked Sarmakh such an earnest question. Though we had full faith in the spiritual powers of The Sant but we were unaware about the depth of his powers. That too to the extent of granting somebody's wish to that level. At once there was pin drop silence and the construction work had momentarily come to a halt. We were all enthusiastically observing Sarmakh and waiting for his reply to The Sant. This situation was rather unique in its own way as Sarmakh was still silent and appeared to be in an impassive mood. After a while Sarmakh emerged from his sombre mood and seriously responded to The Sant, "Yes, I wish her to be my mother in my next birth."

The Sant closed his eyes for a moment and said, "Sarmakh, your wish will be fulfilled."

Instantly all the followers resounded, "BOLE SO NIHAL, SAT SRI AKAL."

Sarmakh now looked calm and contented. We resumed our construction work. Since Sarmakh had been practicing black magic, perhaps he had the ability to foresee the future. We were resting after lunch when Sarmakh joined us. He was in a trance for a while and then enthusiastically wished to share something mysterious with us. He looked at us and presaged three things, "In my next life, I would be the dearest to my mother and she would miss me the most. Secondly, I would get married nearer to my present village and have one child. Thirdly, I would reunite with my soul companion who had longed for me over the ages."

We listened to Sarmakh whole heartedly and were astounded about his vision. Sarmakh passed away after a couple of months. My wife and I were curious about our next child who as predicted, would be the reincarnation of Sarmakh. We believed in the spiritual powers of The Sant and his capability to bless Sarmakh. We were confident that his word would come true about Sarmakh. Our second son was born and as he moved on in his life, we observed that every word of Sarmakh was turning out to be true.

The Gurudwara construction work was nearing its completion and The Sant installed the new Holy Book and commenced holding his monthly gathering there now."

*   *   **

Panth System

I firmly believe that the Panth system is a perennial curse among the Sansi community in some areas. This system had extensively damaged the community rather than cleaning any bad elements from it. In the olden times the elders had sought to streamline and imbibe discipline among the Sansi community and hence imposed some curbs to deter the individuals falling into unethical relationship among the community. Otherwise the undisciplined community would have produced many social criminals in the hamlet as well as in the whole community. Susan was absolutely ignorant about such a system among the Sansis and completely astonished about this extremely complex system. She was incapable of easily grasping this and I had to elaborate the finer details to eliminate her qualms after my father had described the Panth system to us.

Nobody could ever entirely eradicate the social evils from any society but the elders among the Sansis remained vigilant to keep their community under check. They had endeavoured to have strict control over the community so that no individual should go astray and spoil the network of social relationship. This Panth system was unusual but unique exclusively among the Sansi community. My father commenced explaining the most intricate design of this system among the Sansi community.....

"Amongst the Sansis, any person who committed a condemnable felony by violating the social relationship was called a social criminal. One of the major evil doings in this case was, when a person had established a permanent or temporary illicit relationship with a woman within his extended family network. Such an individual was considered a social criminal. For example, an uncle, having an illicit affair with his niece or a person having an illegitimate affair with his uncle's wife, etc., such kinds of abnormal relationships were not tolerable but forbidden amongst the Sansi community. In such cases, only the man was indicted and held responsible for it. He was tagged as a 'social criminal' by the community.

The Sansis have two major clans, Mahla and Beedoo and they marry their children in the opposite clans. If a Mahla man had an illicit relationship with a Mahla or Beedoo niece or aunty, then he would be termed as a 'social criminal' among the Sansi community. Nobody would accept such immoral relationships within or outside their clan. People are always cognisant about such occurrences within the community. The Sansis would call a community gathering to sort out the local disputes or punish the social criminals. The elders of the community would assemble and nominate the jury amongst themselves to decide on such matters. During the gathering the judge would inquire from the social criminal whether he is guilty of his forbidden relationship or not. If the person confessed to it and agreed to break off the relationship, he would beseech the community to pardon him. The judge would discuss the issue with the community members before reaching any conclusion. They would declare the person guilty and bestow a punishment. He would be fined a few rupees and asked to perform some community service. Such a person was then declared 'Sharrey', meaning liberated. After the completion of his punishment, the society would accept him into its main stream. But he would stay blemished for his entire life.

The major problems occurred when the concerned person declined to confess being guilty and raised objections to the allegation. Occasionally the accused would not confess, to avoid humiliation in the whole community but instead rebelled. Then the judge would diktat to the whole Sansi community in the area to ostracise him. They would declare that nobody should have any association with him in the future and he should be shunned by the community. This was far easier said than done. Such a person would have his own family, relatives and other family friends in an extended network. They would endeavour to defend him and carry on maintaining their usual relationship with him. As a result, the community would get divided into two factions, one group in his favour and the other would be against him. Such situations would lead to the creation of a 'Panth', a faction, in the name of the alleged person. As a consequence the community would brand this concerned person and his supporters with a 'Panth' in his name. His supporters would be identified that they belong to the 'Panth' of such and such a social criminal in the community. If there was any doubt then the people would not hesitate and openly ask the other person to which 'Panth' he belongs to. If the person belonged to the opposite group then they would refrain from establishing any relationship with the concerned person. The supporters of the social criminal may possibly belong to both clans of the Mahla and Beedoo because of the extended family network in the community. Hence the community would automatically get alienated into separate faction. Even one or two such cases were adequate to smash the whole community network. People would not marry their children in the opposite factions but within their own circle.

Among the Sansis, the children of a brother and his sister could be given in marriage. Generally most of the Sansis would abstain from it but it was socially acceptable. The narrow network of the 'condemned person' or social criminal and his supporters would fall short especially for the social activity like marriage. People from their own group may not find suitable matches for their children in the same Panth network. Consequently they had to search for better prospects outside their faction.

Now the major question was how to cross the barrier between two opposite factions? Suppose a person in one

Panth found it hard to search for a suitable match for his child in his own group then he would look out for the possibilities in the opposite group. He would often approach through a middleman to initiate negotiations with the person in the opposite group on his behalf. When a person from one group contacted another person in the opposite group, he would make up his mind to pay the penalty without any doubt before approaching the person in the opposite group. If the concerned person in the opposite group approved the proposal then both the families would directly sit together and settle the marriage. But the person who had approached with the proposal would be asked to pay a penalty of a few rupees to the person in the opposite group. By paying the penalty, it now meant that his family had switched over to the opposite group. Such a switch over was never considered a matter of any disgrace and it was openly acceptable in the community. One could switch over to another group without any vacillation but not without paying the price for it.

Crossing over from one group to the opposite group appears to be very simple but it had serious repercussions. The person, who had crossed over to the other group, would have to abandon his relationships with his original Panth including his extended family network. He had to shun his own relatives including his married children, brothers and sisters on his original side. Neither would he be able to invite them for any important family occasions or vice versa. He could meet them without any constraints or ill feelings in day-to-day life but not at any significant occasions. He would be barred from participating in the most important social functions like marriage or any religious function or death in the family.

Later on if the same person resolved to return to his original Panth, he could go ahead at his discretion but again the people in his original group would demand a penalty from him for switching back from the opposite group. Suppose he crossed back to his original group then again he would not be able to sustain a relationship with his present relatives. He had to abandon them as it may be his own daughter or son who had been married into the other group. His daughter or son would now no longer belong to his group.

Practically, the people had no personal enmity between different groups but they got alienated only because of the compelling circumstances based on their personal interest. Unfortunately they had become victims of the circumstances. Many a time none of the individuals would be directly connected to the alleged 'social criminal' but they had been pushed to be a part of this complex system. Though it was simple to cross over to any group by merely paying the penalty, however its consequences had shattered the personal, family relationship both ways. There was no taboo among the community if one switched over the sides but its consequences were too painful.

There were comprehensive repercussions of this Panth system would have its impact during any important occasions. Suppose there was a marriage in the family, obviously both parties would belong to the same group by virtue or by paying the penalty. On arrival, the wedding party at the bride's place, would be scrutinized by the girl's family before being welcomed there. If the girl's family suspected any member who belonged to the opposite group, the welcoming would be put on hold. They would question the groom's father and he had to explain. If he could not prove that the suspected member belonged to his group then he would have to administer the penalty instantly for inviting him. If he agreed to pay penalty, then this would modify the Panth status of that suspected person. He would now be considered a part of the same faction. If the groom's father declined to pay the fine, then either the suspected person had to leave or he would not be honoured during the ceremony. Only after a concrete decision the marriage party would be welcomed and served. This principle of scrutiny is applicable to both the sides. The bridegroom's side too could question the girl's side if they suspected any relative belonging to another group attending the marriage from the bride's side. The Sansis observed this process very strictly and would always be careful not to be caught on the wrong foot. They would avoid paying the penalty unnecessarily and being disgraced at any occasion. People would constantly be vigilant before participating in any kind of function amongst their relatives. They would not wish to be humiliated openly if there was a slightest chance of being questioned about their presence.

Among the community there is no secret as to which family belongs to a certain Panth. When any family crossed over to the other side, the whole community would become aware of it. All the concerned relatives would be on their guard as its impact would affect them in the future when they would personally get involved.

I once participated in a local Sansi gathering which was held in Narangwal in 1937 and I was studying in grade nine at that time. The community discussed about a few social criminals. The Sansis from our village presided over this gathering and my eldest Uncle, Thaman, was one of the judges. The community had assembled in the open place outside our village. The Sansis from the nearby villages would arrive in the morning and return in the evening. Some Sansis from far off villages too had participated in this gathering with the passes. The jury would begin the proceedings and discuss the key issues. Some young boys and I provided community services to take care of our guests. A sufficient number of hookahs were organised for the guests which was a luxury for them while listening to the proceedings. The majority of the Sansis shared hookahs and we rekindled them. They would not permit me to do so because I was studying. They would call some other Sansi boy to serve them. They considered it beneath the decorum of an educated boy to rekindle their hookahs. The Sansis from our village served the guests to our best. At the end of this gathering they punished three social criminals."

This Panth system had wrecked the nucleus of love and affection among families and literally shattered the Sansi community. The elders always wanted the welfare of the society and wished its members to remain under the social ethics, but unfortunately the Panth problem had become a double edged weapon to destroy the human relationship among the community. In general close Sansi families and relatives would normally be friendly with each other but at any vital juncture they would behave more like enemies. A family could be celebrating a happy occasion but undoubtedly there would also be someone in that family who had been banished to join that event because of the Panth system. Unfortunately the Panth system had stood in the way without any personal fault.

The Panth system would not even show mercy to a dead person in the Sansi community. Imagine if someone died in a family, messages would be dispatched to the relatives. Generally every close relative would surface even if they were in the opposite Panth. After everybody had gathered then the family of the deceased would decide as to who would carry the dead body to the cremation ground. Now this moment would be very crucial. Generally to shoulder the dead person on his last journey is considered to be a great honour. Unfortunately if the close relative belonged to a different Panth, he would not be permitted to participate in any of these rituals. If he insisted on partaking, he would be asked to pay the penalty first.

If the fine is paid by the person then his group would automatically be switched over. Such a situation could crop up even between two blood brothers. If a relative had lost the battle in resolving the Panth issue then the family would not even allow him to proffer 'khappan', a piece of white cloth to cover the dead person.

Over the years the educated people among the Sansi community have made efforts to abolish this Panth system but they have failed to gain any success for several reasons. Nearly every family had grievances and their sufferings had piled up and compelled them to become arrogant. The opposite group of the social criminal person would not submit to abolish the Panth system without penalising the accused person. Secondly, in the old times the majority of the Sansis were illiterate and their thinking had not rationalised with the passage of time. The illiterate older generation being in the majority would not listen to the younger educated people. Some of the illiterate younger generation had the same thinking akin to the older generation.

The Panth would automatically gets abolished after the death of a 'social criminal'. Most of the social criminals, old persons had passed away. Thus the system is dying its own natural death. In the recent times no new Panth has evolved so far.

*　　*　　*

Brooms

*T*o visit my mother's hometown was always enticing during summer vacations from the school. My grandmother loved me a lot and we would enjoy chatting with each other for a long time. She had a large family and her sons had their own extended families now and lived independently. Visiting each family of my uncles always filled me with exhilaration. During summer time most of the Sansi ladies would assemble under shady trees and produce brooms from the raw material. In winter they had the luxury to bask in an open space and truss the brooms as well. The raw material of the brooms had a lot of downy flowers on it. When the ladies sorted out the brooms, its flower would keep on flying here and there. Whenever I walked through these feathery flowers, it would invariably stick to my pyjama. The ladies would laugh at me when I struggled to get rid of it. They had no intentions of making fun of me but felt amused when I tried to shake it off. After segregating the brooms, they would store it and the men would transport it on the head,

donkeys or bicycles to sell it in the villages in exchange
for grains or money. Sometimes my maternal uncle would
fetch brooms on his cycle to our village and stay overnight
with us.

My father narrated a very interesting story about brooms
and we recorded it.....

"Brooms were primarily used for sweeping the houses.
The Sansi families in Narangwal were hardly involved in
producing brooms but the Sansis in other villages were
heavily occupied in trussing them. They would procure
the raw material for the brooms which mainly grew wild
in the river beds and on the banks of canals or drains.
The Sansis would store the broom material during the
season and subsequently produce the brooms on a large
scale throughout the year. They would barter it for food-
grains or money. There were specific areas where the
broom material would grow naturally in plenty. Some
Sansi men from other villages would form a group and
travel to far off places for garnering the broom material.
They would establish a temporary camp there to slash
the broom material. After accumulating loads of it, they
would transport it to their village.

A long time ago some of our ancestors had travelled
to fetch broom material from the river bed near Karnal
which is now a district in Haryana State. After the
tiresome journey of a few days, they landed in Karnal
along with their paraphernalia of camels and donkeys, to
transport their stuff used during their stay and bring the

broom material on return. As per the law they reported to the police there. The head constable on duty stared at them suspiciously and asked, 'Who are you? Why have you come down here?'

They got petrified but replied, 'Saab, we are the Sansis from Ludhiana and we have arrived here to collect broom material from the river side.'

They furnished the police authorisation to the chief constable. He scornfully gave them a dirty look and examined the police permission certificate. Abruptly he changed his colour and retorted, 'I am shocked to see that you have travelled during the moonless nights. Who has given you the permission to travel? Go and sit down there.'

The Sansis were stunned and walked away dejectedly. They muttered among themselves and sat down in a nook of the police station. They were discussing among themselves that the chief constable was a very obstinate man. They had no clue what to do next. Under the circumstances they were afraid of landing in jail. They were terrified and had no guts to ask the chief constable as to what their fault was. They believed that even if they dared to enquire, he would not pay any heed to them. At that time the police inspector was not present in the police station. They had apprehensions that if the chief constable behaved in such a manner, then the police inspector would undoubtedly take stringent action against them. They would be penalized and sent to prison. They felt trapped without any cause.

In the evening when the police inspector arrived at the police station, he spotted that a group of dirty looking people were sitting in one corner. He questioned the chief constable, 'Who are these people? Why are they sitting here?'

The chief constable gazed at them and remarked, 'Saab, they are the Sansis from Ludhiana and have arrived here to collect broom material from the river side.'

The inspector seemed to be perplexed with the answer and questioned him again, 'But why are they sitting here? Have they landed here without police permission?'

The chief constable adamantly replied, "Saab, they certainly have police authorization but they are not supposed to travel during moonless nights."

The inspector was now irritated with the chief constable and questioned him again, 'Then what is your problem? This is the responsibility of their area police inspector and superintendent of police to comply with the stipulated restrictions of their travel on moonless nights. What is their fault? Why did you hold them?'

Now the chief constable hung his head down and became speechless.

This group had a glimmer of hope and they appreciated the police inspector who was not unduly prejudiced like the chief constable.

The police inspector turned towards the Sansis. They bowed to give him 'Salaam'. He casually questioned them for some genuine details. After being satisfied he asked them an unexpected question, 'A long time ago there was a police inspector by the name of Haider Ali in Dehlon police station. What was the opinion of the people about him?'

This tricky question was hard to answer as they had no knowledge about him. They believed it was better to admire rather than commenting something else. They cautiously responded, 'Saab, our elders used to have high regards for him. He was supposed to be a really nice gentleman.'

The police inspector then began laughing and said, 'I am Haider Ali. I was posted in Dehlon police station for four years before being transferred to Karnal. I knew your elders very well.'

The Sansis were tremendously relieved and now expected to leave the police station scot free.

The police inspector was in cheerful mood and demanded from the chief constable, 'Where is their police permission certificate?'

The head constable timidly handed over their certificate and the inspector scrutinised it. He appeared to be satisfied with it and ordered the head constable, 'You stamp their certificate with 'Arrived' and 'Returned' stamps right now.'

The chief constable was utterly aghast to hear this and asked, 'Stamp 'Returned' also now?'

Without any vacillation, the inspector ordered the chief constable, 'Yes! There is no need for them to revisit here for the stamp before their departure. You stamp it right now.'

The Inspector further remarked to the chief constable, 'Do you know that these Sansis from Ludhiana are totally different from the Sansis of Karnal? They hardly indulge in any unlawful activities and I can trust them.'

He then asked the Sansis, 'Would you like to have some tea?'

They were so scared and wished to disappear from the police station as quickly as possible. They said 'no' in unison.'

The chief constable quietly took the certificate from the Inspector and stamped it as instructed. With great embarrassment he then returned the permission certificate to the Sansis.

They were contented that lots of unnecessary trouble had been averted. They thanked the Police Inspector and quickly slipped away from there."

*   *   *

JVT Training

"The Independence of India made me and my family dependent on my father once again. After getting discharged from my temporary teaching job, I was now unemployed. I had no other options in the village to earn money. On top of this I had now become a father which saddled me with additional responsibilities. I was unable to save much money from my temporary teaching job as we had to purchase everything in Katani. Whatever we had saved, would not last for very long. My wife too was equally worried as she avoided expecting money from my father because of her differences with him. I desisted to ask money from my father as well. Once again I resumed applying for several jobs but for the time being, the partition of India had blocked most of the job opportunities for me. After waiting for a few months nothing seemed to be working. In the absence of any other alternative, yet again I looked forward to my old reliable profession of grazing buffaloes.

Now I fully realised that if I had to adopt teaching as a profession, then I must undergo a teacher's training course, otherwise I would not stand any possibility. I explored around for admission in the teacher's training course in different schools. But it was already late as the admissions were over and the formal training sessions were about to commence. There was a young man from our village who had recently got admission to the teacher's training course, I enquired from him, "Friend, would you please let me know if there is a new advertisement for the teacher's training course in any school? I am keen on getting admission."

He replied, "Look Natha Singh, the admissions for this year are over and our classes are going to begin soon. But if there is any information, I will certainly let you know."

I was disappointed and it appeared that I would have to wait till next year to get admission. I began grazing buffaloes once again and managed to move forward in life with the help of my wife.

One Rajinder Singh from our village was a retired headmaster of a private school in Kurali village. That school had a Junior Vernacular Teacher training (JVT) course. He had been in-charge there for a long time and still had a good rapport with the present headmaster as well as the school management. In that school there were a few vacant seats left in the training course even after the main selection was over. Earlier he had recommended three other students for the teacher's training course. After that, once again Rajinder Singh got another request from the school to recommend two more students for the same course.

I used to graze a buffalo for Rajinder Singh. One day when I went to return his buffalo in the evening, he was engrossed in reading something. When I went to deliver his buffalo he excitedly said, "Oh, Nathu, come, come. I was waiting for you."

Mentally I thought that my payment was not yet due, so why was he calling me? I apprehensively approached him and said, "Saab, the month is not yet over and I have not requested for any advance."

He guffawed and remarked, "Do you wish to carry on grazing buffaloes lifelong or are you interested in joining some teacher's training course?"

I quickly replied, "You know the selections begin in April and now it is early June. There are no seats available for the training course this year."

He enthusiastically added, "No, no, there is an exceptional possibility but are you interested in going for it?"

I could not believe what I had just heard. This was a God sent opportunity and I hurriedly accepted his offer, "Yes, I am very keen about joining this course."

Rajinder Singh explained the whole situation and asked me to check with my father. I returned home and asked my father. He was ready but had some trepidation, "Look son, you have been out of touch with your studies for many years. Would you be able to manage this course?"

I confidently replied, "Yes father, I would surely manage it without any impediments."

My father agreed to pay for the expenses for the course. I gladly went back to Rajinder Singh and informed him that I was all set to join the training course. Rajinder Singh was pleased and said, "Fine, I will prepare a recommendation letter for you, collect it tomorrow morning from me."

I was excited and looked forward to collect this letter and proceed for training. The next morning when I went to pick up the letter from Rajinder Singh, he was not at home. Only his sister was at home and I enquired from her if he had left any letter for me.

She thought for a moment and said, "No, He has not mentioned anything about any letter."

I was disappointed and wondered how Rajinder Singh had forgotten to leave a letter for me. It seemed to me that my high hopes were dashed and I continued grazing buffaloes.

After five or six days when the wife of Rajinder Singh was sorting out his clothes for washing, as usual she went through his pockets. Surprisingly she found a letter in one of the pockets. She asked Rajinder Singh, "What is this letter in your pocket?"

When he saw the letter, he was extremely shocked. He had forgotten to hand over the letter to me. The next morning when I was assembling the buffaloes in front of our house, I heard someone bellowing to me from a distance, "O Nathu, O Nathu, wait, wait."

I stopped there and turned around to find, it was Rajinder Singh. I didn't approach him but instead waited for him. He asked, "Why have you not collected the letter for the training?"

I was bit upset and crossly replied to him, "Where is your letter? How could I proceed without it?"

He felt a bit embarrassed and took out the letter from his pocket and handed it over to me and said, "Nathu, I forgot to hand over this to you that day. Now take this letter and rush without any further delay."

"Don't you think it may be a little too late now?" I wanted to reassure myself before he left me.

"Don't worry, they will certainly admit you." He enthusiastically answered.

I had a simple principle in life, before leaving from my village if I was uncertain whether on arrival food would be available or not, then I would not hesitate to carry my own food with me. So I decided to carry some homemade food with me as my wife had prepared a sufficient quantity of 'choori', rotis mashed with gur, and ghee. It was semi dry stuff and would last long without getting spoilt.

The next day I went to Ludhiana to board the train to Kurali. When I reached Ludhiana railway station, I found out that my train was running late. Kurali railway station was located in the middle of the jungle and it was feared that the jungle was teeming with dacoits and robbers who would loot the train passengers. The sun had already set when the train departed from Ludhiana. Passengers disembarking at Kurali were twitchy. They were conversing among themselves various stories about how dacoits robbed the train passengers in the night. Most of them stated that they would not be able to make it to their home in the dark instead they would rather stay at the railway station. I was just listening to them but I seriously got concerned as I was visiting there for the first time.

The train arrived very late at Kurali railway station and it was already pitch dark. The platform was dimly lit with kerosene lanterns. About twenty passengers disembarked there. The station master seemed to be perturbed. He was marching up and down on the platform and continued shouting, "I'm not responsible if anything happens in the dark. There is no security here."

The passengers were bewildered and inquisitively looked at each other. At last one man retorted, "Station Master Saab, look, if you are petrified and do not permit us to stay at the railway station then we will camp just outside the station, but we have no other alternative except to spend the night here. We cannot risk our lives if we travel to our villages at this time of the night."

The Station Master was still panicky if something happened in the night, he may get into trouble. But he was warning the passengers in advance, 'I earnestly understand the situation. You can stay at the railway station but I cannot protect you if anything goes wrong in the night.'

One of the passengers firmly replied to convince him, 'You don't worry about it; we won't hold you responsible for anything but we are better sheltered here rather than risking our life.'

The Station Mater had cooled down now and walked away to his room. Gradually the people began locating a comfortable place on the platform to settle down for the night. I also found a place like the other passengers. There was no provision for food at the station. I was hardly feeling hungry under such anxious circumstances but I opened my 'choori' packet and munched a part of it. Some people kept on sitting in the open on the platform. Everybody was attentive in his own way. After sometime there was utter silence in the dark except the various sounds of insects from the jungle. Fortunately that night passed by peacefully.

After dawn people began moving to their destinations slowly. There was no rush for me as I knew the school would not open very early. I had to find out about the school before I left the station. I enquired from a man at the station, "Where is the boys' high school?"

He asked me, "Which one? There are two high schools."

I replied, "The one that has the teachers' training course."

The man instantly said, "Oh, then you should go to the Khalsa High school. If you follow this road, automatically it will lead you to the main road. The Khalsa High school is located right there."

There was plenty of time and I thought of taking a bath before proceeding from the station. There was an oxen-driven well near the station and I headed to the well. After I finished my bath, I wanted to have breakfast with the balance 'choori' from last night. I started from the station and followed the road which connected to the main road. At this intersection there was a bus stop as well as a tea stall. I paused there to have a cup of tea. The school building was within striking distance from there. I finished my tea and entered the school. I asked one of the teachers, "Sir, where can I look for the headmaster? I would like to meet him."

The teacher pointed to the man in blue, who was standing at a distance talking to someone. I approached the headmaster, greeted him and handed over the letter of Rajinder Singh. He read the letter and immediately called one teacher, "Shastriji, please take him to the in-charge of the teacher's training course."

Shastriji led me to a classroom where the teacher-in-charge was busy lecturing the tenth grade students. When I noticed the class was in progress, I decided to wait outside but Shastriji went inside the classroom. Shastriji went away advising me to wait for the teacher. After the class was over the teacher-in-charge came out and I greeted him, "Sat Sri Akal."

He promptly inquired, "Natha Singh, do you know Punjabi?"

I answered, "Yes Sir, Punjabi language was my major subject in Class ten."

Straightway he directed me, "Okay, Natha Singh you deposit the fees and fetch your luggage."

I inquired, "Sir, how much are the fees?"

"Forty rupees", he replied.

I had not carried that much money and I was falling short of funds. I hesitantly asked, "Sir, I have only thirty rupees at hand. I will deposit twenty-five rupees now because I require five rupees to return to my village. When I come back I will deposit the balance money."

He understood my situation but smiled and suggested, "Natha Singh, don't be anxious, your admission is confirmed. You can go back to your village and deposit the total amount on your return."

I thanked him but could not believe my luck. I was extremely pleased that I got admission in the JVT training course. For me this opportunity had come absolutely out of the blue. The recommendation letter of Rajinder Singh had worked wonders. As I was coming out, I met another student and we greeted each other, "Sat Sri Akal." We formally introduced ourselves to each other. His name was Ralla Singh.

He reckoned that I must have come in connection with the teacher's training course. He expressively asked me, "Natha Singh where do you come from?"

I earnestly replied, "Ralla Singh, I belong to village Narangwal near Ludhiana city."

"What happened in your interview? Was it tough?" he enquired curiously.

I innocently replied, "Nothing, I just got admission and was asked to deposit the fees."

He was absolutely stunned and looked at me as if I had said something strange. After coming out of his daze he commented, "Natha Singh, nobody else could be luckier than you. You were simply asked to deposit the fees and fetch your luggage without any test and interview. On the other hand we had been grilled here for three days and had one test after another. Only then were we able to get admission."

After I heard Ralla Singh, I also could not believe that my admission came through so effortlessly. We chatted for a short while and I took leave from him and headed for the railway station to board the train.

I returned to my village and went to express my gratitude to Rajinder Singh at his house. I explained to him what had happened there. He advised me to study sincerely as I would not get such an opening again. My father and wife were glad that I finally had an opportunity to become a qualified school teacher. I requested my father for money and without question he handed over a hundred rupee note for my fees and other expenses.

Since I had to stay there in the hostel, I had to arrange for my bedding and other necessary things required for my daily use. We began gathering old bed sheets as we had no fresh beddings at home. My wife somehow managed to mend a patched bed sheet from the old and tattered ones. My bedding merely consisted of one thin and dirty looking cloth sheet to spread on the bed and one to cover myself. I packed two old sets of clothes for my daily use. We were not in a state to purchase good clothes at this point. I could not afford to demand more money from my father to spend on my clothes. I had to manage with whatever we possessed at home. One could easily gauge that my overall condition was pitiable. At the same time I had an ominous feeling that there could be a strong possibility of discrimination against the lower castes. I assumed that under the present circumstances I might confront an inevitable situation there. There would be many students from different castes and places. So to be on the safe side I asked my wife to pack one glass, one plate and one small bowl along with the rest of my belongings.

I returned to the school with my luggage and contacted the teacher-in-charge. I handed over the hundred rupee note to him. He smiled and looked at me after taking the hundred rupee note. He collected the fees along with the hostel charges. Since the school had its own hostel, no student was permitted to stay outside. I joined the hostel and this was the first time in my life that I was going to stay in a boarding school.

The regular admission process was already over and we were only five or six students who had joined very late. Five students from Rohtak city had also joined late. One of them was believed to be a relative of the Divisional Inspector of Education in Rohtak. As we had joined late, we all were allotted space in one room in the hostel. To adjust all the students in the hostel, the school authorities had put five to six students in each room. Each student was allotted one wooden box to hold his belongings and one bare bed for sleeping. The School charged twenty five rupees a month for the food and lodging. Students were permitted to fetch ghee or other eatables from home if they wished.

We were forty-three students in the teacher's training class. On our first day, we all assembled in the classroom and our teacher-in-charge introduced himself. He first noted the attendance of the pupils. After the attendance was over, he asked the students to introduce themselves individually. When the preliminary introduction was over, he briefed us in short about the whole training programme. After this he asked the students to pay special attention and said, 'Now I would like you to select a Prefect among yourselves for the hostel. His responsibility would be to hold a strict vigil on the other students, ensure that everybody is studying after dinner and maintain discipline in the hostel etc. If the Prefect observed somebody creating any nuisance, he would report it to me.'

He offered the students to volunteer to undertake this responsibility. The students looked at each other; the teacher in-charge gazed at them and eagerly waited for their response. Nobody volunteered to accept this responsibility. Our teacher in-charge waited for some time and ultimately deduced that nobody would come forward for it. He was disappointed with no response but said, "It seems to me that nobody is prepared to carry out this responsibility voluntarily. Now I have to propose any one among you."

There was pin drop silence in the classroom and students looked at the teacher intently. The teacher in-charge scanned the whole class for a few moments and then he suddenly proposed, "Natha Singh will be your Prefect."

I was amazed and could not believe his announcement. I promptly urged the teacher, "Sir, It would be difficult for me to accept this responsibility. I belong to a different district and I am not aware about the local conditions. I request you to select a local student as a better choice."

But the teacher-in-charge was determined and said, "No, I have decided that you will be the Prefect."

The other students clapped and congratulated me. I had no other option apart from accepting it. The rest of the class seemed to be relieved now.

The regular teaching classes had now commenced. Our teachers would give us lessons from the syllabus books. After the classes were over we would return to our rooms. After school hours it was compulsory for all the students to play any outdoor game or take part in any other physical exercise. Since this was a Khalsa school run by the Sikh organisation, all the students were supposed to gather for the prayer in the evening. As a Prefect it was my special assignment to ensure that everybody attended this compulsory evening prayer. By the time this prayer was over, our dinner used to be ready.

The day I began sharing the room with the Rohtak students, I could sense some awkwardness among them towards me. They would stare at me and mumble among themselves in their local dialect which was incomprehensible to me. This whispering would continue among them but they would not utter anything openly to me. I had a creepy feeling that maybe they abhorred me as they could make out that I belonged to a poor low caste. I have read such unambiguous messages in the eyes of hundreds of people who hated the low castes. These Rohtak students would endeavour to circumvent me as well as touching any of my belongings. There was no specific ground for me to rake up any issue without cause unless something practically surfaced. I just remained a silent observer amidst them.

There was no need for me to conceal anything as my living condition itself was evident to enlighten them that I belonged to a poor family and a low caste. Most of the other students had better clothes than me. I had no respectable looking clothes to wear. My bedding was in a shabby state. My old, soiled and patched bed sheet reflected my stark poverty. I was undoubtedly convinced that the Rohtak students as well as the others must be familiar with the fact that I belonged to an untouchable Sansi caste.

My fate had pushed me as well as the Rohtak students into a very rough and tough ordeal. The students from Rohtak belonged to the Hindu Brahmin families. Every day they strictly pursued the Hindu rituals in the morning and evening. Their religion had compelled them to keep a distance from the untouchable low castes. But now a Sansi belonging to the lowest caste was living with them in the same room. Normally they would abstain even from the shadow of people like me. Now, how could they stomach the reality of living with an untouchable? Imperatively they were never supposed to see the face of a low caste person in the morning. But in reality when they opened their eyes every morning, a lowest caste person was amidst them in the same room. They felt religiously polluted with my presence. Unfortunately, under the present circumstances they could not escape from me. But at the same time their sweltering odious eyes had created an aura of hate around me. I had faced situations like this before but this source of hate was too close and unremitting.

The school belonged to the Sikh management and smoking was strictly prohibited in the school premises.

But the Rohtak students would still smoke in the room. They were scared that I may report it to the teacher in-charge but I remained least bothered about it. Initially everybody would have food together at the same large dining table every day. Gradually I could perceive a deep repulsion in the eyes of the Rohtak students while we ate together. They preferred to maintain some distance from me in the dining hall. Finally one evening when we were having dinner together these five students from Rohtak could not tolerate me having dinner together with them any longer. I could discern a flaming odium in their eyes and gloominess on their faces. For unknown reasons they could not dare say a word directly to me. Ralla Singh had also joined us for dinner and sat with us at the dining table. One of the Rohtak students got up and took him aside. He whispered something to Ralla Singh. For a few moments he discussed something with Ralla Singh. After they returned to the table, I could sense some dilemma on the face of Ralla Singh and the student. I clearly discerned that something was definitely amiss. I perceived that their problem was possibly associated with me as Ralla Singh could not make eye contact with me after he returned to the table. I silently continued having my dinner.

After dinner, Ralla Singh and I were returning together to the hostel. He was bashfully laughing yet feeling embarrassed to mention anything. I waited and wanted him to open up and explain candidly whatever he had to say. Suddenly he asked me to stop and cautiously commented, "Natha Singh, I want to say something but I am feeling too embarrassed to verbalize it."

For a moment I felt a shiver slither up my spine, for I perceived that he was going to break some awful news. I retained my courage and asked him frankly, "Ralla Singh, there is no need for you to hesitate, instead speak out bluntly whatever you intend to say."

He mustered up the courage and pitifully said, "Natha Singh, the Rohtak students want you to refrain from sitting with them whenever they are having food at the dining table. They are Brahmins; this is against their religion to eat food in the presence of an untouchable."

I was stunned but not offended when I heard these words. This was not the first time that I had confronted any humiliation in my life. Once again I had to absorb this ache and bury it in the depths of my heart. I promptly choked back my pain and dared to hold Ralla Singh by his hand and led him to my room. I opened my wooden box and displayed my utensils to him.

I explicitly expressed to him, "Ralla Singh, I had anticipated such a situation before I departed from my village. Look I have already carried my own utensils considering such an incident may occur. I came fully prepared in advance to tackle such a situation."

Then Ralla Singh said, "No, no, they are not demanding you to use your own separate utensils. They just do not want your presence when they are eating."

I was now openly naked that I belonged to a lowest caste. There was no fright in my mind to conceal anything

about my caste. I had realised my purpose of being here. I
further added "Ralla Singh, I have not joined this training
to fight with people over my caste but my mission here
is to become a trained teacher. Tomorrow morning I will
carry my own utensils to have food in the dining hall. Let
the whole world know that Rohtak students do not wish
a lower caste to be around them in the dining hall. I will
sit aside and eat food in my own utensils. If my mere
presence is irking them now, then tomorrow they could
cry about the utensils also."

Ralla Singh was speechless, looked at my face and
hesitantly departed without uttering a word further.

The next morning when I arrived for breakfast, I carried
my own utensils with me. Everybody was bewildered to
discover that I had brought my own utensils. Finally one
and all were fully cognizant of the whole episode. There
was a great deal of criticism against the Rohtak students
but nobody uttered a word to them about this incident.

This information had also reached the school authorities.
This was an odd situation for them to initiate any action
against the Rohtak students. Discrimination against the
lower castes was a widespread thing. Nobody had any
antidote to eradicate the hate from the minds of the higher
castes. The school authorities could not demand from
the Rohtak students to stop hating me. So prima facie,
there was no basis for them to take any action. On the
other hand I had not reported the matter to the school
authorities because there was no solid reason for me to
act against them.

The People working in the kitchen felt bad about it and they were very sympathetic towards me. Actually they planned to harass the Rohtak students now. They asked me, "Natha Singh, we will support you in teaching them a lesson. Since you have begun utilising your own utensils, do bring them but you must come along with them."

The staff in the kitchen could not provide three or four rotis to each student at a time. They would initially give just one or two rotis and later on we could ask for more. They described their plan to me, "Natha Singh, you come with them and stand with your plate in the queue in front of them and don't move until you get five or six rotis in your plate. If the Rohtak students object, we will answer them."

After the incident with the Rohtak Students, I now had no reason to lie low and enclose myself in a shell. I decided to participate in the innovative plan of the kitchen staff. I would ensure that I came along with the Rohtak students whenever they visited the dining hall. I would wait with my own plate and it would take a while to receive four or five rotis at a time. During this time if the Rohtak students requested the counter staff to serve them also, then he would advise them, 'You have to wait. Natha Singh avoids asking for more rotis when you are around. We have to give him five or six rotis at one go.' Then the Rohtak group understood that it was the aftermath of their dirty thinking and they could not help it. I would now intentionally sit away from them and eat my food comfortably.

The Rohtak students were ill at ease with my presence amongst them in the room as well. Whilst in the class they would sit far away from me. I presume that they must have discussed this with their parents about an untouchable sharing the room with them. They were looking for a way out to escape from the shadow of a Sansi even after class was over. They earnestly requested the Headmaster to permit them to stay in the Kurali town to elude my presence in the hostel room. Since they had the recommendation from a senior Education Officer, the Headmaster couldn't turn down their request. He authorised them to stay outside but under certain stipulations. He sternly instructed them that he would maintain a vigil on them from time to time. If he found them missing from their place or loitering in the cinema hall, he would take punitive action against them. The Headmaster also mentioned to them that he understood what their real quandary was. So finally they vacated the room and partially got rid of me. I also felt a great relief from their continuous yet contemptuously piercing eyes.

During the class we were given assignments to organize a module for the primary school classes. Now I had a key advantage of my two year stint as a temporary teacher. When I was teaching in Katani, I had come across a small booklet titled 'Guidelines to compose Lessons.' I had purchased a copy for one rupee at that time. So I had honed my teaching skills with the help of that book. Our teacher-in-charge assigned me to devise a writing lesson for the third grade students. Incidentally my first lesson was precisely as mentioned in that booklet. With suitable amendments I transmuted it from that booklet in Urdu to Punjabi. Now this lesson had to be presented in the class in the presence of our teacher-in-charge.

One of my friends, who had one flawed eye, forewarned me that he would pull my leg in the class during the presentation of my lesson. I was confident about my preparation; I laughed and said, "I won't mind at all. You have the full liberty to try your best."

I presented my lesson in the class in such a way that the whole class was impressed. I supposed that the presentation of my lesson was up to the standard. After my presentation was over, there was a discussion and comments from the other students and I satisfied them with my answers. Finally my naughty friend stood up and commented, "Natha Singh, I have a serious doubt about your presentation."

"What is it?" I demanded.

He tried to be witty and alleged, "Natha Singh, there was a flaw during your presentation. You see, the blackboard is black and your complexion is also as dark as blackboard. Consequently the students couldn't distinguish much between the blackboard and the teacher!"

The whole class was now laughing wholeheartedly and I was also amused with his impish comment. Perhaps the teacher-in-charge gauged his implicit remark and he said, "Natha Singh, you hold on I will answer his comment."

I was prepared to confront my friend and I requested the teacher, "Sir, this is my lesson, why should you reply? I will clear my friend's doubt."

The whole class suddenly became silent and looked at me but curiously waited for my reply. I counteracted smilingly, "My friend is absolutely right, that blackboard is black and I too have a very dark complexion. But during my presentation his defective eye was on the same side where I was standing, hence he could not distinguish between the blackboard and me; but the incongruity is that he presumes nobody else could see me and the blackboard."

Laughter rippled through the class and my naughty friend felt a bit embarrassed.

But the fact remained that the colour of my skin had really turned very dark as a result of grazing buffaloes in the scorching sun for years.

The teacher-in-charge was completely satisfied with my presentation and highly appreciated it. He stood up in the class and commented, "Natha Singh has delivered a flawless presentation in this class. I sincerely appreciate his remarkable efforts."

After this presentation I had become very popular amongst the whole class. They carried an impression that I had vast knowledge about teaching but there were some other students among us who had also worked as untrained teachers for some time. When any other student presented his lesson, during the discussion most of the students would make personal comments rather than making healthy criticism about his presentation. I would only make specific comments if required.

During the first half of the session of my training course, the school had charged me the full fees. We had a few students among us who were ex-servicemen from the army. One day they were discussing with the headmaster about the study grant. I was also present there and hence requested him, "Sir, is there any possibility of a study grant or scholarship for me?"

The headmaster enthusiastically replied, "Yes, yes, Natha Singh you will also receive a study grant. You come to my office and fill in the necessary forms; I will forward it for sanction."

After a few days our Headmaster visited the district headquarters and on his return he informed me, "Natha Singh, your study grant has been sanctioned and in a few days you will soon start receiving money."

I then began receiving grant of twenty rupees a month which helped me a lot to cover my school expenses.

The responsibility of being a Prefect was a cumbersome job. I had to spend my own study time to keep a tab on all the students but somehow I managed it.

During our training programme there were lessons on cooking and our teacher-in-charge would create separate groups and ask them to cook together as a team. He had instructed us that there would be practicals for cooking together during our final exams and our performance would be graded accordingly.

Our training course was nearing its end as our theory exams were almost over but our practicals for cooking and other handicrafts were yet to begin. The date for the cooking practical was drawing nearer. Since I had joined late at the time of the admissions, now coincidentally I was grouped with the Rohtak students for the cooking practical. I had waded through an awful experience soon after I joined the course but once again a testing time was looming up ahead. Yet again our fate had brought us face to face with each other without any escape. Everybody in the school was curiously probing as to what would happen now. How were the Brahmins going to participate in a cooking exercise together with a lowest caste untouchable Sansi? That question was ringing in the minds of everybody.

One day Ralla Singh shared the views of the Rohtak students with me as he had inquired from them, what would they do now and how would they eschew Natha Singh during the cooking exercise? He told me that they feel terribly tormented merely with the idea of sharing their kitchen and cooking with me. The circumstances had cornered them once again and there seemed to be no way out to ignore me from this cooking exercise. The participation of each and every student was mandatory in this joint exercise because marks were to be awarded for this practical exam.

One of the Rohtak students who had grumbled the most said to Ralla Singh, 'Now the circumstances have inevitably compelled us to include Natha Singh in our cooking group. We are coerced to compromise our religious sanctity but even under duress we cannot shun the untouchable now. When we return home after the exams, we will go through our purification rituals or even pay the penalty for being under the shadow of an untouchable including cooking food with him.'

Another rigid fellow protested vehemently and strongly argued with Ralla Singh, 'How can we cook with an untouchable? How is it possible? We should proscribe Natha Singh and deny including him during the cooking exercise.'

The others abruptly cut him short saying, 'What nonsense are you talking about. You are forgetting that this is a joint exercise. We would unconditionally be disqualified in the exam.'

On the other hand the Rohtak students now had no nerve to talk to me directly. They were feeling embarrassed to discuss this issue with me. At the same time I was also making my assessment to resolve this intricate problem. I had come to a personal understanding that I would not achieve any objective by blemishing their religion. They detested, eschewed and disregarded me, it was their problem. I was sensible enough to comprehend the complexity of their situation under this dubious caste system. They were grown up in this strictly controlled environment and it was impossible for them to shed it off overnight.

Finally Ralla Singh wanted to gauge my opinion and asked me, "Natha Singh, then what have you contemplated about this cooking practical with the Rohtak students? There are only a few days left before the exam."

I answered indecisively, "Ralla Singh, so far I have not come to any conclusion. Let's us wait and see how those students interact with this problem. I have not planned anything yet."

Ralla Singh deferred to discuss this issue and departed without uttering a word.

One day I happened meet one of the Rohtak Students who was more rigid about his religious sanctity. I asked him, "Friend what have you people decided about the cooking exercise for the final exam? Is there any possibility by which you could shield your religious consecration?"

He was absolutely dejected and replied in a distressed tone, "No, Natha Singh, we have sincerely thought about it from various aspects but there is no solution to safeguard our religious sanctity. When we return home, we would be widely condemned among our community."

"You know the date for the cooking practical is approaching shortly; please let me know whatever you decide." I wryly told him.

With anguish he replied, "Actually we are in an absolute fix and unable to seek any possibilities to wade through this cumbersome exercise."

He counter reacted promptly but doubtingly asked me, "Natha Singh, by the way have you thought of any solution to solve this convoluted muddle?

I merely smiled and casually replied, "Don't worry; I will look for a viable solution to this issue."

I marched away leaving him speculating about my answer.

Of course I was also fretful how to work out a plan to get through this cooking practical. Luckily a genuine idea popped up in my mind to tackle this problem. I mentally visualised a cooking scene and tried to perceive how everybody could be seen working together during our exam at the time of inspection. I virtually assigned the duty of each person and realized that I could suitably fit myself in that perfect scene without blemishing their religious inviolability. A crystal clear view emerged in my mind and I was delighted with this flawless design.

The next day incidentally I came across the same fellow and hinted to him, "Friend I have a workable plan and if you all are interested then we can discuss it."

All of a sudden his face brightened up and he was curious to know about it. Still unbelievably he asked me, "Natha Singh, do you actually have an answer to solve our problem?"

I beamed confidently and replied, "Yes, it is an effectively workable solution."

Their group had lost all hopes but now he was desperately eager to know and quickly asked me, "Natha Singh would you please let me know of your plan?"

I decided to unveil my plan and expounded to him, "Look, on the exam day you people cook the food according to your religious dedication, and I will not impede all of you at all while you are preparing the food. Rather I would stay away from you. Only at the time of inspection I will position myself just outside the marked boundary of your cooking area and push just one dry piece of wood into the hearth at that moment. This way it would appear that our cooking has been a joint-venture exercise. Do you think that plan would be passable for you?" I inquisitively enquired from him.

He was astonished when he listened to my adaptable plan and could not believe that I had designed it so immaculately. He was extremely thrilled and expressed his enormous relief, "Natha Singh if you could assist us to implement your plan then we will be highly obliged to you forever. We would be spared from undergoing a taxing process of religious purification."

He immediately informed my plan to his other friends and they were absolutely thrilled. All of them came to me and said, "Natha Singh we are out rightly satisfied with your impeccable innovative method. Now tell us what should we cook during the practical exam?"

In life I had eaten simple cooked rotis with chillies or onions. I hardly ever relished any delicious dishes at any occasion. I casually replied, "You may cook whatever you like. I do not have any particular preference."

On the day of our cooking practical, the Rohtak students marked a boundary of their cooking area and washed it with mud and cow dung to sanctify it. They were engaged for more than an hour preparing their kitchen area. The cooking material had been purchased in advance and I too contributed to the expenses. I quietly sat away and extensively observed them executing their rituals before they started cooking. I had candidly declared to them that if they wanted my assistance, I would be available at any time. They were now pleased merely with the fact that my annoying presence did not interfere with their cooking process. They chopped and cooked some mixed vegetables which were to be served with some boiled rice. Their favourite sweet dish 'kheer', rice cooked with milk and sugar, was also on the cards. When they were cooking 'Kheer' I noticed that the examiners along with our teacher-in-charge were heading towards us for inspection. I alerted the Rohtak students and instantly positioned myself outside the limit of their marked kitchen. When the examiners arrived there, all of us pretended to be occupied and I just picked up a piece of dry wood and thrust it into the fire. Our teacher-in-charge just smiled at my act and the examiner asked us, "Have you prepared the food together?"

We replied in unison, "Yes Sir, we are cooking the food together."

Then the examiners scrutinised the cooked food closely and tasted a morsel of it. Subsequently he noted something in his booklet. Immediately after this they were on their way to inspect the other students. The Rohtak students were elated to get through this exercise smartly. After the food was ready they jovially said, "Natha Singh, in the homes people generally serve the Brahmins first but today you deserve to be served first. We shall eat afterwards."

The Rohtak students first served me and waited till I finished the food. Soon after that they ate separately.

After the practical was over, later on Ralla Singh evidently questioned the rigid fellow from that group, 'So now what is your opinion about Natha Singh? Has he not sagaciously dragged you out of the sinking sands of your religious confinements?'

The fellow hardly had any answer but replied, 'Yes, Ralla Singh, now we all confess that we were wrong. Natha Singh was seldom against us but we were incapable of understanding him then.'

Fortunately all the students passed in the final exam in the JVT training course. The school had to forward the certified list of the bona fide trained JVT teachers to the district education department. Our teacher-in-charge was specially authorised to issue the certificates in this connection. He had an aversion towards the Rohtak students and protracted issuing them their credentials. He deferred to oblige them under one pretext or another. Finally he gave out the certificates to them without any approving comments. When I requested him to inscribe the certificate for me he politely advised me, "Natha Singh, you wait for some time, I will let you know when I am in a better frame of mind."

One day he was sitting alone after issuing the certificate for Ralla Singh. He appeared to be in a good mood and called me, "Natha Singh, you also fetch your form, I will certify it now." He thought for a moment and then endorsed a distinctive remark in my certificate.

Quote:

> 'Though Natha Singh belongs to a criminal tribe, he does not illustrate any characteristics which portray any propensity towards criminal activities.'

Unquote.

In addition to this certificate, the headmaster also issued a character certificate to all the students. The headmaster also specifically mentioned propitious comments in my certificate as follows.

Quote:

> 'With great pleasure I certify that Sardar Natha Singh is qualified in Hindi and Punjabi in the JV teachers' examination held in March 1950. Nature has gifted Sardar Natha Singh with all the essential qualities of a good teacher, in his head as well as heart. I testify the nobility of his personal demeanour and character.'

Unquote.

Signed/Nanak Singh

I concluded my JVT training in the session of 1949-50.

*   *   *

My father had secured the right of admission at par with the other students for this training course by passing class ten. This training period would have been an exception in the life of my father if he had not experienced the wraith of being an 'Untouchable' during his Teachers' Training course. He had been explicitly pushed to the wall by the high caste Brahmins. His five classmates from Rohtak belonged to the premier privileged class of the Hindu Brahmins and instinctively felt affronted by observing equality between the high and the low caste, the rich and the poor during their stay in the room with my father. Despite being rich and from the highest caste, they had not practically extended any assistance or favour to my father so that they could always make him feel inferior to them. But fortunately they were born and grown up in the culture of dominance over the lowest castes, hence could not digest the presence of my father around them. Under normal circumstances in life, untouchables like my father would stand with heads down and folded hands in front of their house and they would hardly talk to them. They would not permit them to get into their homes. But by living with them in the same room there was a direct invasion on their supremacy on all borders by an untouchable, which was way beyond their unexpected dreams.

Without any imagination my father must have felt a deep stab in his heart each time the Rohtak students had overtly begrudged him. But time had tamed him to stomach such humiliation as a part of his life and created a tested and trusted character in him to endure such scathing attacks. He had envisaged the state of affairs before he departed from his village and hence carried his own utensils. He openly declared to the world around him that even though he was an untouchable, he had no shame in eating in his own utensils. He had no vacillation in standing in the line by carrying his own utensils to have food. Let it be known to the whole world that he is a Sansi however he firmly held his ground where nobody could demean him any further. I consider this episode with the Rohtak students was the worst kind of dehumanization in his life.

As a human being, my father must have experienced a mind blowing tempest in his heart irrespective of being used to endure humiliation quite so often in his life. Innumerable questions must have arisen within him when the Rohtak students had maltreated him. Was it his fault if he was born into the Sansi caste? He had never touched the food of the Rohtak students, then how could he blemish their so called religious sanctity merely by his presence? If the Rohtak students were supreme because of their caste, then what was the objective of education, a mere tool to get a job after this training? If education could not entrench improvements in a person to be civilised to respect other human beings, then what exactly was its fundamental objective? What kind of training would be doled out by the Rohtak students as teachers, to the coming generations especially to the lower caste children at the primary school level? Unlimited unrequited questions must have spun through his mind. The other upper caste students in the class could not express their antipathy as bluntly as the Rohtak students because of his physical propinquity to them. In their own way the other students would maintain an unnoticeable coldness towards him. The most laudable component of this episode was that under such torn apart conditions, my father did not overlook his crucial aim of being at that place. He did not contemplate abandoning his training to run away from further squalor, but rather remained steadfast to complete his training programme. He had swallowed a bitter pill of candid mortification as he was not in a position to strike back at the Rohtak students. May be the teachers and the school administration might have sympathy with him; but they could not take any action against the Rohtak students. Nobody raised their voices against this unjust and inhuman conduct. Only the staff working in the kitchen dared to avenge them.

If we look at the broader perspective then both sides were victims of the prevailing social norms and had undergone the undue tremendous mental agony because of social precedence.

*   *   *

Permanent Job

"After Independence, the government was able to resolve the issue of settling the refugee teachers on priority basis, yet there were additional vacancies in the government schools. The Education Department had reconciled the list of all the qualified teachers from various training institutions in the state. Eventually they initiated the process of filling up the pending vacancies in the schools. I was eagerly waiting for my posting because some of the newly trained teachers had received their fresh appointment letters. Ultimately I also received my appointment letter to join as a permanent teacher in the Burundi village. On June 3, 1950 I reported to the headmaster there. After a brief introduction to him and the staff, he asked me to take charge of grade one pupils. This school was up to the eighth grade only. My family and I were very pleased with my appointment.

Burundi village was twelve miles away from my village. I would walk as there was no conveyance accessible at that time. As it would require almost two and a half hours for me to reach the school, therefore I had to leave very early in the morning from my village. I had no reliable source to wake me up except a train that arrived in the nearby village Kila Raipur at four o'clock every morning. I would hear the whistle and then get out of bed. After some time I got used to waking up early every morning. My wife would then cook my breakfast and lunch and in the meanwhile I would take bath and get ready to depart for school. In the beginning I would get tired walking twenty five miles every day, but gradually I had built up the stamina to complete this distance at ease.

As soon as I reached the school, first I would ink my attendance in the staff register. Shortly after the Morning Prayer, I would take attendance of my class. After examining their handwriting, I would direct the students to sluice their wooden boards and in the meanwhile I would quickly have my breakfast. I would mostly remain engaged with my class and seldom moved out to mingle with the other teachers in the school. I would meet the headmaster only if necessary.

I had purchased two sets of new clothes exclusively for attending school and always kept it neat and clean. Now I could afford to wash them properly with detergent every week.

During this period my wife was pregnant and we were soon expecting our second child. At that time we had run into grave trouble with another Sansi lady from our neighbourhood. Her name was Santi and she lived across the road. As usual I had gone to school during the day and Santi accused my wife of a baseless issue and picked up a scuffle with her. Initially they were verbally at loggerheads with each other but at the flash point Santi hurled a brick at my wife. Providentially it did not strike my wife but nevertheless she had a narrow escape. Somehow the neighbours interceded to prevent them from fighting further. Regrettably Santi's husband was not present at home when this episode had taken place. In the evening when I returned from school, my wife narrated the happenings to me. I unerringly listened to her and determined to take up the issue with Santi's husband Jogi.

Generally by nature I would avoid interfering with the trivial issues amongst the ladies. But this matter had now taken a serious turn and before the situation could cross the limit, I decided to step in to end this unnecessary clash. Since there was hardly any point in talking to Santi, I considered discussing it with Jogi directly. He was a like a 'Brother' to me as we were from the same generation among the Sansi community. In the evening I approached him and asked, "Jogi, I trust you are aware that your wife had quarrelled with my wife today. There is no sense in accusing her on any unfounded issue. You inquire from your wife why she picked up a clash in this fashion."

Jogi was of a very humble nature and found it awkward to reply. He was feeling a bit embarrassed, so instead of demanding an explanation from his wife he replied, "Nathu, Why are you asking me? My wife is sitting right here and you can ask her directly."

I was exasperated and said, "No, you being her husband should question her why she had gratuitously alleged my wife."

Now Jogi had no other way and he questioned his wife, "Santi, why did you pick a fight with Nihalo and hurled a brick at her?"

She was in no mood to answer and remained quiet. But Jogi repeated his question sternly this time and she ambiguously answered him, "Don't ask me, why don't you go and enquire from Nihalo?"

Jogi asked her more questions and she declined to reply at all. This unbecoming attitude of Santi seriously offended Jogi. At last she spoke vehemently with a vague answer and both of them had a heated argument with each other. During this verbal duel, Santi passed some imprudent comments to Jogi and he got enraged with her. In a fit of fury he promptly began thrashing his wife. Santi was quite a hefty woman and Jogi was very thin and lanky. In his fury he repeatedly kicked her in the chest with his knee. She was writhing with pain and lying on the ground. She desperately struggled to protect herself from his blows and beating. This happened so rapidly that I was bewildered and unable to make any decision whether to interfere or not to stop Jogi from beating her. In this chaos Jogi accidentally pummelled her in the heart with his knee and she collapsed to the ground. Jogi then stopped hitting her thinking that she was pretending to be quiet. Some people from the surrounding neighbourhood had gathered there. The bystanders also got the impression that she was deliberately lying there. I returned home without uttering a word to Jogi and the other onlookers also gradually scattered away.

After some time Jogi was concerned when he noticed that Santi was motionless. He attempted to move her but Santi was absolutely motionless. Now he was utterly terrified to observe her in this unmoving state. Then he realised that something had gravely gone wrong. He became frightened and shouted to the Sansi families to come quickly. We all dashed to his place and Santi was lying immobile on the ground. One of the neighbours checked her pulse but was surprised to find there was no sign of life in her. Ultimately he announced that she was no more. There was an unexpected turn of events and the situation had suddenly become very serious.

This incident had happened late in the evening and most of the people in the village were unaware about this unfortunate episode. The Sansi community in our village clandestinely determined to bail out Jogi from the police case and they planned to organise her cremation that night itself. They were frightened lest anybody would report to the police if they waited for her funeral the next morning. After midnight in the darkness they quietly carried Santi to the funeral ground and cremated her. Our family was so terrified that we avoided participating in the cremation. The Sansis had their separate cremation place which was away from the rest of the village. This place happened to be in close proximity to the fields of our village Numberdar.

The next day before sunrise some people from our village were going to Mehma Singh Wala village on their bullock-carts to transport bricks from there for the construction of the Narangwal girls' school building. Our village Numberdar was accompanying them. By chance the Numberdar perceived that something was aflame near his fields. He curiously asked one of the other fellows, 'What is that fire near my fields?'

The fellow promptly replied to the Numberdar, 'Don't you know that Santi died last night because Jogi thrashed her up? The Sansis have hurriedly cremated her in the night itself.'

Our Numberdar was a shell shocked, 'Oh I see, the Sansis had burnt her dead body to eliminate the evidence to avoid the police case. How come nobody had tipped me off about this incident? Now I must immediately report it to the police.'

To his good luck, when they arrived in Mehma Singh Wala, he bumped into an Assistant Police Inspector there and reported the death of Santi to him. The Assistant Inspector immediately rushed from there to Narangwal to investigate the Santi case. He rounded up all the Sansis and started preparing his report. To gather some evidence he dashed to the cremation place but her body had already turned into ashes. The police inspector recorded the statement of my wife along with the other people in the neighbourhood. We were scared that we would be entailed in this police case now. There were various contradicting statements from different people. Hence the real cause could not be ascertained without an actual post-mortem.

The police was unable to execute any arrests in the absence of concrete evidence. This case kept on lingering for a long time. Ultimately the case was referred to the Superintendent of Police. He personally paid a visit to our village and held an open public inquiry. People in the village were now keen to save Jogi. Someone said that Santi used to eat mud from the walls of the hearth. She already had a heart problem and she was likely to die. Another person said that she hardly had any blood in her and she always appeared pale and frail. People from the village cited various reasons for her possible death. Then one man from the public commented, 'How could Jogi kill Santi? He is too skinny to murder anybody and she was much heftier than him.'

This comment stuck in the mind of The Superintendent of Police and he now began wondering how Jogi could possibly kill such a hefty woman. After the death of Santi, Jogi was terribly frightened and appeared even poorer in health. He was very nervous and terrified with the shocking turn of events. The Superintendent doubtfully stared at Jogi and ordered him to be weighed. They weighed Jogi and he turned out to be merely forty seers, thirty seven kilos. Luck favoured Jogi and it was concluded that such frail man could not possibly murder a hefty lady. She must have possibly died of a heart attack. Eventually the case was dismissed on that ground and we all heaved a tremendous sigh of relief.

When I joined as a permanent teacher in Burundi, my appointment was against the post of a teacher who had been under suspension at that time. The post office in Burundi was located in the school and the suspended teacher had been in-charge there. It was believed that he had been seriously involved in some embezzlement of funds in the post office. He had been charge-sheeted and put under suspension from the post office duty. An official investigation had been initiated against him. As a consequence, the education department had also put him under suspension till the outcome of the case. There was a general impression that he would not be able to shake off the punishment. This incident had occurred a few years back before I joined there. Finally the investigation was concluded and surprisingly he was not found guilty. A copy of this judgement from the post office case was dispatched to the education department and as a consequence he had been reinstated as a teacher again. He rejoined the school but I had to quit.

I had become jobless once again. My family and I were depressed with this loss of my job. Being a trained teacher my hope was alive that sooner or later I would get a job. Luckily in those days our former headmaster Niranjan Singh from Gujjarwal School was posted to the district headquarters of Education. I approached him in his office and he was already aware of my case. He enquired from his assistant if there was any vacancy in any school in the district.

The officer promptly asked me, "Natha Singh, do you have your service book?"

I said "Yes Sir, I do have one."

They scrutinized my service book record and calculated that the total tenure of my service in Burundi was one year and four days only. According to the regulation, anybody who had completed the service for more than one year then his services could not be terminated. He had to be treated as a confirmed and permanent employee in that department. Opportunely I had marginally qualified as a permanent teacher. Now the education department was liable to provide a job to me. Former Headmaster Niranjan Singh approached the district chairman on my behalf and apprised him. The chairman approved my case and regularised my service. They searched for a place to accommodate me and discovered that an untrained temporary teacher was posted in Machhiwara village. They terminated his service and consequently released my transfer order to village Machhiwara. This village was quite far off from my place. It was not feasible for me to return every day to my village, but there was no other option except to join there.

I subsequently requested Niranjan Singh to look out for a nearby place for my posting. He prudently suggested to me, "Natha Singh, don't worry, you accept this transfer even if it is far away. As soon as there is an opportunity, I will transfer you closer to your village. You are extremely fortunate that you have barely qualified to continue your service, otherwise you would have been sitting at home and waiting for the next available vacancy."

I also sensed that he had a strong point in his advice and I discussed it with my family. They too were of the same belief that I should not dismiss this opportunity. Now I was determined and joined in Machhiwara.

The headmaster of that primary school was very kind and helped me to make arrangements for my accommodation in one of rooms in the school itself. I established a contract with the owner of a small 'dhaaba', a road side food stall, for my food on a monthly basis. He charged me twenty rupees a month, for a meal consisting of dal, vegetable and rotis. If I desired to relish fried dal then I would carry my own desi ghee. I would visit home once a fortnight to meet my family as well as to replenish my stock of desi ghee among other requirements."

My father now had to protect his esteemed dignity by plugging the holes which could tarnish his image. In the early phases of his life, circumstances had compelled my grandfather into the acts of stealing like all other Sansis. But the times had changed because my father now had a permanent job as a teacher. He strongly detested and resented the stealing acts by my grandfather. Even though his salary was low, yet he refrained from indulging in any activity, personally or by his family where he would feel ashamed later on. He was frightened each time when my grandfather would fetch stolen stuff from the fields.

My mother equally shared the views of my father and supported him to prevent my grandfather from stealing. In the beginning, when my father asked him to quit stealing, my grandfather did not consider it sincerely. He continued stealing despite the strong resentment from my parents. To assert more pressure on my grandfather, my parents had to adopt a different approach now. At one stage my father and mother evidently conveyed to him that if he brought home any stolen goods, they would not utilise it. At last my grandfather realized and said, 'If you are not going to use it, then why should I undertake this risk? Then for whom and for what am I filching?' At this stage my grandfather relinquished stealing.

*   *   *

Transfer to Narangwal

"While teaching in Machhiwara, whenever I visited my village, I would often remind our former Headmaster Niranjan Singh about my transfer. To my good luck a teacher had retired from our own village primary school. Niranjan Singh lost no time issuing my transfer orders from Machhiwara to our village Narangwal. At that time our second son was born in August, 1951.

An advance copy of my transfer order had already arrived at the school in Narangwal. I reported on September 5, 1951 to the headmaster, Harbans Singh prevalently named 'Mahi'. He belonged to our village. Besides him there were two other Jat teachers in the school. All three of them had a lower standard of education as compared to me since they had studied only up to class eight. I was the only qualified JVT teacher who had joined this primary school. The headmaster Mahi allocated me the charge of class two.

I had now returned to my school where I had expended my monotonous childhood as 'Nathu'. What a climax it was that a Sansi boy, whose father was coerced by the superintendent of police to admit him in the school to study, would now be educating the children of his own village. For the people of the village, this untouchable Sansi who had earlier grazed their buffaloes for years had now joined as a school teacher. My father proudly held his head high because he had toiled hard in his life to make me capable of what I was today. There were mixed feelings among the Jats and they had their own speculations about me.

On my first day in the school, I deliberately signed the teacher's attendance register in English instead of in Urdu or Punjabi. My style of signature in English piqued the other Jat teachers when they noticed it. They could not help revealing their own discomfiture and attempted to make fun of me saying that I was an 'angrez', an Englishman. I didn't pay any heed to their mockery and continued signing in English. For me it was rather a matter of great pride and not of any disgrace. By any standards I was decidedly better educated than any one of them.

There had been hardly any improvement in the school since the times when I was a student. The same two big rooms with a veranda in the front and a black wooden door at the main entrance were intact so far. There was no sign of electricity as yet, the two classrooms with high ceilings provided good cross ventilation for adequate comfort in summer. The big courtyard with a well in one corner and the space along with the boundary walls to plant flowers had remained untouched. The teachers would move their classes to the courtyard during the winter and the big Pipal tree in one corner would provide shade to the teachers and students during the summer season. A few wooden chairs for the teachers were in a dwindling condition. The children would either sit on the bare ground or would carry gunny bags from their homes even now. The old records of the school were stored in one big wooden box and a built-in cupboard was still in its original shape and place. There was a medium size room in one corner which was allotted to the post office. Generally in the rural areas the post offices were situated in the schools in those days.

I had sensed that it would not be trouble-free for me to work as a teacher in my own village. People involved in the village politics which had trickled into the school as well, posed a greater challenge for an untouchable to work among the Jats. The other teachers were deeply implicated in the school politics and I had specifically identified the teachers in the school who were for and against whom. Mahi was the ringleader of one political group in the village. His opponents from the village had made their way into the school politics through the other teachers who were against Mahi. My survival under such uptight circumstances was uncomfortable. Within a short period I had appraised that to side with any group was unmistakably inviting trouble. I was completely conscious that being a low caste I would be the first one to be targeted. To spurn every possible peril and not to be caught between the two sides, I adopted the best possible strategy to remain nonaligned in the school as well as in the village politics. Both the political parties in the village intently monitored me to determine if I had any inclination to side with either group. They attempted to associate themselves with me to solidify their presence in the school in order to have a stronghold over their opponents but I offered no opportunity which would indicate my sympathy with any group. Later on I had bluntly proclaimed to them that I would not side with either group.

I regarded all the students at par, irrespective of them being rich or poor, belonging to the high or low castes. I had to be extra cautious while giving punishment to the pupils in the class so that nobody should point a finger at me. Later on even when my own children joined the school, for the same reason I always punished them a little more than the other students.

I emphasised a little more on teaching science to the students as compared to the other subjects. Perhaps Mahi had been persistently observing what I was teaching the students. I could not figure out why Mahi got irritated and one day he came to my class and said, "Natha Singh I have frequently observed that you are putting more emphasis on teaching science as compared to the other subjects. Stop teaching science and concentrate more on the other subjects."

I circumvented responding to him but instead stayed unruffled. Incidentally a few days later we received intimation that the education inspector was visiting our school for an annual inspection. Mahi gathered all the teachers and advised us to prepare our classes for the inspection. Once again I apprised Mahi, "Sir, you know, these inspectors are JVTs' and they are familiar with the science subject. I assume that they would certainly raise some questions about science to the students. Hence our students should be conversant with science."

But Mahi got incensed with my suggestion and scorned me. He said in an irritating tone, "Natha Singh, I do not know why science is wedged in your mind. You always speak about teaching science. You are ignorant about school inspections yet, I know better than you."

I remained quiet.

Mahi had an exceptional characteristic of preserving the school by keeping it neat and clean. As preparatory measures for the school inspection, the courtyard was mud washed and suitable slogans were being written on the school walls etc. To gain appreciation during the inspection he made serious efforts to decorate the school. In fact I had never witnessed such a high standard of sprucing up the premises at any other primary school. The inspector, Sudarshan Singh Kahlon, visited our school for inspection. My class was sitting in the porch and I was delivering a lesson to them. The Inspector proceeded directly to Mahi's class and after exchanging pleasantries, he positioned himself in the middle of the class. There were three rows of the students. He questioned the students about mathematics, the Punjabi language and then science. This whole exercise was an oral questions and answers. Unfortunately the Inspector directed his questions to the students who were poor in their studies. He quizzed some students with science questions and none of them could answer a single question. Mahi was feeling humiliated in this particular state of affairs. When there was no response from the students then the Inspector cautioned Mahi, 'It appears to me that you have not suitably concentrated teaching Science to the students. Science is also an equally important subject.'

Mahi was speechless.

The Inspector proceeded to examine the other classes afterwards. After the inspection was over, the Inspector registered his comments in the school log book. He explicitly specified in his report that in class four the other subjects were all right but proper attention was not paid to teaching science. The Inspector proceeded from our school and the other teachers were anxious to find out what annotations had been registered in the school log book. We rushed to Mahi to know about the inspection status report. Mahi was very upset with the remarks about his class. He agonizingly uttered to us, 'My hard labour is lost as he has not specified a word about the upkeep of the school. He has predominantly pointed out to me about the lack of emphasis in teaching science to the students.'

Now it was my turn to prove my point and I said to Mahi, "Sir, I had cautioned you in advance that he would definitely ask some questions about Science."

Mahi was thunderstruck for a moment and then stated, "Natha Singh you were correct but I underrated your advice."

We continued concentrating on our classes and once again I discovered that most of the students in my class were incapable of writing numbers up to ten thousand. I considered it essential to revise it and re-started teaching the Numbers to them. Perhaps the previous teacher had not handled this section of the syllabus properly. One day Mahi enquired from me why I was repeating the chapter of Numbers. He raised a serious objection and issued a official memorandum seeking my explanation.

In his memorandum, a part of it read, 'What is the necessity to repeat the chapter of Numbers when this portion had already been covered by the previous teacher?'

I was ignorant about the procedure or protocol of replying to such an official memorandum. I just replied in simple words, "It could be possible that the previous teacher had covered the chapter of Numbers but the students still cannot write figures up to ten thousand proficiently. Hence I have decided to revise this chapter to the whole class."

The basic motive behind this episode was a mystery to me. Was the Mahi group on a look out to shunt me out from Narangwal by creating an official record against me about my inefficiency or lack of intelligence? Perhaps my presence was worthless to them; otherwise Mahi had no reasons to meddle with my teaching. I was just left to guess the main cause of this game plan. When I replied in this fashion, perhaps it was not exactly what he had expected. Now he was probably wondering how a junior teacher like me was replying to him in this fashion. Conceivably he felt offended but avoided uttering a word to me after my reply. He discussed this issue in his political circle in the village.

After this incident, one day I met the former headmaster Niranjan Singh while he was going for his evening walk.

As usual I greeted him saying, "Sir, Sat Sri Akal."

He too replied "Sat Sri Akal."

He then asked me, "Natha Singh, wait, I want to speak to you."

I was surprised when he straightway asked me, "Why do you and Mahi have a tussle in the school?"

I replied point blank, "Sir, if you really wish to know the fact, please tell me who is accountable for the class in the school? Is it the teacher-in-charge or the headmaster?"

Niranjan Singh looked at me in surprise and said, "Of course, the teacher-in-charge is responsible."

Then I elucidated the whole story about how Mahi had pointlessly interceded when I was teaching the students and on the top of it, he issued a memorandum to me.

I do not know what transpired between Niranjan Singh and Mahi, but after that Mahi never commented or meddled in my style of teaching in the school."

After my father finished this story, I was telling Susan that my brother and I had a disadvantage of studying in the village primary school. I was generally good in studies but sometimes when I was punished along with the other students, I would get at least two or three extra whips of the cane from my father. May be my father was justified in his own way, but consequently we became the victims of his justification. I would always wonder about this little extra caning each time. At that time I did not grasp the purpose behind this. But I realised now after my father explained it in his story.

*   *   *

A Scuffle in the School

"In the primary school I was also in-charge of admissions and discharges of the students. Every year I would update the school records after the admissions were over. One day I was occupied with the updating of the school records when one Gurbaksh Singh from our village hurriedly appeared in the school. He was a headmaster at a high school in a nearby village. He straightway demanded, "Natha Singh, you take this list of the students and immediately write out the discharge certificates for them. They are looking forward to take admission in my school."

I was extremely occupied and wanted to finish my work first before I could take up his work. I gazed at him with surprise and answered him in a casual way, "I am sorry, I have to finish my work first and after that I require sufficient time to check the school records and then issue the discharge certificates."

Perhaps he had not expected this response from me and again insisted, "You may leave your work at hand but as

I am in a hurry now you must attend to my requirement first."

I felt piqued and finally answered, "Sorry, I cannot do it right away. If you wish, you may contact me later on."

He was exasperated yet he said in satirical tone, "Then wishing me 'Sat Sri Akal' had no meaning?"

He was bristling with rage and eventually moved out from the school in a huff. I could not believe what he had uttered but I continued with my work. He was annoyed because I had not obeyed him. He had envisaged that I would instantly comply with what he had asked me to do. The bottom line was that he was vexed because he belonged to the Jat community and me being a Sansi, I had not listened to him. He had taken it for granted that I as a Sansi was supposed to follow his instructions at any time and under any circumstances. He had a fancy that I greeted him 'Sat Sri Akal' because he belonged to a higher caste. He considered it not as a matter of respect for him, but as a right that I being a low caste was supposed to wish him. But I merely respected him because he was a school teacher and elder to me. Unfortunately even the educated people like him had such a low mentality towards the lower caste people.

Our headmaster, Mahi, was grossly implicated in the village politics. I had often clarified my stand to him that my association with him was solely up to the main door of the school. Outside the school premises I would not politically involve myself with any side. Whenever there was any scuffle in the village, he would discuss it in the school. But in the end he would always laugh and say, "Natha Singh, you are our companion only up to the 'kala phatak', the black door, the main entrance of the school."

I would laugh and reply, "Yes Sir, you are correct; I am with you only up to the 'kala phatak'."

To encounter Mahi and expand more influence in the school politics, the opposition party in the village managed to bring another teacher to the school. His name was Karam Singh and he lived in another nearby village. The main purpose was that he would kick off a fight with Mahi and register a case against him. As a consequence Mahi would be transferred to another school. The basic game plan was to throw Mahi out from the school. Mahi being from my village, I had a natural affinity for him rather than with the new teacher. People from both the political parties would visit the school and be with their favourite teachers. They would spend time with them at their own leisure.

As the frequency of the outsiders had considerably increased in the school, I sensed something obnoxious was brewing. As Karam Singh was new in the school and not being conversant with our village politics, I genuinely wanted to alert him. One day while in conversation with him, I said, "Karam Singh, you should be vigilant of the people who frequently contact you in the school. They belong to this village and live here but you could get trapped between the two parties."

Before I could finish my conversation, he ignored me without paying any heed to my advice. He abruptly cut me off and arrogantly replied, "Natha Singh, you are ignorant about such political games. Don't try to lecture me; I am capable of handling this without your advice."

Possibly he misunderstood me and contemplated that I was friendly with the opposite group. That is why I was discouraging him not to mingle with his people. Perhaps now he had a grudge against me after this conversation. He had stopped talking to me and behaved indifferently in the school.

Karam Singh was in-charge of the post office also. Every month the Treasury office dispatched our salaries as a money order through the post office. One day Karam Singh commented to another teacher saying, 'This time I will not distribute the salary money order to the Sansi for five to six days. Let the Sansi starve this month.'

I was in a close proximity and overheard his comment. I was not ready to accept this gratuitous remark. He was not paying my salary from his own pocket. I said to the other teacher, "Tell him that everybody in my village knows that I am a Sansi, there is no mystery about it. He is not my employer. Even if I die of hunger, I will not go begging for my salary."

Mahi noticed that we were going to clash and therefore to nip the issue in the bud he arrived there. He asked me what was happening and I described to him what Karam Singh had just commented.

He ogled at Karam Singh and indirectly avowed, "Let me see, who can stop your salary. I will make him face the music if he dares to do so. You be calm about it."

To goad Mahi, Karam Singh dared not to utter a word after this.

One day a student found a small iron rod and brought it to the classroom. Mahi asked him, 'What is it? Where did you get it?'

The child innocently replied, 'Masterji, I found this on the roadside.'

Mahi asked him, 'You hand it over to me; we will use it to sound the school bell.'

So Mahi stored that iron rod in the closet which was adjacent to his seat.

The monthly function of The Sant was due the next day. I applied for one day leave and departed to visit The Sant.

When I returned from The Sant, there was turmoil in the village. It was said that Karam Singh had entered the classroom and assaulted Mahi and battered him devoid of any provocation. When Karam Singh was grappling with Mahi, the children got scared and made a hue and cry. The other teacher came running to find out what happened. In the mean while Mahi strived to defend himself and thus reached out for that small iron rod and hit Karam Singh over his head with it. Karam Singh was badly hurt and they fell apart. The other teacher intervened to stop them. Both Mahi and Karam Singh bellowed and shouted at each other in the presence of all the students in the class.

Then Karam Singh straight away dashed from there to his post office room. He quickly opened up the money bag and scattered the money all over. After that he began hollering at the top of his voice and pretended as if Mahi had sneaked into the post office and attempted to loot the money bag. Karam Singh wasted no time and lodged a complaint with the police that Mahi had endeavoured to burgle the post office.

The people in the village speculated their own outcome of this incident. Both the groups in the village were hyper active to deal with this situation effectively. Each side pulled up the strings through their political and official mentors. They prepared their own game plans as how to tackle the police inquiry. The Karam Singh group was making every attempt to establish that Mahi had practically endeavoured to snatch the money from Karam Singh in the post office room. On the other hand the Mahi group had a solid ground to falsify their accusation. They were sure that Karam Singh would not be able to provide evidence as stated in his complaint. This issue had become a sizzling and fervent topic in the village.

The police sprang into action and began their investigations without any delay. This case was vital as it was associated with the post office, a central government undertaking. On the following day, an assistant sub Inspector of the police entered the school premises for the investigation. I used to sit with my class out in the veranda, near the main entrance of the school. So he came up to my class but the students got petrified after seeing a policeman. He posed some questions to the students directly about the incident but the young students remained silent.

I advised him, "Look Inspector, there's no point in making your investigation with these young children. Do not anticipate any information from them as they are scared of you. You should go to the class four students where the incident had actually occurred. They are a little more mature than these children, thus they will be able to describe it in better details."

He asked me if I had any knowledge about this episode. I bluntly informed him that I was on leave that day. I directed him to Mahi's classroom. He wanted to listen about the incident directly from the students and requested Mahi to leave the classroom for some time. He took the students into confidence and then asked them to candidly describe what had occurred the previous day in the classroom. The students in their simplicity and innocence, chronologically described the whole incident to the Inspector, 'Karam Singh Masterji entered our classroom and without cause attacked our Masterji. Our Masterji tried to protect himself and therefore pulled the bolt from the closet and hit Karam Singh Masterji. Both of them hit each other and in the meantime the other teacher arrived and separated them.'

Then the Inspector questioned the students, 'Where was your Masterji after the fight? Did he go to the post-office?'

The students promptly replied, 'No, he was sitting right here with us nurturing his bruises.'

The police sent the report of the whole incident to the postal and education department simultaneously. The police Inspector had undoubtedly stated that Karam Singh had cooked up the entire story and there was no truth in Mahi looting the post office.

There was a mixed reaction from the people in the village. Most of the people were in favour of Mahi as the strategy of Karam Singh had miserably flopped. Karam Singh's party began changing their colours now because there was no strong base for them to act against Mahi. Instead they were now accusing Karam Singh and wondering why he had cooked up the post office story about which he was incapable of providing concrete evidence. They were cursing his stupid plan. He should have organised it in a more systematic manner to seriously entangle Mahi.

To craft a fictitious report and lodge a police complaint on behalf of the postal department was also a major offence. Karam Singh had invited grave trouble for himself. His mentors in the village could not side and shield him from any action that would be taken against him. The Education Department took immediate action against Karam Singh after receiving a report from the police department. He was instantly transferred from the school in Narangwal.

When Karam Singh was finally leaving the school, he apologetically said to me, "Natha Singh, you were right. Now I regret not having listened to you. You told me that one day they would join hands and that I would be in trouble and that is what ultimately had happened."

I simply replied, "Karam Singh, I know these people better than you, because I live in this village."

My father was very excited while telling this story. We were surprised he wished to continue with his next story without any stop. He continued narrating.......

"Karam Singh was replaced by another teacher named Chaman Lal from Ludhiana. He had also been assigned the additional charge of the post office. He had a very peculiar nature of developing contacts with all the renowned people in the village. Perhaps he had contemplated that by this novel gesture he would win the goodwill of all the reputed people. By nature he would elevate the significance of the concerned person through flattery. A few days later after joining the school, he planned to launch a campaign to create his contact base in the village.

One day he played the same card with me and said, "Natha Singh, I infer that you are very popular in the village. I need your help."

I was slightly taken aback by this undue comment, yet I replied, "Chaman Lal, I will certainly be happy to assist you within my limits."

Without any formality he straightway said, "Natha Singh, I would like to become proverbial with all the important persons in the village by personally delivering mail to their abodes. I wish to ascertain a close rapport with them."

I laughed at him and commented, "Chaman Lal, this is not Ludhiana city, everybody is important here in this village. Don't start off this practice otherwise you would be delivering letters only and then forget about teaching."

He strangely gaped at me but still he insisted to know the influential people and pleaded, "Natha Singh, basically I am interested in the really important ones."

I sincerely advised him again, "If you deliver the mail to the important ones, then the others would feel affronted. They would turn against you because you have not considered them at par with your so called important ones. You will run into trouble for nothing."

He was not yet satisfied with my reply and still asked for the names of the most important ones.

I realised that he was bent upon getting in touch with the prominent persons. I decided to highlight those people whom I believed to be important. So Finally I said, "Look Chaman Lal, your choice and my penchant may not match but if you still insist then there are only two important persons in this village for me. There are two saints and one of them is Sant Bhai Randhir Singh. During his annual programme in the village, some money orders pour in for him. The other saint is in the Gurudwara near the village hospital. In my opinion only both of them deserve to be served."

Chaman Lal was not actually elated with my succinct list but he did not further compel me for more names.

One day Chaman Lal seemed to be excited and came rushing to me saying, "Natha Singh, would you accompany me to deliver the money order for the Sant Bhai Randhir Singh? I have not met him as yet."

A money order for thirty one rupees had come for the Sant Bhai Randhir Singh. The annual religious function had already started in his place. I was primed to visit him with Chaman Lal. But at the last minute Chaman Lal altered his mind and said, "Natha Singh, it would be better if you could go alone this time. Next time we will go together."

Now I had no alternative and agreed to proceed alone.

Though I was acquainted with the Sant Bhai Randhir Singh yet I seldom had an opportunity to have a word with him individually. When I was studying in Gujjarwal, I would meet him on the way and I would just greet him 'Sat Sri Akal'. He was a legendary person who had actively participated during India's freedom struggle. He was a true nationalist but as a saint had plenty of followers. I picked up the money order from Chaman Lal and headed for the saint's home. I decided that if I come across his sevadar, his helper, I would hand over the money order to him. He would deliver it to the saint and obtain his signature. As I reached there, luckily his sevadar Mal Singh was standing at the door.

I modestly conveyed to him, "Mal Singh, I have come to deliver the money order to the saint. Would you please pass it to him and obtain his signature?"

Instead of obliging me rather he directed me and said, "Masterji, you may go upstairs, the saint is there."

I was a wee bit diffident to go alone and therefore asked Mal Singh again, "You know, I have never met him personally, so I think it would be better if you take this pen and money order to him."

Mal Singh then took my pen and money order from me but he asked me to follow him upstairs. There were two rooms and I sat down on one side. One preacher was reciting the Holy Book and the saint was listening to it. Mal Singh presented the money order to the saint. The saint had sensed that I must be the person who had come to deliver the money order. He took the money order and signed it.

The saint asked Mal Singh, 'Who has come to deliver the money?'

Mal Singh replied, 'Natha Singh is sitting there.'

The saint directed Mal Singh, 'Go and convey to him that he should have come personally to me to ensure that the right person was collecting the money.'

Mal Singh returned with my pen and paper simultaneously communicating to me what the saint had said."

*   *   *

Mahi in a Mess

"Generally people who have lived in the cities do not prefer to work in the villages. I had no knowledge under what circumstances Chaman Lal had been transferred from Ludhiana city to Narangwal. He had rented a room from Raagi Harnam Singh but he was finding it uncomfortable to manage alone in the village. He was not used to village life and cooking food was another major problem for him. He would often remain edgy. After spending a few months in the village, he initiated his efforts to return to Ludhiana. In addition to it, Chaman Lal could not develop a cordial relationship with Mahi.

Chaman Lal was also mulling other connections in the Education department in Ludhiana for his transfer. Somehow Chaman Lal had strong apprehensions that even if he received his transfer orders, Mahi could stall his efforts. Mahi could easily decline to release him without a replacement. So he sought his transfer order to reach when Mahi was not present in the school.

One day Mahi had gone to attend a marriage in another far off village and Chaman Lal had prior information about it because Mahi had applied for one day out-station leave. Chaman Lal pulled his strings and informed his people to dispatch the transfer order on that particular day. In the absence of Mahi another senior teacher Karnail Singh was officiating as headmaster in the school that day. Chaman Lal seemed to be cheerful that his plot had finally worked. He came rushing to my classroom and said, "Natha Singh my transfer order has come. I have this excellent opportunity to depart today. What should I do now?"

I doubtfully asked Chaman Lal, "You know that the headmaster Mahi is out of the station, who then will sign your relieving order?"

Chaman Lal felt a little disenchanted and half heartedly replied, "You know that Mahi would not sign my relieving order easily and I would never be able to leave then."

Anxiety reflected on his face and he was now terribly worried about his fate. I sympathetically suggested to him, "Under the present circumstances you may request Karnail Singh who is in-charge today to relieve you."

Instead of consulting Karnail Singh, Chaman Lal attempted to act smart. Without any further discussion and delay he promptly made an entry in the school order book and mentioned there, 'I have received my transfer order. I may please be relieved immediately.'

After making the entry he handed over the order book to Karnail Singh.

Karnail Singh was bewildered to see the note in the order book. He came running to me and asked, "Natha Singh, Chaman Lal has made an entry in the order book to be relieved immediately, what I should do? He has put it on record now."

Obviously Karnail Singh was under pressure, still I steadily advised him, "Don't worry, you just mention in the order book that he should hand over the charge of his class to me before he is relieved."

Officially Karnail Singh was not the competent authority to relieve Chaman Lal. As such there was no emergency to decide this matter right away and take immediate action. But on the other hand Chaman Lal was pleading, insisting and pressurising him for his immediate release.

Finally Karnail Singh noted in the order book, "Chaman Lal, you may hand over the charge of your class to Natha Singh. Then I will sign your relieving order."

When Chaman Lal read this note in the order book, he was ecstatic. He instantly came to me and displayed the order of handing over the charge of his class to me.

I smiled at him but asked, "Chaman Lal, I am willing to take charge of your class but what about the charge of the post office?"

He now held his head in despair. He had not realised about the post office at all. He read the order book again and there was nothing mentioned about handing over the charge of the post office. It was impossible for him to leave without handing over the charge of the post office.

As Chaman Lal contacted Raagi Harnam Singh and narrated the whole story. He requested him to search for some way to get out from this muddle. Raagi accompanied Chaman Lal to school in the afternoon and asked me, "Natha Singh, you know Chaman Lal is under too much anxiety. Is there any possibility for you to take charge of the post office as well?"

I respected Raagi a lot and explicated him, "Raagi ji, I am not officially eligible to take charge of the post office from him because Karnail Singh is senior to me. He is the only one eligible to hold this responsibility."

Since I owed some obligations to Raagi ji, now I had an opportunity to return the favours. I appealed to Karnail Singh to work out some way to help Chaman Lal. Then we decided that Karnail Singh would take charge of his class as well as the post office. I would unofficially assist Karnail Singh with the post office work until some permanent solution was reached. Eventually Karnail Singh issued the relieving order to Chaman Lal and a copy of it was attached in the order book for Mahi's referral. Now Chaman Lal was immensely delighted to receive his relieving order that evening. Shortly after all the formalities were undertaken, it was time to close the school for the day.

The next morning Chaman Lal was all set to leave after saying goodbye to Mahi. He came to school in the morning but Mahi had not reported for duty as yet. We were expecting Mahi to arrive at any moment as by and large he was never late for school. Chaman Lal was getting disappointed and impatient with each passing moment. Now he was in two minds whether to wait for Mahi or proceed without bidding him goodbye. Gradually the whole day went by and yet there was no sign of Mahi. He finally decided to wait for Mahi till the next day.

On the third day Mahi reported for duty in the school and Chaman Lal was cheerful when he observed that Mahi was present there. He cautiously approached Mahi and greeted him 'Sat Sri Akal'.

As usual Mahi responded to him. Then Chaman Lal enlightened Mahi, 'Headmaster Saab, I had received my transfer order the day before yesterday and I have already obtained my relieving order from Karnail Singh.'

Mahi was quite taken aback and asked, 'Chaman Lal, how can anyone except me give you the relieving order? Does it mean that you have regarded me as 'Absent' from the school yesterday?'

Mahi was literally perturbed with this new development.

Actually Mahi had applied for only one day leave from the school but his vehicle broke down on his return journey. There was no possibility for him to reach school the next day. When Mahi finally came to school, he had marked himself 'Present' in the school attendance register for the previous day as well. Chaman Lal was unaware of this fact because he had not signed in the attendance register. In his excitement he had not given Karnail Singh and me any time to brief Mahi regarding the latest development which had occurred in his absence.

Chaman Lal played his favourite master stroke to flatter Mahi. He requested in a pampering tone, 'Well headmaster Saab, I know you are the appropriate official and competent authority to sign my relieving order. If you think Karnail Singh was incompetent for it then you can do it now. After all you are the bona fide headmaster.'

Mahi was pleased with this compliment and said, 'Chaman Lal that makes some real sense. I will issue your relieving order.'

Then Mahi issued a backdated relieving order with his own signature and handed it over to Chaman Lal. Chaman Lal was ecstatic and he departed for Ludhiana on a happy note.

Evidently Chaman Lal reported for his duty in Ludhiana and visited the district education office to express his thanks for helping him with his transfer. They asked him why it took so long for him to get relieved. He described the whole story to them that he had to wait for the headmaster as he was 'Absent' for one day. The other teachers were ineligible to officially relieve him. When the headmaster reported for duty, he marked himself

'Present' in the school attendance register for that day and gave me a backdated relieving order as well.

A junior officer from our village was present there in the education department office when Chaman Lal narrated this story. He was also instrumental in the transfer of Chaman Lal. He belonged to the anti-Mahi group in the village. After listening to Chaman Lal, he discussed this whole incident with his group in the village. They now had the God sent opportunity to take revenge on Mahi. They were dead sure that Mahi would be suspended. The officer asked Chaman Lal to give it in writing that Mahi was absent from the school for one day. On that basis a departmental investigation was initiated against Mahi.

Even in his wildest dreams Mahi had not imagined this turn of events but he was in grave trouble now.

Mahi asked Karnail Singh and me to somehow protect him; otherwise he would face severe consequences of his stupid mistake. In fact there was a double mistake. Firstly to mark himself as 'Present' for the day when he was actually 'Absent' from the school and secondly on the top of it issuing a backdated relieving order to Chaman Lal as well. Chaman Lal had gone beyond his reach and he was absolutely dependent on both of us who could vouch for him to be 'Present' on his missing day. His job was at stake and he heavily depended on our statements during the investigation. We did not desire that Mahi should lose his job or face any disciplinary action as he was close to his retirement. We discussed amongst ourselves regarding our statements during the inquiry. So I sought from Mahi, "Sir, what should I explain in my statement?"

He had no clear line of action and casually said, "Natha Singh, you say that I was here around 12 o'clock."

The investigating officer came to our school. First he asked Karnail Singh about the sequence of events regarding Mahi and asked different questions to Karnail Singh.

In the end Karnail Singh told him, 'Mahi was there in the morning when I arrived at the school. Later on I was engaged with my class and other work. I remained occupied and did not have a chance to meet him again.'

Later on the inquiry officer summoned me and asked various questions. I endeavoured to defend Mahi as much as I could. Finally I said, "I had met Mahi around 12 o'clock."

The inquiry officer retorted, "Karnail Singh says that Mahi was there in the morning and you say he was there around 12 o'clock. What is the truth?"

I was now in a fix. After a quick thought I replied "You know, during the prayer in the morning, he wasn't there. After that the students had gone to their classrooms and I was attending to my class. Approximately around 12 o'clock I wanted to discuss something with him and when I went to his room, he was there."

The inquiry officer assumed that I was protecting Mahi and said, "Natha Singh you are acting smart now."

The officer returned to the district headquarters. I don't know what he had described in his report but Mahi got bailed out unscathed from this intricate state of affairs and his job was protected.

* * *

State Elections

"**M**ahi retired from the service, and a new headmaster Kishori Lal had taken over the charge in our school. He was a pundit, a Brahmin. The State assembly elections were coming ahead soon. The government generally deputed the school teachers for election duty. This time too, the teachers were assigned election duties to various stations. Luckily Kishori Lal and my duty turned out to be in our own village. The election officer convened a meeting with all election duty staff in Ludhiana for a briefing and other compulsory arrangements. He distributed the election material and inquired whether there were any other problems. After organizing the election issues he checked regarding the food arrangement for the election staff on duty.

The election officer asked Kishori Lal, "Masterji, how can food be arranged for the staff? Is there any hotel or dhaaba, a road side eating place, nearby?"

He thought for a while and then answered, "Sir, there is no such arrangement in the village."

The officer asked again, "Any likelihood in the neighbouring villages?"

Kishori Lal replied, "Nearby there is another big village Gujjarwal but there is no possibility to obtain cooked food from there."

The officer seemed apprehensive and asked Kishori Lal, "Masterji, could the rations like wheat flour, lentils, vegetables, cooking oil, spices etc. be arranged for?"

Kishori Lal resided in Kila Raipur and had barely any information about the shops in Narangwal. He inquiringly looked at me. Then I informed the officer, "Yes, Sir. There is a feasibility to organize the rations."

The officer was at ease now and said, "Fine, then you organise the rations and we shall send a cook."

We returned to our village and planned to arrange the rations. Kishori Lal being senior to me had more accountability than me. The next day Kishori Lal suggested to me, "Natha Singh let us get in touch with our village Sarpanch, Zaildar Pritam Singh, regarding the election arrangements." He was a rich farmer and had a big mansion. I accompanied Kishori Lal and we marched to meet the Sarpanch, village headman.

The younger brother of the Sarpanch bumped into us at the main gate and he light-heartedly asked Kishori Lal, "Oh, Panditji, what brings you here? When a pundit is at the door, then he would be seeking something or the other."

Kishori Lal also laughed and replied, "Well, you people have always served pundits so it's nothing new! Now we look forward to meet your older brother, where is he?"

"You can go inside, he is unoccupied at the moment", he answered.

Zaildar Pritam Singh was partially impaired of hearing. He would always carry a hearing pipe with a mouthpiece at one end. We both greeted him. He gave the mouthpiece end to Kishori Lal and inserted the other end in his ear.

The Sarpanch asked Kishori Lal, "Masterji, how come you are here."

Kishori Lal bluntly replied, "We require your assistance during the elections. You would be providing food to the election staff. I have given my word to the Election Officer in Ludhiana."

The Sarpanch began laughing and said, "I was expecting this to happen."

Kishori Lal further made it clear, "We would require rations only for the election staff but not for the police on duty."

The Sarpanch laughed again and responded, "Yes, I appreciate that these police people would consume food at my house as well as at your place. So it would be a double loss for me."

Kishori Lal was contented that he had taken the responsibility to provide rations for the election staff but further casually remarked, "Well, I assume that the police force would surely rely upon you."

The Sarpanch had more than enough potential to feed a large number of people at a time. He assured Kishori Lal, "Masterji, don't worry about the rations, I will organise it for everybody."

The Sarpanch asked me, "Natha Singh, you inform Bakhtawar Singh, the shopkeeper, he should provide grocery according to your requirement and tell Ismail Khan to supply dry wood for cooking. I would settle their bills later on."

Our problem was resolved. There were no complications in getting rations during the election days. The election staff and the police people freely enjoyed the food."

*   *   *

Demise of My Father

"In the middle of September, 1959. My father had grown quite old and had been ailing for the past few months. He had turned feeble and unable to move with ease. One afternoon when I was at school, my wife sent a message that my father had breathed his last. I could hardly believe that he would pass away so soon. When I hurriedly arrived home my cousins were around and they had followed the old ritual of placing his dead body on the ground on a sheet of cloth. I discussed with my cousins about the funeral and we concluded that it was late now. There was hardly any time to perform the funeral rites because the sun was about to set. Secondly, there was barely any time to inform our relatives. Persons close to the deceased would always be keen to have a glimpse of the deceased for the last time. I consulted my wife and we dispatched messengers to our relatives that the funeral was set for the following morning.

Word had spread in the village and among our Sansi community about the demise of my father. People began visiting my house to share my grief. The Sansi families also started arriving to pay their condolences. The men sat around the dead body and shared their memories of my father with me. The ladies were wailing loudly making the atmosphere even grimmer. My cousins chatted with the other Sansis about the happenings in the life of my father. Late that night the people had gradually left and only my cousins and I were sitting alone. The memories of my father began reeling through my mind. I remembered how my father was nearly beaten up at the police station when he had initially refused to admit me in the primary school. I recollected how living in utmost poverty, he had faced numerous hardships while bringing me up. My father suffered for me by sacrificing the hookah and other things in his life. I could sense his agony when he perceived that his educated son could not get a job and continued grazing buffaloes. There were unlimited vivid memories floating in my head. I was aware that tomorrow his body would be burnt but the memories of my father would always stay with me.

The next morning all the relatives began trickling in. The Sansi men from the village collected the heavy logs of wood and prepared the pyre in the cremation ground. My cousins and I placed my father for his last bath and after this we wrapped him in 'khappan', white piece of cloth. His body was placed on a bamboo stretcher and his face was uncovered for the last glimpse. A copper coin was inserted in his mouth and then his face was covered. It is said that the man who stumbles upon this coin at the time of collecting the ashes, was dearer to the deceased person. My cousins, another relative and I carried the stretcher of my father to the cremation ground and men and women trailed us. When we moved from our home, the head of my father was towards the cremation ground. My eldest son carried a water pitcher in front of the procession. The gathering following us was chanting, "Satnam Waheguru, God is Truth.

When the procession reached half the way to the cremation ground, we placed the stretcher on the ground and my eldest son smashed the water pitcher in front of the dead body. We picked up the stretcher again now with his feet towards the cremation ground. This signified that the dead person had an attachment to this world when his feet were facing towards his home. But now he had detached himself from this world and was ready for the final journey after death. The ladies returned home from this point. After we reached the cremation ground, we placed his dead body on the pyre. I lit the pyre with a heavy heart. The flames engulfed the dead body rapidly. People sat down at a distance and stared at the glowing embers amidst the cracking sound of bones and burning flesh. When more than half of the logs were burnt, one man pricked the skull with an iron rod to check whether it had burnt or not. It is considered that if the head was burnt then the rest of the body was also burnt. When the man confirmed that the head was burnt then everybody picked up a piece of straw, broke it and threw it on the pyre. This meant that they had emotionally detached themselves from the dead person.

I did not pursue any Sansi rituals afterwards. In his memory I performed Sehaj Paath, the recitation of the Holy Book, at home and this concluded the mourning rituals.

*　　*　　*

An Impressive Visit

*M*y father would generally be dressed in simple but clean clothes every day when he attended the school. He had only two sets of white clothes especially for this purpose. He would always dress with a white turban to the school. In winters he would put on neutral coloured but thick cotton clothes. When he visited his in-laws, he would wear a bright coloured turban. Perhaps he had taken a cue from his past that his clothes would also reflect his personality.

When my father was jobless he could not afford to purchase respectable looking clothes at that time. When he acquired a permanent job, only then he realised the dire necessity of buying new sets of simple cotton clothes. For exclusive occasions also he had spent money to buy just one brown colour suit. Along with that he had bought one special brown pair of Bata shoes. He would only make use of this exclusive set of clothes whenever he visited his in-laws. He had never utilised this trouser suit in the school.

Otherwise it would remain neatly packed in an iron trunk. Perhaps he got that suit stitched before I was born. A son-in-law was given incredible importance in those days by the in-laws. They would provide the very best for him whenever he visited there. The son-in-law would also call upon there in style with the best of clothes, even if he had to borrow it from others.

My father disclosed another very interesting tale when he was in the prime of his youth.....

"Once when I was visiting my in-laws, I dressed in my special trouser suit and a very bright parrot-green coloured turban. It would distinctively stand out even from a distance. I would go there on foot as there was hardly any regular transport then. On the way I was passing through a village Nathu Majra, which was quite close to my in-laws village. Outside the village there was a farmer irrigating his fields with his oxen driven well. As I walked through a long and dusty road, I desired to freshen up before arriving at my in-laws house. I moved towards the well to wash my hands and face. As an old practice, I began washing at a little distance from the well, with the water from the drain flowing into the fields. I refrained from washing at the well itself. The farmer driving the oxen at the well looked at me and was astonished to observe a well dressed person like me washing away from the well. He could not hide his curiosity and asked me, "Young man, why are you washing there, why don't you come to the well for a wash."

"I am supposed to wash away from the well", I replied candidly.

His curiosity had amplified with my reply and he questioned me again, "By the way who are you?"

"I am a Sansi."

He was utterly dazed and commented, "A Sansi!"

He became a little more inquisitive and asked, "Where do you come from?"

"I belong to village Narangwal."

Perhaps he had some notion about the villages around Narangwal. He seemed to be satisfied and remarked, "I can believe you as a lot of people are educated in that area. Where are you going?"

"I am visiting my in-laws in Ramgarh Sardaran."

I finished washing and went on my way with a great feeling of dignity.

My father-in-law really loved me and he was proud of me. He would pamper me whenever I visited there. When my mother-in-law served food to me, he would sit beside and fan me. She would vehemently preclude her husband from mollycoddling me but he would proclaim with great pride and tell his wife, "Don't you know, there is no other Sansi boy as educated as my son-in-law."

After this she would not criticise him anymore and I could sense that she was equally proud of me.

One day while at my in-laws place I was returning from an evening walk. I was decked out with a nice shirt and an expensive dhoti which cost me two rupees fifty paisa. A man from the village passed by and greeted me 'Sat Sri Akal'.

I too replied, 'Sat Sri Akal'. I was surprised that an unknown person was wishing me. Perhaps he considered me an affluent man as I was well groomed, but when he noticed that I entered my in-law's house, he was flabbergasted."

The inferiority complex was ingrained very deeply into the psyche of the low caste people like my father. Whether in his village or outside it, he never contemplated to over step the specified boundaries chalked out for the untouchables. He remained confined within the safe zone irrespective of the time, place and the people. He avoided being caught on the wrong foot to face unwarranted humiliation. He strictly applied these restrictions on himself.

In certain cases if a low caste person obtained a good job far away from his village, he would attempt to conceal his low caste to avoid any open discrimination there. He may pretend as if he belonged to a higher caste. He may even acquire some fake surname of a higher caste. But such things seldom remain veiled from the people. They would detect the fact one way or the other. When the reality was exposed in his work place then the word would also spread to his village. Then he would face severe humiliation in both places. People would make fun of him and he would not find a place to hide his disgraced face. Fortunately my father never committed this blunder; he put up a brave face by accepting the ground reality that he belonged to the Sansi caste.

* * *

Vast Responsibilities

"The headmaster Kishori Lal retired in 1959. I was the next senior most among the other teachers in the school so I was acting as a headmaster. Generally the post office charge was also held by the senior teacher consequently I also took over the charge of the post office from Kishori Lal. I had considerable knowledge and experience of the post office work which I had gained when Mahi was in-charge of the post office. He would often request me to lend a helping hand to complete his paper work. In a few months I had achieved a comprehensive working knowledge of the post office. I studied about its rules and regulations from its working manuals to acquire extensive information.

One family from our village had their business in Calcutta. The head of the family would send a money order to his family almost every month and his wife would receive the money order from our post office. On one occasion that man arrived from Calcutta and came to meet me in the school. We were just chatting for some time and when he was about to depart he unexpectedly said, "Natha Singh, I have forgotten to talk to you on a specific issue."

I was surprised but said, "Yes, why not."

He seemed to be in a slightly irksome disposition now. He remonstrated, "Natha Singh, I dispatch a money order to my wife almost every month. When she approaches you to receive the money order you always demand for a witness."

I peacefully listened to him and then replied, "Sorry friend, but I just comply with the post office rules only. There is a rule that in a branch post office, whenever someone comes to collect a money order, he must bring along a witness. I demand it within the post office rules."

Now I observed a frown on his face. He seemed to be visibly perturbed and said, "You know, we deal with big post offices in Calcutta and there nobody solicits us for a witness. Do you have your own separate rules here?"

The way he complained made me irritable. He endeavoured to demonstrate his high handedness as he was a Jat. Perhaps he did not believe what I just told him. I had the copy of the manual on the post office rules and was fully conversant with it. I remembered that in the rules book, the rule number was 110 and it was also on page 110. I was cognisant of the fact that all and sundry may attempt to find fault with me on such issues.

I now insisted and asked the man to follow me to the post office room. I pulled out the rules book and remembered that rule and page by heart. I turned the pages and handed over the book to him.

I said to him, "Now you read the rule yourself."

The rule clearly stated that, 'Whether the payee is literate or illiterate, the postmaster in a sub-post office must ask for a witness to certify that the person has received the money in his presence.'

The man read it, looked at me and muttered, "Yes, you are right. A witness is essential."

The man was now speechless and walked away without uttering a word.

Being the headmaster now, I was keeping abreast of the information regarding government grants for the students belonging to the lower castes. Sometimes there were special funds meant for tribal students only. The Sansis were termed as 'Vimukat Jatis', denotified tribes. I wanted the Sansi children to study and take advantage of the government assistance.

Once there was a special grant from the government for the Sansi students only. This aid was, two rupees for the primary class, five rupees for the middle class and ten rupees for the higher class students per month. This was the first time that special forms were printed for such kind of grant. I procured the forms for the Sansi children in our school and submitted them for its sanction to the education department.

Initially I was ignorant about the procedure how to withdraw the money from the Treasury office. I enquired from a clerk who worked in our village high school, how to process and obtain the sanction. He advised me an easy working formula. If the student was absent from the school for more than seven days in a month, there was a proportionate deduction from the grant money. I would prepare the statements accordingly and generally there was no problem in receiving the grant money from the Treasury office.

Once I had a bitter experience while withdrawing money from the State Treasury office. After the sanction was granted, the Education Secretary had to countersign the forms before submitting them to the Treasury office. Gurdial Singh was the Education Secretary and I knew him personally. On that day he was not in his seat, so I handed over the forms to his clerk for counter signature. He signed and handed them over back to me. When I presented the forms at the Treasury office, the cashier there just hurled the forms back at me in an inappropriate way and demanded, "Masterji, you produce the witness otherwise I refuse to make the payment."

I was annoyed at his gratuitous rude behaviour but I controlled myself.

He then unceremoniously added, "You make sure that your witness should be known to me."

I was in a quandary as to where I would look for such a witness. I had no other contact except the Secretary Gurdial Singh. I decided to return to the Secretary's office. Fortunately by that time he had come back to his seat. I narrated how the cashier there had admonished me. He replied to me, "Don't bother about it Natha Singh; you give me your forms."

He signed the forms with a green pen and put his rubber stamp. He returned the forms to me and assured me that this time the cashier would not dare to question me.

I was still a little shaken and asked, "Sir, what about the witness?"

The Secretary smiled and replied, "Natha Singh, you challenge the cashier that your witness won't come."

I regained confidence with his assurance now and reappeared at the cash counter. I pushed the forms to the cashier. He stared at me and grumbled, "Where is the witness?"

I retorted, "There is no need for me to bring any witness."

He was stunned at my reply and immediately closely scrutinised the forms. He observed the personal stamp and signature of the Secretary.

He now stepped down from his high horse and meekly whispered, "Yes, now I understand why your witness will not come."

He quietly counted the money and handed it over to me without any further query."

*   *   *

Theft in the School - I

*T*he fighting spirit of my father was remarkable when he was absolutely confident about himself. He would not get bothered about the outcome but stick to his point. The passage of time could never dampen his fighting spirit even though issues were settled after a prolonged period. He would not relent under any kind of pressure. He struggled for years and tackled the odds with an extraordinary courage. His strength to rise against the unjust was admirable even when the people against him were in a more powerful position. He dared to challenge them explicitly and stood his ground even when the world around was attempting to prove him wrong. He fought for a cause but not for any personal achievement. His zeal to encounter the unfair state of affairs had never diminished. His capability to compose extensive correspondence was incredible. Fighting for the school theft case had developed into an obsession for him. This episode highlighted that sometimes if small things are ignored in life, they could *later emerge like a volcano with serious repercussions and abandon us with nothing to fall back upon.*

I was grown up when the theft had occurred in the village primary school. I had closely observed the happenings that occurred during the whole incident. Susan and I commenced recording another tantalising long episode of his life.....

"Once our BEO, Block Education Officer, had provided stationery for the school and I was making entries in our school inventory register. When I was casually scrutinising the record register, I noticed that there was an entry in the register of a theft in the school way back in 1938. It was a minor theft of one metal bell, one glass and one mug. But there was an important remark in the register that the theft should have been reported to the police and a copy of First Information Report (FIR) should have been attached in the record register. At that time the school inspectors had the authority to waive off or delete the old entries of the obsolete items from the school record register. They could write off the list of condemned articles from the school records but could not nullify that theft entry.

Being in-charge of the school, things were working fairly smoothly. Everything was running peacefully without any major happenings. Unfortunately on June 6, 1962, when I reached school that morning, I was stunned to see the teachers and students waiting for me outside the main gate. The teachers informed me that a theft had occurred in the school and they had held back the students outside to avoid tampering with the evidence. I noticed that the bolt of the main door was wrecked. We commanded the students to remain outside. Along with the other teachers, I undertook an inventory of the missing articles. We established that only three items were missing, one glass, one jug and three mugs. We protected the suspected foot prints in the open area if it could help the police to identify the thief. After completing the inventory, we permitted the students to enter the school premises.

The total value of the stolen goods was approximately about four rupees and fifty paisa. I consulted the other teachers and decided to inform the police. Our first priority was to report this matter to the village Sarpanch, Zaildar Pritam Singh. Along with the other teachers, I went to our village Sarpanch.

He was astonished to see why all the teachers had approached him together. We met and greeted him. He handed over the mouthpiece end of his hearing pipe to me and inquired, "Natha Singh, what brings you here with the other teachers? Is there any serious problem?"

I briefed him about the theft in the school and reported to him, "Sarpanch Saab, you know that the government property has been stolen from the school. Though the loss is insignificant yet we cannot disregard it. We have to lodge a FIR, first information report, with the police."

He was shocked to hear about this theft and replied in surprise, "I am unable to understand what the thief had expected to steal from the school. There are hardly any valuables in the school. But you are right to inform the police for investigations."

I again asked him, "But I expect you to accompany me to the Dehlon police station to report this theft. Are you free today?"

He appeared doubtful about coming along with us. After some serious thought he reluctantly replied, "Natha Singh, I have already promised someone to be present in the court today. I personally would not be able to accompany you to the police station. I will prepare a reference slip and you go to the police station to register the FIR."

He wrote a reference note to the Police Inspector and handed it over to me. I asked the other teachers to go back and manage the school and I proceeded to the Dehlon police station alone.

I walked to the police station and when I reached there I could not find the Police Inspector in his room. Only the 'Moharram', the clerk in the police station, was there and he was engaged in registering another case.

The 'Moharram' casually stared at me and asked, "Yes, why have you come here?"

I replied, "I have come from village Narangwal to lodge a FIR for the theft in our village primary school. Our village Sarpanch has forwarded a note regarding this."

He casually glanced at the reference note and directed me, "Masterji, you sit down here and let me finish this report."

The 'Moharram' carried on registering the case and at one stage I overheard 'that bottles of country liquor and some snacks were confiscated from such and such person during the police raid.' This statement unconsciously got registered in my head. When he finished with that case he received the slip from me and studied it. He returned the slip to me and said, "Well, Masterji, I have seen this slip you may go now. Your complaint will be registered. Our officer will visit to investigate your school theft."

I was surprised how he would register the case without asking me a word. I could not help asking him anything further and returned to the school.

I shared my experience in the police station with the other teachers and they too were confused about it. I also informed the Sarpanch Zaildar Pritam Singh what had happened in the police station. He thought it was advisable to watch and wait for some time.

Since I remembered about an old remark regarding a theft in the school records, it immediately struck me that I should report this theft to the police in writing. I primed a theft report and posted it to the Dehlon police station. At the same time I marked a copy of my report to the Block Education Officer. I mentioned in my statement that I had personally visited the police station to register the theft and the 'Moharram' had verbally advised me that he would register the FIR. I attached copies of both the letters in the school record register. I had used government service stamps on both the letters.

There was no response from the police department as more than two weeks had gone by. It was obvious that my letter remained unattended at the police station. We were surprised that there was no reaction from the police. The other teachers were unsure whether the police would even investigate the case at all. I intended to dispatch a reminder but contemplated to wait for a few more days.

On 28th June, almost twenty days after the theft, one Assistant Sub Inspector (ASI) visited our school. He inquired about the details of the theft and examined the broken door etc. Finally he asked me, "Masterji, do you suspect anyone who could have committed this theft?"

I realized that he was simply executing the formality. This delay had already exhibited their commitment to investigate the case. I reluctantly responded to him, "I do not doubt any person."

The ASI wanted to elucidate the reason of their delay to initiate the probe. At last he excused himself and said, "Masterji, you know we were busy with a very important case. We have to take action on priority basis. It does not matter if such cases like this are investigated a few days later."

I remained silent but understood his intention to justify their delay.

When he got no response from me, he further added, "Masterji, would it make any difference if we show that the theft had occurred only two days ago? We shall cover up the rest. You don't have to worry about it."

Obviously he wanted to protect himself by recording that the theft had taken place on the 26th June instead of 6th June. Then he could justify the investigations after two days. He had no grounds to justify the delay of twenty two days. I was extremely alert to avoid any commitment. I replied, "Inspector, this is not my problem. I have already dispatched my report to the education department regarding this theft."

The Assistant sub Inspector attempted to pacify me to change the date of the theft. He suggested various ways and means how to cover up this delay. I carried on listening to him but paid no heed to his lecture. To end his useless speech I firmly proclaimed, "Look Inspector, I will not amend any records now as there is no ground for me to do so. You may take whatever action you wish."

Now he comprehended clearly that he was trying to pacify me in vain. He asked for my pen with an excuse to note down something and subsequently inserted it in his pocket. He intentionally carried it with him when he departed in a hurry. Later on I suspected that he had probably taken away my pen with the intention to modify the date on my original letter with the same ink and pen. Now I had to act fast to safeguard myself and clip the wings of the police if they attempted foul play with my pen. I immediately mailed the complaint letter to the higher authorities in police department stating that the assistant sub inspector had deliberately taken away my pen with him. I assume that my pen could be misused for official purposes. I also marked the copy of my complaint to the education department as well. The police had invited trouble for themselves but surely my complaint had prevented them making any amendments on my original letter. The police people were in dire straits now. They could not find any way to get out of their self created trap.

The Inspector Raghbir Singh was in-charge of the Dehlon police station at that time. He must have been informed about this initial goof up. He had never approached me personally nor replied to any of my letters. Once he came to our village for some other inquiry. He called me there and tried to impress me, "Masterji, you have mailed several complaint letters to my higher authorities regarding the theft in your school. It would not make any difference to me. I am due for my promotion very soon as DSP, Deputy Superintendent of Police. My promotion orders should be on the way shortly. It would not impinge my career at all."

He wanted to play police tactics with me by this irrelevant statement. I simply replied, "Inspector, I am concerned about the theft in the school. I have no intentions of becoming the inspector in your place, once you are promoted."

He could hardly swallow my scathing reply but avoided to continue any further conversation in front of the others. This attitude of the police people fuelled to push me into writing more letters. There was no sign of any probe for the theft. I would write to the highest authorities in the State and even to the State Home Minister and Chief Minister. They would forward my letters back to the police higher ups and reply to me about their action. When there was no convincing answer from the State authorities, then I began writing letters further to the Central Home Minister, the Prime Minister then finally to the President of India. They followed the same protocol to redirect my letters to the State departments and ultimately it would land in the police department. Then I would mention the cross reference of those letters and write to the local police authorities about any action taken by them with reference to the letters from the higher-ups. Eventually everything would land on the desk of Inspector Raghbir Singh. I would mark the copies of my letters to the education department to update them with the latest development of the case. Sometimes my letters would expand to at least five pages.

Actually there was a case without a case. Because the police had not registered the theft case hence there was no case nor any probe from their side. But on the other hand the theft had occurred and I had initiated the case, hence a case existed from my side. The negligence of the police had put them in a peculiar situation."

* * *

Babaan

A mong the Sansis, carrying the dead body on a decorated stretcher to the cremation ground is called 'Babaan'. At the death of an old person, they would beautify the stretcher with flowers, balloons and coloured paper etc. On the way to the cremation ground they would shower puffed rice mixed with some coins over the dead body. The four individuals called 'kannis', who carry the dead body on the stretcher to the cremation ground. They are the privileged individuals during the funeral rites.

I vividly remember when my uncles had organised 'Babaan' for their father, Gaata. Two days after the funeral of Gaata, my father and uncles along with the other community people collected his ashes. They decided to immerse the ashes in the village canal instead of going to some specific renowned places. I had witnessed certain Sansi rituals performed by my uncles. They wished to perform the ritual called 'theekri'. There are two kinds of theekris, one is kachi theekri and other is pacci theekri. To perform *kachi theekri*, my uncles had prepared a mixture of boiled rice, sugar and ghee and put it in a small earthen pot. They carried a portion of this mixture to a field near the cremation ground. My elder uncle had dug a deep hole in the ground, placed some mixture in it and then closed the hole. After reaching home, they served the balance rice and sugar with ghee mixture first to the 'kannis' and afterwards it was served to all the other visitors.

At the end of the mourning period of thirteen days, as a concluding ritual my uncles had planned to serve *pacci theekri*. For that they had cooked goat meat and prepared boiled rice separately. When both the things were ready, they began layering the boiled rice with ghee and the cooked goat meat. They repeatedly thickly layered it three more times. When this foodstuff was all set, they took out a small portion of it in an earthen pot and now this time they had dug a hole in the ground under a shady tree near their home and inserted the foodstuff in it. They said a small personal prayer and the covered this hole. After this ritual was over then the balance food was served to the 'kannis' first and then to the other people. Though it was expensive for my uncles to provide *pacci theekri* but they had to prove that their father was a prosperous person because they had exhibited it by 'Babban'. It was considered a matter of great pride to serve *pacci theekri*.

Now the new generation does not believe in the 'theekri' rituals. There is a transformation in their thinking. Generally nowadays they follow the Sikh traditions to end the mourning period by performing 'Sehaj Paath'. On the closing ceremony of 'Sehaj Paath', they serve vegetarian food to the whole gathering. Though the Sansis are better off now as compared to the old times, it is rare to witness 'Babaan' nowadays.

*   *   *

Organising Marriages

We could understand that my father was a real well wisher of Baggoo's family. He continued being in touch with Baggoo's family even after his death. My father was profoundly concerned about Baggoo's unmarried children as people may refrain from giving their children in the marriage to a widow's family. He enlightened us how he was involved later on to settle the marriages of Baggoo's children.....

"Baggoo was our family friend in the Sansi community and his ancestors had a healthy association with my uncles. He resided with his family on the other side of our village. He and his wife, Bachni, would frequently visit and share their family problems with us. Both of them would do errands in the village to sustain their large family. Like other Sansis, poverty flashed from their lifestyle without asking. Baggoo was fairly aged now and often remained unwell. His children were still young except his eldest daughter who had been married. The whole responsibility fell on Bachni and somehow she would run the family.

After a brief illness one day Baggoo departed from this world. The whole burden was on Bachni to manage her family. She constantly remained in contact with us even after the death of Baggoo and shared her struggle in bringing up her family single-handedly. She was seriously concerned about her marriageable son and two daughters. She was on the lookout for suitable matches for them but nothing had clicked so far. She would often request me to search for reasonable matches for her children.

Unfortunately the eldest brother of my wife, Beeru had expired long back leaving behind a large family. His youngest brother married Beeru's wife later on. My mother-in-law was still alive and she would also exchange her views regarding the marriageable grandchildren of her deceased son. She was also quite enthusiastic to arrange the marriages of her grandchildren as early as possible. Once I visited her and she casually asked me, "Nathu, I understand that Bachni has a grown up boy in your village, why don't you check with her and see if there is a possibility of him marrying the eldest daughter of your brother-in-law, Beeru?"

I thought that it was a genuine query but I deemed it vital to brief her about the back ground of Bachni's family. I replied to her, "There is no problem in talking to Bachni but I would like to inform you that the boy is illiterate and generally works as a manual labourer in the fields. There is no other source of his income. Bachni also has a large family with other unmarried children. I inform you that the family is very poor and later on I should not be blamed that I have not advised you about it."

She smiled and said, "Do not worry Nathu; I promise that we shall not hold you responsible for anything."

I assured her that I will raise this issue with Bachni and get back to her shortly. I returned home and first had a discussion with my wife because her niece was involved in this matter. Her consent was mandatory before I could proceed any further. She would be the first one who would be answerable from both sides. She approved it positively and we decided to call Bachni to our place. She hurriedly arrived and was surprised to know about this unexpected call from us. She promptly asked me, "Baba, you have called me at such short notice. Is there anything serious?"

She always addressed me as 'Baba.'

I placed the proposal on behalf of my in-laws for her eldest son with the eldest daughter of my deceased brother-in-law. The frown of her anxiety had instantly evaporated from her face and she was now in a cheerful mood. She immediately responded, "Baba, I am excited about this offer and wholeheartedly give my consent to this proposal."

She had sufficient knowledge about the family of my brother-in-law. She also knew that Beeru had two marriageable boys. After a moment she appeared more composed and then added, "Baba, if you judge it appropriate then it prompts me to share another proposition which I have in mind."

Now I was astonished about her impulsive remark and encouragingly asked her, "Bachni, without any hesitation you can explicitly express your opinion."

She immediately interrupted me and asked, "Baba, I wish to convey you an unanticipated proposal from my side. I propose that if your in-laws are primed to offer one daughter in marriage to my son, then I look forward to offer my two daughters in marriage to their sons."

I could not believe this enticing offer from her and appreciated her remarkable suggestion. My wife and I were extremely pleased that there was a sincere opening for both the families. I realised that if this proposal could materialise then each family would have three children married at one go. Their burden would considerably be reduced from the marriage point of view.

Both my wife and I were delighted about her proposal. I said, "Bachni, this appears to be a magnificent proposition for both the families. I will discuss it with my in-laws and hope that it would soon become a reality."

I returned to my in-laws and briefed my mother-in-law about Bachni's novel aspirations. She eagerly informed her youngest son and he considered it a promising development. Afterwards he visited our village and discussed it with Bachni. They mutually agreed and settled the dates of the engagements and the weddings of their children simultaneously. There was no issue involved from the Panth point of view as both the parties belonged to the same Panth. Everything was progressing peacefully and smoothly. On the day of the wedding, Bachni accompanied the marriage party of her son. I was regularly monitoring these developments sans too much interference in their general affairs.

The next day my brother-in-law arrived for his sons' wedding and the marriage party was scrutinised to verify if there was any suspected person belonging to the other Panth. Suddenly there was uneasiness in the family when they detected that there was one person in the marriage party belonging to the other Panth. Unfortunately he was one of the closest friends of my youngest brother-in-law. Bachni righteously enquired from me, "Baba, there is one member in the marriage party who has a connection with another Panth. What is your viewpoint about it?"

Actually I received this information before Bachni disclosed it to me. I had no legitimate justification to defend his presence even though he was a dear friend of my brother-in-law. I had to remain unbiased under all circumstances. I frankly answered her, "Look Bachni, we have no intentions to disgrace anybody in the marriage party but as per our community rule you can deny to honour him if my brother-in-law demands 'Sardari' for him. You have the right to decline it."

Bachni accepted my practical advice and treated this man as a respectable member of the wedding party. They were well taken care of at the time of the reception.

My brother-in-law was also uncertain about 'Sardari' for his friend. During the ceremony when the members were about to be honoured, my brother-in-law requested Bachni to handover the total number of 'Sardaris' to evade the direct insult to his friend publicly. Bachni was predetermined to distribute Sardaris individually. My brother-in-law again insisted on total Sardaris but Bachni refused to yield under pressure. She was absolutely right in her own way; else in future she would have faced the consequences of this one wrong step. I had no role to play in this exercise and remained a silent observer. Ultimately my brother-in-law began announcing the names of the individual members for Sardaris. When he asked Sardari for his friend, then Bachni point blank refused it. My brother-in-law and his friend felt openly affronted in the gathering. My brother-in-law got furious and looked at me, but I was helpless to defend him.

I questioned my brother-in-law, "Why did you take this risk bringing your friend along when you were fully aware about the law of our community regarding the Panth issue?"

He did not reply as he was evidently upset without realising his own mistak."

*   *   *

Theft in the School – II

"The primary school theft episode continued for a few years and there was no let up in my writing letters to the various authorities. I had still not received any direct reply or reaction from Inspector Raghbir Singh. The police was active in their own way as Inspector Raghbir Singh was operating behind the scene. He approached The Sant to persuade me through one of the followers, to find a solution to this muddle. He wanted The Sant to pressurise me to alter the date in the record. During the monthly function I would regularly brief The Sant about the progress of this case. The Sant did not respond to that follower because he was fully cognizant of the dire consequences if I modified any record at this stage. As a result I would straightway lose my job.

When the police people in Dehlon could not discover any means to intimidate me and then they adopted a policy to attack my personal affairs. I had organised a special 'Saptah Paath', a weeklong religious function at home at the behest of The Sant. It was like once in a life time event for me. The Sant had promised me to bless the occasion with his presence at the closing ceremony. The recitation of the Holy Book had started and I would spend maximum time in attending to it. This programme was progressing peacefully. I wanted to celebrate the concluding ceremony in style and decided to use a loudspeaker. In those days special permission was mandatory to use the loudspeaker. This authorization was granted only by the District Collector's office in Ludhiana. I deputed my cousin Gurdial to make the necessary arrangements for the permission in advance.

A day before the closing ceremony, in the morning Gurdial went to Ludhiana and applied for the authorization to play the loudspeaker. He came across a constable there who was posted in Dehlon police station. He recognized Gurdial and enquired, 'Gurdial, how come you are here in the district collector's office?'

Gurdial naively replied, 'Natha Singh has organised 'Saptah Paath' at his residence. Tomorrow is the final day of the ceremony and I am waiting for permission to use the loudspeaker.'

After getting this news, something impish cropped up in the mind of this constable and he lost no time in returning to Dehlon police station. He updated the station in-charge about my function in the village.

I attended school in the day and that evening as I was about to close the school and I saw a police constable approaching me. I was apprehensive and wondered why this constable was heading directly towards me. As the constable drew near he said, "Masterji, our Inspector Raghbir Singh intends to meet you today. You must ensure to be there without fail. He has something important to discuss with you today itself."

When I heard this, momentarily I had an ominous feeling and replied, "Look tomorrow there is a religious function at my home and it would not be feasible for me to come there today."

The constable immediately reverted, "Yes Masterji, I know it very well. I met Gurdial in Ludhiana today. But the Inspector wants you to be there today."

He quickly moved away without waiting for my further reply.

Now I presumed that their intention was merely to harass me. They premeditated that if they summon me to the police station today then under duress I may agree to amend the records as they desired. Beyond doubt they were well aware that this religious ceremony was exceptionally important for me.

I hurriedly reached home. I was very upset and told the people at home that the Inspector wanted to meet me today itself. As we were discussing this latest development then one of my close friends bluntly said, "Natha Singh why do you worry? You're not a criminal? You go there, show your face and come back. In the meantime we will manage here."

I was still uncertain but unenthusiastically decided to proceed to Dehlon police station. I went on foot and by the time I reached there the sun had already set. Before I entered the police station, an old man was standing in front of its main gate. He possibly recognised me and said, "Masterji, I had stolen three mugs from the school."

I was absolutely stunned when he stated this. Then I asked him, "If you have the three mugs, what about the glass and the jug?"

He plainly denied, "No, I do not have the glass and the jug."

I wondered about the set up of the police people but I shot back at the old man and asked, "But why are you confessing it to me, you go and tell the police."

He remained silent.

When I went inside, I found that the police inspector Raghbir Singh seemed to be deeply absorbed in some paper work. I greeted him and asked, "Inspector, you have summoned me to appear urgently, what is so important now?"

Without even looking at me he stated, "Masterji, you sit down there. Don't you see that I am very busy?"

I quietly sat down on a wooden bench in a shocked state and observed that he was not interested in me at all. I had no option except to sit and wait. It gave an impression that the Inspector wanted to clear his whole backlog of paper work today itself. Every moment weighed heavily on me as my mind was back home, engrossed with the tensions of the ceremony tomorrow. The Inspector did not even bother to glance at me. I was helplessly fuming and very upset with the indifferent attitude of the Inspector. There is a religious programme at my home and here I was, sitting in the police station. Why? I had gauged their mean intentions and understood that their basic plot was to harass me by just making me sit in the police station. After about three hours the Inspector called one sub-inspector, "You inform Masterji that I do not have time to talk to him today. You reach Masterji home on horse."

The Inspector walked away without even looking at me.

I was furious when the sub inspector conveyed this message to me. I out rightly rejected his offer to reach me home on horseback. There was no possibility for me to walk in the dark night through the remote area. I grumbled at sub inspector, "Anyway it is too late, I don't need your horse ride to go home now. I would prefer to spend the night in the police station."

Then the sub inspector pretended, "No, no, Masterji then you stay at my home."

Another sub inspector also offered, "Masterji, you stay with me."

I observed this drama and plainly affirmed, "I am not going from here. You tell me where I may lie down in the police station for tonight."

They gradually scattered away without a word after that. I lay down in one corner of the police station that night. There was no arrangement for food inside the police station. The eating place outside the police station had already closed down. I had to remain without food that night. I could not sleep as my mind was in turmoil, thinking about the ceremony at home. The next morning after I got up, I asked the sub inspector on duty, "What do you want me to do now?"

He meekly replied, "Masterji you see, the Inspector has not uttered a word to me. I cannot suggest anything to you. If you wish you may see him again."

I retorted, "I have already seen him yesterday. He had no time to discuss anything with me and I know that there is nothing to talk about."

He remained silent but before departing from the police station I conveyed to him, "Listen and tell your Inspector that I will not change the records for his sake."

By the time I departed from the police station for my village I had lost hope of reaching in time for the closing ceremony. My reaching home would require almost three hours. I was silently cursing the Inspector in my heart. I felt disgusted at the way the police people had ruined my dream ceremony. My family was equally worried at home. In the morning they sent a person from the village to Dehlon to find out what had happened to me. When we came across each other, we began laughing. I asked him, "Kaolu, why did you come?"

He was a very jovial person and remarked in jest, "Masterji, I came in search of you whether you are still alive or gone forever."

I laughed and replied, "Don't worry I am not going to die so soon."

He then asked me what happened at the police station. I narrated the whole episode on our way back to the village.

When I arrived home, the religious ceremony was already over. As planned, The Sant had arrived and performed the closing ceremony with full fervour. Everybody condemned the police people when I described what had happened there. Then the Sant advised me not to take it too seriously as lost time could never be regained. The rowdy behaviour of the police people had made me antagonistic and I began writing letters more often. Once I directed my letter to the Governor of the State with a headline, "Who will listen?"

I must have dispatched about more than sixty letters to various officials in a short span.

More interestingly at one point, the police people even denied that I had reported at the police station to lodge the FIR. They assumed that there was no proof because I was not asked to sign any document there when I had gone to lodge the FIR. I only had a verbal conversation with the 'Moharram' in the police station. But luckily my memory bailed me out and I recalled that line '...that some bottles of country liquor and snacks were confiscated from such and such person...' I quoted those lines in my letters. It proved beyond doubt that, yes, I did go to the police station and the above statement was being recorded in the police records at that time. This truth was wedged in everybody's mind and they suspected that the police people had endeavoured to craft a false assertion. I guess that even police people must have verified this fact from their own records because there was no reply from them afterwards.

During that period our new BEO, Block Education Officer, had joined our block education office. He must have scanned my correspondence about the school theft. One day he called me to his office and questioned me, "Natha Singh, how had such a situation arisen?"

I clearly explained to him, "Sir, this had happened due to the sheer negligence of the police department. They had completely ignored me when I initially reported to the police station regarding the theft."

Finally he said, "Masterji, whatever you have said and written in your reports, if it is true, I will definitely get that police inspector suspended."

His colleague who was sitting beside him interrupted, "Officer, the sky may fall but the report of Natha Singh cannot be wrong."

The BEO's office was located in a small town called Raikot, quite a distance away from our village. The police in-charge in Dehlon contacted his counterpart in Raikot and requested him to apply pressure on the new BEO to help him out somehow or the other from the school theft case. The BEO agreed to oblige them. He lost no time and initiated an inquiry against me to verify whether my theft report was true or false. The inquiry officer visited our village and met some people. In a few days, he submitted a concocted report and mentioned in his findings, 'I had contacted the village Panches and Sarpanch and they have said that the theft had not occurred.'

The BEO was in search of some excuse against me. He dispatched a copy of the inquiry report to me along with a memorandum seeking my explanation. I was appalled to study the report of the inquiry officer. He had distorted the facts in his statement and accused me instead. I was not perturbed at all with this report but decided to strike back vehemently.

Unfortunately the Sarpanch then, was no more in this world but I had preserved his slip which he had given me at the time of the theft, to present in the police station for registering the FIR. I wrote back to BEO fervidly, "I have received your letter and regret to learn that you have doubted my integrity. As far as the theft is concerned, I am enclosing a copy of the slip which was handed over to me by the then Sarpanch, to report the theft in the police station. The Sarpanch had addressed this slip to the police inspector. It is clearly evident that the inquiry officer had submitted a fabricated report for reasons best known to him."

Now I did not desire the BEO to sit quietly on my explication. I marked a copy of my explanation to the CEO, Central Education Officer as well. I was in no mood to spare the BEO and wanted him to face the music as well. I despised his double standard attitude and decided not to allow him hushing up this inquiry at his level.

I do not know what was cooking between the BEO and the inquiry officer but the BEO's move to accuse me was thwarted. The BEO was in a tight spot and he had created trouble for himself. Now stringent action could be taken against him too. The BEO never reverted to me after he received my explanation. He probably was wondering how to save his own skin.

After some time I received intimation from the CEO'S office that he was visiting a school in the nearby village Mehma Singh Wala for inspection. I was asked to be present there. I really appreciated that the CEO was concerned about this school theft case.

When I arrived there I was astounded to note that the BEO was already present there. He ignored me and turned his face away. When the CEO was free from his inspection, he called us together inside the room. He opened his bag and pulled out a copy of the enquiry report and my reply.

He demanded from the BEO, "Why have you created this needless muddle? On what grounds have you initiated an inquiry against Natha Singh? Secondly, your inquiry report says that the theft had not occurred but the then Sarpanch had given the slip to him to report the theft in the police station. Why did you act against your own department?"

The BEO was speechless now. He could not mince words to explain anything. But again the CEO insisted for an answer. The BEO tried to make some excuse but the CEO was not willing to listen to his baseless explanation. The CEO again bellowed, "No, no, nothing doing. This is absolutely inappropriate on your part. I am certainly going to take stern action against you and the inquiry officer."

The BEO was on his knees and begged to be pardoned. He was profusely asking for mercy and pleaded to be forgiven this time. I was simply watching this whole scenario.

Then CEO roared again, "Had I acted on your false report, Natha Singh would have lost his job. Who would have been responsible for it? Your irresponsible behaviour is most unbecoming for an officer like you holding such a high rank."

The BEO continued listening to him holding his head down. The CEO questioned him again, "You explain to me, what personal interest had he to lodge a fake theft report? On the top of it you have put up an enquiry against him. What coerced you to behave like this?"

Finally The BEO broke his silence and said, "Sir, the police people had pressurised me to help them."

The CEO was furious and asked both of us to leave.

The BEO was immediately transferred."

*   *   *

Helping Hand

*W*hen we were listening to and recording my father, he asked us to wait for a while as if he was refreshing something in his memory. He desired to share a few remarkable stories where he had facilitated the people in awful situations. He recounted the most significant instances where he had stretched out his helping hand without any self interest. He believed that such timely help had played a crucial role in the dire situation.

In the old times the people did not consider it essential to record the date of birth of their children as most of the deliveries were performed at home. Generally people in the village would casually notify the village watchman regarding the birth and death in the family. He would in turn convey it at his own convenience to the area police station to maintain the records. There was no permanent authentic source to issue a birth certificate in the village. Later on when this certificate was officially or legally *required, then they would look for a possible source to issue an authentic certificate. One of such convenient source was to get in touch with the primary school. Actually the schools were not meant for issuing birth certificates but they could attest what was observed in their records if the child had got admission in the school. To search for an old record was really a Herculean task.*

After a short break he set the ball rolling again.....

Episode - I

"While teaching in the village school, if someone approached me for any assistance within my limits, I considered happily. I owed some social responsibility towards my village. This school had established the foundation for my capability of today. The generous families had played a key role and contributed in conferring favours to me in shaping my career. Now I had an opening to repay its debts in my own way. I had not contained any ill feelings against anyone who had discriminated me. The Government was disbursing my salary for teaching the students but there were certain areas where I could voluntarily opt to help out the people. The School was unlike the government offices where people would approach every day with their problems. My field was specific but I had to take a step forward to help the genuine cases. There must be many occasions when I had assisted the people in general but I remember a few memorable incidents during my teaching career in the village.

Kishori Lal was the headmaster in the school during those days when this incident had taken place. He was obstinate by nature and would take any issues in his normal routine but not under any kind of pressure or persuasion. One of our neighbours, Pritam Singh, had migrated to London long back. After living there for many years he had applied to obtain British citizenship. The authorities there had necessitated his date of birth certificate. He requested his relative to contact the village primary school to certify his date of birth. When the relative received this information, he immediately rushed to Kishori Lal at his home in Kila Raipur. Kishori Lal directed him to contact in the school. The next day the relative approached Kishori Lal in the school for the official document. Kishori Lal reluctantly asked me to get the old admission register. I searched for it and handed it over to him. He asked me to join him and locate the name of Pritam Singh. All three of us sat down together and began searching the entries in the register, page by page. We searched in the register up to the last page with our wholehearted attention but we were unable to trace the name of Pritam Singh. We were disappointed because our efforts had gone futile. The relative required this certificate desperately as Pritam Singh would lose this opportunity to become a permanent citizen there. The relative hesitantly requested Kishori Lal, "Masterji, if you don't mind could we have another look as we might have missed it."

Kishori Lal out rightly refused to delve into it once again and said, "You have seen all the entries one by one with us and we could not locate it. You want me to go through it once more, sorry I will not do it now."

The relative looked helpless as he needed the document badly but there was no other way. He took a last chance and asked Kishori Lal, "Masterji, if you allow, may I request Natha Singh to have another look once again?"

Kishori Lal unwillingly replied, "I don't mind if he wishes to."

I agreed to go through the entries once again and began scrutinising the entries but in vain. In the end we felt weary and I plonked the register in the wooden box. I asked this man to try his luck tomorrow and assured him that I would definitely strive to help him.

I surely remembered that Pritam Singh had enrolled in the school and this notion repetitively got stuck in my head. The next day when I went to school, I wished to look for the name in the register once again. I called one of the students, "Bring me the admission register from the wooden box. I have just kept it on the top yesterday."

The student asked, "Is it the same register which you were looking at yesterday?"

I said, "Yes".

When I opened the register, to my revelation the first name on that page was, Pritam Singh son of Ghota Singh. I was delighted that I had finally succeeded in my efforts. I prepared the certificate and Kishori Lal inked it with his signature and seal. He was also amazed as to how all three of us were not able to locate it yesterday.

Pritam Singh's relative arrived at the school with a grim look on his face and again hesitantly requested me, "Natha Singh, Let's try once again. You know the worth of this certificate for Pritam Singh."

I smiled at him and said, "Relax, I have already located it."

He could not believe it and profusely thanked me. I handed over the certificate to him.

I presume that without this certificate, Pritam Singh would not have gained the British citizenship to settle there with his entire family."

* * *

Episode-II

"Boota Singh was a bachelor and resided in our village along with his two young nephews and a niece. The youngsters had spent their childhood in the village before Boota Singh admitted them in the primary school. After completing their primary school education from Narangwal, they moved out for higher education. The niece of Boota Singh continued staying with him till she got married and settled down. After this Boota Singh was living alone but his nephews would occasionally visit him.

Boota Singh owned an adequate piece of land in our village but he was not interested in cultivating it himself. He had rented his land to a village farmer on a contract basis for farming. He received enough revenue from this contract to live his life comfortably. That farmer continued farming his fields for many years and Boota Singh did not bother to update the records in the land revenue accountant's books. This land book had to be updated every four years. But that farmer had crossed all time limits without any update and could have filed for possession of the land by law if desired. The other farmers in the village would provoke this farmer, 'You have cultivated this land for ages why don't you just grab it? Boota Singh would not be able to stake any claim.'

The farmer was a gentleman and had no intentions to be greedy. He would simply reply, 'Boota Singh has faith in me and I would never shatter his trust.'

Boota Singh had grown quite old now and was ailing for quite a while. From time to time some distant relatives besides his nephews and niece would visit him. He remained unwell and ultimately one day he passed away. Unfortunately he had not registered any title deed in the name of any particular person. After his death, his distant relatives and nephews both made their claim separately for his land and other property. Actually his niece and nephews was the closest kith and kin to inherit his assets. But his distant relatives claimed to be his nearest relatives and contended for the whole property. Now there was a dispute between both the parties and his relatives could not succeed in grabbing the property because the nephews had already occupied the house and taken possession of the land. The other relatives had no alternative except to file a court case to inherit his assets.

The court proceedings commenced and both the sides attempted to prove their close relationship with Boota Singh. The nephews contended that they had lived with Boota Singh and studied in Narangwal. But the relatives refuted this argument and contested that they had never lived with Boota Singh. But the nephews informed the court that they could prove it. The court consented and asked the nephews to produce the evidence at the next hearing.

One day the father-in-law of Boota Singh's niece came to meet me in the school. He introduced himself to me and said that he is posted as a Secretary controlling all the police stations in the State. He then asked me, "Masterji, you know the property case of Boota Singh is in progress in the court. I must have the copy of the admission certificate of Boota Singh's nephews that they had studied in Narangwal."

He briefed me about the whole court case.

When I was young, Boota Singh and I had a good relationship and we would often come across each other in the village. I was fully aware that his nephews had studied in the village primary school. I vividly recalled those days and replied to the Secretary, "Boota Singh was my good friend and I was acquainted with his nephews. I would be glad to facilitate you but there is an official hitch."

Probably the Secretary had not anticipated any difficulty in obtaining the certificate hence he asked me with surprise, "Masterji, what is the anomaly in issuing the certificates?"

I pondered over it from the legal point of view. There was a legal possibility that I could officially be questioned on this issue. To avoid any legal implications for me I advised him, "Look Saab, you are not the legal heir of Boota Singh; it would not be appropriate for me to issue the certificate and hand it over to you. Later on I could officially be queried by my department."

He was amazed at my reply but subsequently asked me, "I had not realized it that way. What is the way out then?"

I replied, "In this case you have to obtain special permission from the District Education Officer to issue the certificates and hand them over to you. Only then will I be authorized to take necessary action."

"That should not be a problem; I will procure the authorisation letter and get back to you." The Secretary replied enthusiastically.

I remembered when I was in the primary school, the elder nephew of Boota Singh was one year ahead of me and the younger one was one class after me. I knew that the nephews belonged to village Raean. A few days later the secretary fetched the permission from the District Education Officer and furnished it to me.

I examined the authorization and advised, "Secretary Saab, I have to go through the old school records and for that I need some time. You may contact me after two days."

I didn't know the father's name of the nephews but the Secretary had handed over complete details on a piece of paper before he left. I looked for their admission dates and prepared the certificates accordingly.

Before the Secretary returned to collect the certificates, there was a sudden turn of events. The other relatives of Boota Singh were not sitting quiet. They were also engrossed in doing the ground work and exploring the possibility to find an effective link to contact me. To establish an efficient channel, they contacted a former teacher Karnail Singh who at one time used to teach with me in Narangwal.

Subsequently I received a message from Karnail Singh that he would visit me the next day. I was wondering what compelled Karnail Singh to have a word with me. I had no clue to his unexpected necessity to get in touch with me. Karnail Singh arrived early in the morning when I had barely opened the school. He pretended to be very friendly now. He asked me, "Natha Singh, I have approached you for a special favour. I absolutely rely upon you and anticipate that you will not let me down."

I could still not deduce what he was hinting at and his amenable attitude towards me was deceptive. I was instantly on my guards and questioned him, "Karnail Singh, don't beat around the bush. Tell me straightway what you are expecting from me."

Without wasting any time he opened up and said, "I am sure that the nephews of Boota Singh would certainly approach you for the school admission certificates. I want you to decline from issuing the certificates at any cost."

Before I could utter a word he further added, "Look, there is a message for you from the other relatives of Boota Singh. They are ready to proffer anything for this favour. Please do not furnish the certificates at any cost."

I was stunned by his stipulation about the school certificates. I had not anticipated this luring deal from Karnail Singh. My mind immediately began stirring to seek a solution and escape from this tempting deal. I was least interested in this offer. I pretended and replied to him, "Karnail Singh, you are rather late as I have already handed over the certificates yesterday."

He was gobsmacked and regretted his delay. He meekly uttered, "Natha Singh, I cannot blame you; I admit my mistake and regret not contacting you earlier."

I timidly responded, "Sorry, Karnail Singh it is too late now."

He was extremely disappointed and cursed himself for being late. He walked off in despair.

The next day the Secretary came to collect the certificates. He impatiently asked, "Masterji, are the certificates ready?"

I smiled and said, "Yes, please sign in the register to confirm receipt."

After he signed in the register and I handed over the certificates to him. He was very glad and thanked me. When he was about to go, he pulled out a five rupee note from his wallet and held out his hand offering it to me.

I stared at him and said, "Secretary Saab, What is this? Why are you offering this money to me?"

Perhaps he had not expected this rejection but lamely repeated, "Masterji, this is nothing, you just keep it."

I was rather annoyed now and resented, "Secretary Saab, no thanks, I don't need it, put it back in your wallet."

The Secretary felt humiliated at my refusal and reluctantly put back the five rupee note in his pocket. He then remarked, "Masterji, you are the first person who has declined to accept money. Otherwise people gladly accept it when they favour others."

I actually felt offended and responded; "Secretary Saab, now you listen to me very carefully. I have extended this favour just because of my friendship with Boota Singh and his nephews. I have honoured our amity but not for your five rupee note."

The Secretary was amazed when I revealed the purpose of extending my help to him. Finally he said, "Sorry Natha Singh, if I could be of any assistance to you at anytime, please let me know."

Initially I wished to remain quiet about the attempt made by their opponents. As he had instigated me, now it was necessary to highlight to him regarding the alluring deal offered by the opponents. Before he could step away, I strongly put it into words, "Look Secretary Saab, you are unaware of the facts; your opponents were here yesterday and were prepared to offer me 'anything' not to provide the certificates. I declined it by stating that I had already handed over the certificates when actually these certificates were still lying in my drawer."

The Secretary was stunned when I uncovered this truth to him. He was speechless now and walked away quietly. The nephews of Boota Singh won the case in the court and could claim the property on the basis of those certificates."

*   *   *

Accident

I *had joined the wedding party of my second uncle, Jeet, when he remarried. A few days before his marriage, unfortunately his mother was accidentally, seriously injured. I can still visualize the dent and scar on the right side of her forehead. The poor people were always petrified to move their patients to the big hospitals in the city. They were incapable of paying for the expenses. Their helplessness would force them to accept the death of a person instead of ruining the life of the whole family in debts. My uncles had faced such a situation with their mother. My father was seriously concerned when this accident had occurred. He was ready to recount the whole story in his own words and we began recording......*

"The 'jungle' girls had parted their ways with my cousins. My elder cousin, Gurdial was staying alone and his mother Bachni was staying with my younger cousin, Jeet. My cousin Jeet was almost close to forty when his mother organised his second marriage. The date of the engagement was already fixed and a few days before this, some guests had already arrived. She was busy with the preparations and noticed that the Chillum of their hookah was damaged from one side and was difficult to use. Without any delay she considered it necessary to replace this Chillum with a new one. She headed for the shop to purchase new one but unfortunately could not obtain it from one shop. She did not wish to postpone it and proceeded to another shop. On the way the electricity people were installing new electrical lines in the street. When they were stretching the wire, an iron angle popped out from the wall and hit my auntie on her forehead. She began bleeding profusely and the workers were shocked by this unexpected accident. That iron angle had severely injured her forehead. Immediately they carried her to the village hospital and informed us at home. Everybody became panicky and the men folk rushed to the hospital.

We arrived at the hospital and observed that Dr. Malvia, a senior doctor, was attending to her. After he finished with the first aid he came out. I personally knew doctor Malvia and asked him, "Doctor, what is her condition?

Without waiting for any other question he immediately replied, "Masterji, She is in a serious state and it would be very tough for me to handle this case here. Most likely we have to shift her to CMC, Christian Medical College hospital in Ludhiana. I have dispensed first aid to her and the bleeding has stopped."

I enquired again, "Doctor is she conscious? Can we see her now?

He replied, "Yes, she is conscious and you can see her for a short period."

We entered the room and she glanced at us. I asked her, "Auntie, are you Okay?"

She was unable to utter a word but nodded affirmatively and simultaneously raised her hand towards Ludhiana and signalled 'no'. Perhaps she must have heard Dr. Malvia talking about transferring her to Ludhiana. I understood what she meant and we came out from her room. Dr. Malviya had gone to his residence.

Her son, Jeet, had gone out when this accident had occurred. A message was sent to him to return quickly. We were anxiously waiting for him as we could not take any decision on our own to move her to Ludhiana. After some time my cousin Jeet also arrived at the hospital in a very nervous state of mind. He instantly enquired from us, "How is my mother? What is her condition?"

We asked him to calm down and conveyed to him what was advised by the doctor. We further added, "She is of course serious but we were waiting for you. Dr. Malviya has recommended referring her to CMC Ludhiana. But she has signalled that she does not want to go there."

Jeet was perplexed now and unable to make up his mind whether to move his mother to Ludhiana or not. At last he decided to keep her here at his own risk because it would be disastrous for him to meet the expenses in CMC. The CMC hospital in Ludhiana was well known to the people for being very expensive, especially for the poor. It was beyond the reach of the common man to get treatment there. Unfortunately there were hardly any other good hospitals around, particularly in the rural areas.

Finally we all decided that it would be advisable to meet Dr. Malvia at his residence and apprise him of our intentions. We headed for his residence but he met us on the way to the hospital. He was not amazed to see us but instead asked me, "Masterji, what have you people decided now? I understand the wound is deep and it is better to avoid taking any risk. There is a possibility of complications; hence I advise to transfer her to Ludhiana."

I briefed him hesitantly, "Dr. Malvia, I understand your sincere concern but she is dependent upon her younger son. He is getting married in a few days. He cannot afford the expenses in CMC. He makes his living by doing manual labour in the fields. He has refused to move her to Ludhiana."

He promptly asked me, "Masterji, who is her younger son?"

I pointed towards Jeet and Dr. Malvia explained, "Jeet, your mother is in a serious condition, shall we send her to Ludhiana?"

Jeet was puzzled and replied in a worrisome tone, "I cannot afford to spend money on her if she is admitted to CMC Ludhiana. I would prefer her to die instead of sending her there."

We were all traumatised by the way he had replied in a baffled condition. Dr. Malvia got really exasperated with him and retorted, "Why do you speak like this? There is no guarantee that she will die here and there is no assurance that she would survive there. But you should not have spoken in this crude manner."

I endeavoured to calm down Dr. Malvia, "Dr. Saab, he is an illiterate person. Please do not mind what he has said."

Dr. Malvia cooled down after some time and then expressed his intentions, "Masterji, if the situation is so desperate then I will retain her here and do my best to treat her."

We all heaved a tremendous sigh of relief at his assurance. Jeet was in tears and profusely thanked Dr. Malviya.

Then Dr. Malviya personally attended to her and commenced appropriate treatment. He monitored her progress on a daily basis and after a week or ten days she had become stable. He discharged her from the hospital to avoid unnecessary expenses and advised her to get the bandage changed in the hospital after every two days. Ultimately she was able to participate in the marriage of her son."

*　　*　　*

Dedication of The Sant

"Ever since The Sant had started performing 'Akhand Paath' in the Gurudwara, he had never skipped it to the best of my knowledge. I am not aware when The Sant had originally commenced this monthly ceremony. Ever since I came in contact with him, he had never skipped this programme. Decades had gone by and The Sant had continued holding this monthly ceremony in the Gurudwara month after month. He was absolutely dedicated to this ceremony with full fervour. Things had been going comfortably and once a testing time had occurred when The Sant performed this ceremony under almost unfeasible circumstances.

In 1965, this monthly function happened to fall during those days when the war had occurred between Pakistan and India. The Indian Air Force aircraft would continue perambulating round the clock. Sometimes anti aircraft guns would boom unexpectedly when there was an air raid by the enemy's aircraft to attack the Air Force base station in our area. The sirens would blare at a high pitch to alert the people to run to safety. People in the surrounding villages would abandon their houses and hop into trenches. The doors and windows of the houses would jangle when a bomb was dropped. There was an overall blackout in the night and nobody would put on any lights to avoid being bombed. People would finish their dinner early and remain alert the whole night. The people in the villages had voluntarily stepped up their vigilance especially in the night, to guard their villages from any suspected spies. The military had also surrounded the Air Force station area. They had set up observation posts in the area and installed one post near The Sant's Gurudwara.

This Gurudwara is situated right at the foot of the Air Force station. The war was in full swing and there was no indication as yet for cease fire. The Sant was profoundly anxious about his monthly programme. He had no intentions to defer this age old tradition. He was determined to execute this function come what may. At the same time he was absolutely aware about the prevailing conditions, but his sincere devotion hard-pressed him to go ahead under any circumstances which appeared virtually impractical.

We, the closest followers of The Sant assembled at The Sant's place a day before the beginning of the function. The Sant discussed with us and he was determined to hold this programme without fail. We planned to converse with the in-charge of that army post. We along with The Sant convened a meeting with the in-charge there. Incidentally he was also a Sikh. The Sant informed the army officer, 'Saab, our monthly gathering is continuously taking place over many decades. I do not wish to interrupt this tradition but we are prepared to create any infra structure to ensure the safety of everybody. You may instruct and supervise the necessary arrangements and guide us from the safety point of view.

The Sikh in-charge understood the significance of the function and finally agreed to grant us permission under certain conditions. He firmly instructed us, 'First you must camouflage the Gurudwara and then ensure that no inside light was emanating from any angle. You may proceed with the arrangements and after you complete it, then I will scrutinize it.'

Under the supervision of The Sant, we began masking the Gurudwara. We veiled the doors and windows with banana leaves and other tree branches. We erected another small wall in front of the main door to obstruct any direct light from inside. A small side passage was created with just enough space to enter the rooms. The camouflage looked so perfect that nobody would even guess there was any Gurudwara within. When we completed our ground work, The Sant requested the army officer to visit and examine the arrangements and advise us if any further modifications were required. The officer minutely inspected the place and he was completely satisfied with the arrangements. After the inspection was over the army officer informed The Sant, 'I am convinced with your perfect cover up. You may go ahead with your function. I will re-examine it during the function to perceive if any further modifications are necessary.'

We were indeed grateful to the officer who had taken a calculated risk under such dangerous conditions. The Sant directed us to take all precautions especially in the night while moving in and out of the rooms. The people from the village were scared when they discovered that the programme would be on. They were apprehensive about their safety but no one dared to question The Sant and prevent him performing this function. When the people noticed that Gurudwara was undetectable after camouflage, then their fear had abated.

The function commenced in its normal course with a few selected followers who were essential to manage this programme. Continuous recitation of the Holy Book was going on smoothly. In the evening, The Sant in the presence of the Army Officer, asked us to put on the lamps and re-examined the setup to check if any ray of light was visible from outside. But our arrangement turned out to be absolutely perfect. The Army Officer seemed to be totally satisfied with the arrangements and departed after giving us a few more instructions. Late in the evening The Sant left for his home. His house was about a hundred meters away from the Gurudwara. The first night remained peaceful and luckily there was no air raid.

The Sant again joined us early in the morning after his routine individual recitation. He monitored the progress of this function and spent most of his time with us. He was contented that the programme was progressing in its customary way. There was no siren warning about an air raid in the day except the routine sorties of the Indian Air Force aircrafts for nonstop vigil. We had no trepidation in our minds and carried on with our regular course. We cooked food in the Gurudwara during the day and had an early dinner before sunset. The Sant re-checked the arrangements minutely once again and then returned to his home.

During the second night, I was on recitation duty along with another preacher. In the middle of the night, we suddenly heard the sound of an aircraft flying overhead. Our other followers who were resting at that time immediately got alert. The Sant also heard the sound of the aircraft and rushed to the Gurudwara from his home. We were all amazed to see him with us in no time. He was composed and counselled us, "Don't be anxious, you carry on with the recitation."

The next minute the aircraft plunged a bomb and the Gurudwara trembled like a dry leaf. We were jolted up in the air for a moment. I observed that we were safe and the Gurudwara was also intact. The Sant and other followers did not panic either. We were all pleased that there was no loss of life or property. The anti aircraft guns began booming and they sounded the siren. This commotion sustained for a few minutes and after that everything fell silent once again. It appeared that we were out of danger now. The army officer dashed to the Gurudwara to ascertain if the situation was under control. He asked The Sant if everything was in order. He heaved a sigh of relief and returned to his observation post.

In the morning The Sant rejoined us for the closing ceremony. Some people from the village came to participate in the final ceremony. They revealed the true story about the bombing of the previous night. Some people were irrigating the fields from the small canal in the moonlit night. One of them felt a strong urge to smoke a cigarette. He ignited his cigarette without realizing that an aircraft was flying overhead. Perhaps the pilot noticed this light. The aircraft moved in swiftly and released the bomb there. They were lucky to escape as the bomb had missed the target. The splinters of the bomb had hit a big banyan tree and its branches flew into the village. The bomb had created a large crater in the field.

We all considered ourselves to be extremely fortunate that we had survived."

*   *   *

Theft in the School – III

"**O**ne day the delivery man of the sub post office of Gujjarwal was carrying the dispatch bag to the post office in Kila Raipur. While he was passing through a deserted place, he was robbed and murdered. The police swung into action and promptly began their investigations. Since this case was concerned with robbery and murder, a high level police officer was deputed to probe it. The DSP, deputy superintendent of police, initiated the investigations. Inspector Raghbir Singh was still in-charge of the Dehlon police station. Since village Gujjarwal fell under his jurisdiction, he accompanied the DSP. The DSP convened a meeting with all the Panchayats from the nearby villages in Gujjarwal including our village. When the DSP arrived in Gujjarwal, he had an open discussion with the Panchayats from the different villages. Since the DSP was visiting, Inspector Raghbir Singh wanted to exploit this opportunity to solve his own problem regarding the school theft case in Narangwal. He wanted to get out of the tangle of the school theft case and resolve this problem once and for all. During this period Raghbir Singh had a word with the

DSP to help him and close the school theft case. Only a high ranking officer could possibly disregard his gaffe.

It was said that the DSP had told Raghbir Singh, 'If the present Panchayat of Narangwal could testify that the theft had not occurred in the school then he would think about it.'

Raghbir Singh pressurised our village Panchayat to speak in his favour in front of the DSP. To find favours from the police from time to time, our village Panchayat agreed to speak in his favour. Raghbir Singh sent a message to me to appear in Gujjarwal in front of the DSP.

The next day I reached there. At that time Dilip Singh was the new Sarpanch. The DSP called our village Panchayat first and enquired from the Panchayat about the school theft. The Panchayat stated that we are not sure whether the theft had occurred or not as this incident seems to have happened a few years back. They gave a vague reply to the DSP.

There are some reserved seats for the lower castes in the village Panchayat. One Panch, belonging to the lower caste was present there when the DSP had called them in. After their meeting was over with the DSP, the Panch belonging to the lower caste requested me, "Natha Singh, let us have a cup of tea."

I was amused when he invited me for tea. I rejoined, "Fine, let's go."

Then the Panch from the lower caste regretfully said, "Natha Singh, I am not worthy of sharing a cup of tea with you because today the Panchayat has told the DSP that the school theft had not occurred. It is shameful that we have spoken against you."

I was not startled at his revelation but coolly replied, "What you have conveyed to the DSP doesn't make any difference to me. The reality would never change."

After this, the DSP called me in and asked some irrelevant questions. He enquired, "Masterji, the total cost of this theft is around three or four rupees. Why have you wasted so much government money using government services stamps for your letters?"

I strongly resented, "DSP Saab, I have not wasted any government money while mailing letters to all concerned. I have spent money from my own pocket. If you have any doubts, you can verify it."

He refrained from asking me any questions regarding the theft as he was already aware of the facts.

In the end I candidly proclaimed, "DSP Saab, the police people have crossed the limit when they crushed my personal religious sentiments. I had a rare religious ceremony at my home and they deliberately spoilt it by keeping me in the police station and harassed me there without a cause. Otherwise I have no personal grudge against any individual. The theft case is an official issue."

The DSP glanced scornfully at Inspector Raghbir Singh and then asked me to leave. I don't know what he had riposted to Raghbir Singh about our school theft case but surely a few days later the cleaver had fallen on Raghbir Singh. He was transferred from the Dehlon police station to the Ludhiana police lines (on beat duty) as a punishment.

A new station in-charge had joined in place of Raghbir Singh. May be he wanted to stay aloof from this theft case because he had not reacted in any manner.

My cousin, Gurdial, was a frequent visitor to Ludhiana for one reason or the other. Once he bumped into Raghbir Singh in Ludhiana. Then Gurdial asked him, "Inspector Saab, how are you? How is life treating you now?"

Raghbir Singh regretfully stated, 'Gurdial, the fact is that your brother has blocked my career. There is no ray of hope for me and now even the DSP has abandoned me. If Natha Singh writes one more letter, I would straightaway lose my job.'

Gurdial returned home and narrated the pitiable condition of Raghbir Singh. He narrated that the sheen of a police inspector had now absolutely vanished from the pompous Raghbir Singh. He was feeling totally marred because none of his seniors were interested in listening to him anymore. He had virtually surrendered now.

At that stage, I decided to relent from my stand as there was no point in pushing this case anymore. I was not going to gain anything personally and there was no way for the police to unravel this petty theft as several years had already elapsed. The police people had already paid the price for their negligence.

I finally decided to call off this case.

I was a government servant and had executed my duty to report the theft of government property. If there was any dereliction of duty on the part of the police, I was not responsible for it. I stayed on the right course from the very beginning.

At last one Assistant Sub Inspector came to our village and met one Panchayat member. I was called over to meet him. He took out my pen from his bag and said, "Masterji, you had written complaints about your pen. Please take your pen and give me the receipt for it."

After I received my pen, I remarked, "It would be needless to say that the police could have misused this pen to change the dates and I could have lost my job."

He had no answer for it but politely replied, "Masterji, let's forget the old story. Your pen has written off the destiny of some stalwarts in the police department."

This theft case remained unresolved forever but it had literally traumatised the police department."

*   *   *

"A few months had hardly passed by after I had stopped writing about the school theft case when an assistant sub inspector of police from Dehlon illegally wanted to search my house.

My cousins used to brew country liquor. Off and on the police would often conduct raids to search their houses and the surrounding areas. My house was adjoining to my cousins. A police sub inspector from Dehlon along with some constables stormed into the houses of my cousins. They searched their houses but could not discover any illegal material. There was some fodder stacked on my roof. That inspector and his constables searched the pile of fodder also. Perhaps the police informer had concisely reported that my cousins had concealed their liquor on the pond side. Only my house was on the pond side where some wild shrubbery had grown. Parenthetically I was at home when this search was carried out. The people from the village had gathered there to observe the raid.

To explore the pond side, the police had to cross through my house. When they entered my house, I objected to it. I asked the inspector, "You cannot trespass my house without permission. This is against the law as well. Do you have a search warrant for my house?'

He could not believe his ears and he was absolutely stunned when I challenged him. Perhaps the sub inspector thought, 'Who could he be to stop me in this manner?'

He felt embarrassed in front of the villagers. To show his authority, he ordered his constables, "You search his house also."

I strongly protested, "Inspector, how can you rummage around in my house without a proper search warrant?"

The Inspector did not listen to me and asked the constable to proceed with the search.

I confronted him again, "But let me tell you that you will pay the price for this high handedness. if you are bent upon illegally searching my house I have one condition for it."

The sub Inspector directed his men to hold on and asked me, "What is your condition?"

"If you insist then only one of your constables should enter my house that too with just a loin cloth. I have my doubts that your men could implant something illegal if they go inside in their full uniform. How do I know what they are carrying in their pockets?" I strongly argued.

The sub Inspector looked at me awkwardly but considered my stipulation. He asked one of the constables to remove his uniform and wrap a piece of cloth around his waist and then searched the house.

The constable followed the orders and reluctantly began searching my house. He searched one room and before entering the second room he suggested to the sub inspector, "Saab, there is no point in searching further. There seems nothing objectionable in this house."

The sub Inspector asked, "Now it's on record that we have searched his house. You conduct the search thoroughly."

The constable searched the house for formality sake and came out. After this they searched the pond side but could not trace anything objectionable.

I was determined not to spare this sub inspector now. I complained to the Superintendent of police, 'Your police sub inspector has searched the house of a government servant without a proper search warrant. What authority had he to do so? He had attempted to malign me without any valid reason.'

There is an old proverb 'Once bitten, twice shy.'

There was an instant reaction to my complaint. The sub inspector was immediately removed from the Delhon police station and sent to the police lines."

*   *   *

"In its own way my correspondence on the Narangwal School theft case had left its conspicuous impression in the various police offices. One person working in the office of the superintendent of police in Ludhiana were familiar with an unseen person, Natha Singh. My correspondence regarding the school theft was enough, that the staff engaged in filing my letters remembered the name of one Natha Singh very well. I came across one such person during the State assembly elections. I was assigned for election duty in village Sakhana along with one of my friends Mohan Lal from Gujjarwal. We were supposed to join the others in a school there. As usual I marched on foot from my village. They had bicycles and reached there in advance. The police staff arrived in their own vehicle.

One of the police personnel asked Mohan Lal, 'Who is Natha Singh among your staff?'

Mohan Lal was astonished when he enquired about me. He became curious and asked, "Why are you looking for Natha Singh?"

The police personnel replied, "I am interested in meeting him."

Mohan Lal replied, "He has not yet reported. He would soon arrive by foot taxi."

Mohan Lal was a quite a jovial person. He saw me approaching when I was about hundred yards away from the school. He dashed into the school and excitedly called out to that policeman, 'Come out quickly, the foot taxi is arriving!'

Both of them appeared outside and were waiting for me. Mohan Lal was laughing and introduced me to the policeman. Then the policeman exclaimed, "So you are the great Natha Singh!"

I did not understand what he meant by it. Out of curiosity I inquired from him, "I do not know you but why were you on a look out for me?"

He asked me not to take it seriously and subsequently he added, "I am employed in the office of the Superintendent of Police in Ludhiana. When I received the list of staff on election duties, I read the name of Natha Singh. I presumed that you could be the same person who had written numerous letters regarding the school theft case. Hence out of my curiosity I looked forward to meeting you personally."

After that we both sat down and chatted for some time regarding the theft case. During our conversation he elaborated, 'Your school theft case file contained more than two hundred and fifty pages. We were amazed that such a small case had blown out of proportion due to the sheer negligence of the police.'

He ended up saying, 'The police should have registered the FIR when you had first reported to the police. Secondly, the Inspector should not have ruined your religious function.'

* * *

My father never hesitated to walk to any place. He would not wait for public transport for a short distance of ten-fifteen miles. He would only seek public transport for a long journey. When he got a job as a permanent teacher, he would easily walk ten to twelve miles one way, every day. Bicycles were rare at that time. He didn't have enough money to buy an expensive bicycle. He purchased an old bicycle for us when we were studying in the high school. He never made any attempt to learn cycling. We persuaded him to our level best but he was too scared of falling from it. He feared that he would break his bones if he fell from the bicycle while learning. When I used to accompany him to The Sant he would comfortably sit on the bicycle carrier seat. Otherwise he would not touch the bicycle at all.

In very old times having a bicycle, was a matter of great pride. People could not afford to purchase a bicycle easily. To show off, some people would borrow a bicycle and walk with it to their in-laws. My younger uncle, Jeet, was very fond of bicycles. He had saved enough money to buy a brand new Raleigh cycle. He was very proud of it.

* * *

Appearing in court

My father was closely associated with the happenings in the village but at the same time he remained aloof. He would walk to and from the school for his duty. He would never spend time in chatting with people on the way or made any courtesy visits in the village. We raised a buffalo most of the time and he was fond of grazing her. During the summer he would rest after returning from the school and subsequently drive the buffalo out for grazing and bring her back in the evening. He had another companion, Master Harcharan Singh, who would join my father with his own buffalo. Besides this he had never attended other activities in the village except some religious programmes. He would not participate in any general gatherings in the village. He was excited to recount another interesting story to us.....

"I remember when Dilip Singh had accompanied his son for admission in the village primary school. His young lad was a bit nervous and clinging to him. Dilip Singh said to me, "Masterji, he is my younger son Tejinder Singh and I have brought him for admission in the primary school."

I was well acquainted with Dilip Singh as he was the the Sarpanch of the village now. To ascertain the age of the child, I casually asked Dilip Singh, "What is his age?'

"About five and half years", he replied.

"Then he is eligible for admission", I answered.

I pulled out a blank admission form from the drawer and asked Dilip Singh to fill it. He filled in the entries and returned the form to me. Before accepting the form back from him I inquired, "Dilip Singh, did you read the instructions carefully?"

"No", he promptly replied.

I returned the form and asked him to read it carefully.

There was a clause in the admission form stating 'it is mandatory that the parents must read the admission form thoroughly or have it read to them at the time of admission.'

He laughed and took the form from me and went through the instructions.

"Yes, Masterji, now I have read it but I must appreciate that you follow the proper procedure for everything", he commented in a lighter vein.

I admitted Tejinder Singh in class one and charged the stipulated fees from Dilip Singh.

Dilip Singh and other farmer had a dispute over a piece of land in our village. The land was said to be registered in the name of Tejinder Singh. This matter could not be resolved locally as the other farmer also claimed for this. Ultimately a court case was filed. This case stretched on for a long time in the court. It was believed that at one stage the farmer asserted that Dilip Singh had no son named Tejinder Singh.

I had no information about the exact background of this case and design behind this ridiculous argument. The judge demanded from Dilip Singh to provide evidence for his younger son Tejinder Singh. He had no hesitation and agreed to substantiate the evidence. He appealed to the judge to permit him to present the primary school records in the court. Dilip Singh urged the judge to instruct the village primary school headmaster to exhibit the school records. The judge accepted his plea to exhibit the record on the next hearing and directed his clerk to dispatch the summons to the headmaster to be present in the court with the school records.

I received the summons from the court before Dilip Singh visited me in the school. He mentioned to me that the court had sought the school record for Tejinder Singh. He just wanted to reconfirm if there was any glitch in bringing the records to the court. I informed him that I have already accepted the directive from the court and assured him that there was no problem. He felt a tremendous relief and departed after briefing me about the case.

On the date of the hearing, the elder son of Dilip Singh arrived on his motorcycle at my home to take me to the court. I had not anticipated it but I was against accepting favours from any side. He requested me, "Masterji I will give you a ride on my motorcycle to the court."

I had no intentions to ride on his motorcycle. I replied, "Look, both the sides are at par for me and I am least concerned about this case. I am only supposed to present the school records in the court. I am not appearing as a witness in favour of any side which would affect the final decision."

He insisted that his father had instructed him to bring me to the court. He felt helpless and a bit embarrassed when I declined his offer. Once again he attempted to pacify me and requested, "Masterji, I understand what you say but it would not make any difference if I drive you on my motorcycle."

But I flatly refused, "No, I would reach there by bus. Do not worry, I will not be late."

When I reached the court, Dilip Singh and his party heaved a sigh of relief. The advocate of Dilip Singh succinctly counselled me about the court proceedings as I was appearing in the court for the first time. We were called into the court and the advocate of Dilip Singh requested me to display the school records to the Judge.

The Judge glanced at the records and handed it over to his clerk for noting. Instantly the opposition advocate appealed to the judge to allow him to cross examin me. The Judge granted him the permission to proceed.

I was surprised about this unexpected development but I could not overrule the decision of the judge. Mentally I was getting equipped to face cross examination. The advocate shot the first question at me, "Masterji, have you admitted Tejinder Singh in the school?"

"Yes".

"Did Dilip Singh accompany Tejinder Singh to the school for his admission?"

"Yes, he escorted his son to the school."

"Did he personally read the instructions in the admission form or not?"

"He read it personally as noted in the record."

I glanced at Dilip Singh and he was smiling now.

Then the advocate intended to corner me beyond my role and asked, "Masterji, you are from the same village and must be familiar with more details about the family of Dilip Singh."

I resented at this and replied, "I have appeared here to exhibit the school records and not as a witness."

The advocate was stunned at my reply. The Judge gazed at me and said, "Natha Singh, let him try, you may answer his questions."

I had no option now but to answer the next question from the advocate. He queried, "How many children does Dilip Singh have?"

"Dilip Singh has four children."

In fact, Dilip Singh had two marriages. His first wife had expired and later on he remarried. He had two children from the first wife and two from the second wife.

The advocate satirically enquired, "What was the name of Dilip Singh's father?"

I was not confident about his father's name and avoided to answer incorrectly. I replied, "I don't exactly remember but I recollect that his grandfather was Narain Singh and he was a famous man in our village."

The advocate now intended to acquire more details about Tejinder Singh. He cunningly questioned me, "Did you visit the house of Dilip Singh when Tejinder was born?"

I was quite perturbed at that question and replied, "I am not the village Dai that I should attend every delivery in the village."

The Judge and the audience began laughing and the advocate had befooled himself. The Judge observed that this was a ridiculous question so he banged the gavel and asked the advocate to stop questioning me anymore.

I asked the Judge, "Sir, if he wishes to inquire about some relevant information then he should pose some sensible questions. Otherwise is it the duty of a school teacher to visit every house in the village where a child is born?"

The Judge was laughing and postponed the case for the next hearing. I collected my record register and returned home by bus."

*   *   *

A New Tradition

"The Sansis are always enthusiastic about their children getting married on top priority basis but for me it was the last one. The majority of the uneducated Sansis would seldom consider sending their children to school. They would endeavour to get them married as early as possible to wash their hands off from their responsibility. My brothers-in-law and other Sansis from our area would often criticise me when I had turned down their requests to accept their girls for my sons. Since my children were studying, hence the Sansis were fascinated to give their daughters in marriage for their bright future. But I had no exigency to seek alliance for my children because my preference was to establish my kids to be self reliant before their marriages. To get them married while they were studying would have been a suicidal act hampering their progress in life. When I paid no heed to their requests, their optimism had vanished and they would not raise this subject for discussion with me anymore.

Since I had embraced Sikhism and being a devotee of The Sant, I was determined to perform the marriages of my children according to the Sikh customs. My eldest son had finished his education and got selected for a permanent government job. My wife and I intended to search for a girl for him. Some Sansis approached us with several proposals for him but they would not assent to a Sikh marriage. We were prepared to wait and watch but committed to perform 'Anand Karz' for our children by following Sikh rituals. This mandatory stipulation became a hindrance for Sansis in our area and they turned away with their proposals. We were not anxious at all because my son had a job and we were confident that someone or the other would step forward to acknowledge our condition for brighter prospects for their daughter.

In 1971, Tulsi, a Sansi from village Gagra visited us with his son-in-law. Tulsi had a distant relationship with us as our ancestors knew each other very well in old times. He had served in the Indian Railways for a short period when he was young. He was in search of an educated boy and sought an alliance for his marriageable daughter. His son-in-law had informed him about my eldest son.

After they settled down then his son-in-law addressed Tulsi, "Uncle, my duty is over to guide you up to this house. Now you may further discuss it with them directly."

My wife and I were sitting around and Tulsi laughed and responded to his son-in-law, "Son, I was not confident about the location of the house otherwise I am acquainted with this family."

It appeared to me that Tulsi was not certain whether I had recognised him or not. Before he could proceed any further, he casually enquired, "Nathu, first of all do you recognize me or not?"

I had seen him long back when he was a young boy of around ten or twelve years old. He used to live in a nearby village with his relatives. I smiled and replied, "Yes, I remember you are Tulsi."

Tulsi felt relaxed and resumed his conversation, "Nathu, I have approached you to discuss the proposal of my marriageable younger daughter to your eldest son."

I glanced at my wife and she nodded in affirmation to consider this proposal. Since our families were unfamiliar with each other, Tulsi considered it crucial to express about his daughter and family. He openly spoke to us, "My younger daughter is uneducated and mainly occupied with the household work. My eldest son is married and has kids. The younger son is still a bachelor and my eldest daughter is still unmarried. Besides this if you have any demand for a dowry etc. then you can openly tell me."

My eldest son was also around and Tulsi solicited to corroborate it from my son. He wanted to know his personal choice and frank opinion before this proposal would materialise. He advised me to formally ask my son.

I asked my son, "Bhajan, what is your opinion about this proposal? Is it suitable for you?"

He shyly replied, "It is not important for me if the girl is uneducated but she should be humble by nature."

Tulsi promptly responded, "Yes, my daughter is modest by nature and you would find it comfortable to adjust with her."

I exchanged my views with my wife alone and together we decided to accept this proposal. After a while I conveyed it to him, "Tulsi, your offer is acceptable to us but we have one condition."

Tulsi was taken aback by this unpredictable condition. His face turned grim and looked at his son-in-law. He mustered the courage and seriously enquired, "Nathu, what is your demand?"

"Look Tulsi, we do not seek any dowry or money to confirm your proposal. But we wish you to perform the marriage according to the Sikh traditions. We desire to sanctify this marriage with 'Anand Karz', a Sikh marriage ceremony, instead of 'Phere'."

Tulsi was swept off his feet by this unforeseen strange condition and he was quite uncertain how to react to it. There were not enough educated and well settled boys available for his daughter. He was apparent in his mind that if he said 'no' directly, then he would lose a chance to engage his daughter. He thought deeply for a while and then reluctantly replied, "Nathu, this would be setting a new tradition among the Sansis. I have to discuss it with my family and all our relatives. I cannot immediately decide of my own."

I could appreciate his helplessness and uncertainty at this crucial juncture. He was worried whether his all relatives would endorse his decision or not if he jumped to an instant conclusion. I left it open for him. I encouraged him and said, "Tulsi, I absolutely realise your situation. You take your relatives into confidence, convince them and then decide. We shall await your reply."

Our demand was peculiar as no other Sansi had performed the Sansi marriage with Sikh customs in our area or perhaps anywhere else too. Tulsi was not disappointed but uncertain about the consent of his relatives. He got up and said, "Nathu, I will come back with an answer after a few days."

They immediately departed from our place.

Tulsi assembled his relatives at one place and briefed them about the marriage proposal for his daughter. He informed them that the whole thing is almost finalised except for one condition. The family desires to consecrate the marriage with the Sikh traditions.

Incidentally a person from my in-laws side was present there. He heard their conversation and conveyed to Tulsi, 'If Nathu has demanded it then he will not deviate from this condition. He had rejected several proposals from his own brothers-in-law. He won't diverge from his stand.

This solely depends upon you whether to accept or refuse his demand.'

Tulsi replied to him, 'I am ready to concur but my major concern is if I carry on with the Sikh marriage, would my relatives support me or not?'

At this stage his relatives debated amongst themselves. Sensibly they realised that basically there was nothing wrong with it as it was a sheer matter of faith. They appreciated that as I had embraced the Sikh religion, it made more sense for me to perform the marriage accordingly. They unanimously agreed and supported Tulsi not to worry but instead to go ahead with this proposal.

After a week Tulsi returned to us and now he was in a cheerful disposition. He excitedly conveyed to us, "Nathu, my relatives have unanimously agreed to support me to honour your condition. My family too has positively endorsed it."

We were extremely contented. The Sant also appreciated this development as he was expecting this to happen. This news had spread among the Sansi community about this new transformation. I delightedly said, "Tulsi, we are pleased as you have assisted us to fulfil our dream. We are ready to support you in making necessary arrangements for 'Anand Karz' if you foresee any difficulty in your village."

Tulsi was satisfied now that the situation had come under control but he was uncertain about the arrangements in his village. To ensure that the ceremony should be followed in its true spirit, he requested me, "Nathu, we have never experienced such an event among the Sansis. It would be an immense relief to me if you can organise the preachers to solemnise this function. I would be able arrange for the 'Holy Book' in my village."

I assured him, "Tulsi, do not worry at all. There are preachers available at The Sant's place who would eagerly be waiting for this occasion. I would request them to be present at your place in advance."

Tulsi Ram was at peace and fully satisfied that his mission had been successful. He departed happily after settling everything with us.

The wedding date was confirmed and I requested The Sant and other preachers to perform the ceremony of 'Anand Karz' for my son at Tulsi's place. They were all set to solemnise it.

Though this was the first marriage in our family we decided to celebrate it modestly. The Sant accompanied the wedding party and solemnised the 'Anand Karz'. This was the first ever marriage accomplished according to the Sikh traditions among the Sansis. This marriage was solemnised on 26th June, 1971."

*   *   *

The Mad Man

"One family from village Kila Raipur owned a transport business in Calcutta. The head of the family had settled down there with his two grown up sons. His wife lived alone in Kila Raipur to look after the farming. She would visit Calcutta a few times in a year. Her husband sought to expand the business further but his elder son wanted to establish separate business in his own way. His father was not in favour of it and declined to split the business. Gradually the rift began widening between them and ultimately it lead to petty daily fights. The father became more sympathetic towards his younger son. The elder son turned more jealous and vehemently began demanding his share. The situation turned brasher when his father decided to disown him and transfer the whole business to his younger son. The elder son strongly refuted it and threatened his father with dire consequences if he attempted to deny him his share.

Their father realised that this dispute could lead to an awkward situation. He planned to search for another alternative to get rid of his elder son without any fight.

As he was determined to sideline his elder son, he sought the help of a Tantric. It was said that Calcutta was notorious for Tantrics and black magic practitioners. He came across a Bengali Tantric who was very popular and dominant in the field of black magic. He made a deal with the Bengali Tantric to cast a hex on his son for whole life. The Bengali agreed to it and handed over some powder to administer to his elder son. He came home, mixed that powder in the food and gave it to his son. Within a few days his son began behaving like a barmy person. He would shout hysterically with bizarre movements. With each passing day his condition turned into a horrible state. People would often get frightened of him. Some days he would stay calm and sometimes he would turn so aggressive that he had to be chained. His father was least concerned about this as he had nattily executed his plan. Once and for all he had sidelined his perpetual hindrance. He further played safe and called his wife to inform her about the condition of their son. He wanted nobody to doubt him. His wife got extremely worried about her son and rushed to Calcutta without any delay. She was traumatized when she saw the horrible plight and the behaviour of her son. She asked her husband about how he reached this state but he gave some vague reply. She strived to look after her son and called some doctors. There was no improvement at all in his condition. Since she could not stay for a long time in Calcutta, she asked her husband to make arrangements to send him back to the village with her. He readily agreed.

If anyone visited her house in Kila Raipur, her frenzied son would shout and act in an eccentric way. The whole village was aware about his insanity. People were frightened and avoided passing by their house. His mother was troubled and endeavoured all possible ways and means to bring her son back to normal. Besides seeking medical assistance, she also began conferring local Tantrics as advised by her friends. The doctors were unable to discern why his condition was not improving with the medicines. The local Tantrics had miserably failed to rein him. His mother now strongly assumed that her son was under the spell of some potent evil spirit which could not easily be trounced by the local Tantrics. She had remained desolately unsuccessful to seek out any effective means for the treatment of her mad son.

Another lady from Kila Raipur was a follower of The Sant. One day the mother of the mad man bumped into this lady. The mad man's mother recounted the unfortunate tale of her son. She defined her endless woes to her that she could not find any remedy so far. The other lady informed her about The Sant and suggested that she should contact him at the monthly gathering. The mother of the mad man considered it worth taking a chance with the hope of finding some solution. She reached there to attend one monthly function. She explicated the whole story about her son to The Sant and requested him to make her son well. The Sant observed silence for a moment as if he was making some sort assessment of this tedious case with his divine vision. I was around and noticed that The Sant had become very sombre for a few moments.

The lady was intently looking at him with some hope and waited for his response.

After a few moments he emerged from his oblivious frame of mind and broke his silence, "Lady, look this is an extremely convoluted case and I would be able to handle it. Your son would become normal once again but it could take some time."

The lady was glad with assurance from The Sant.

The Sant asked me to give a bottle of holy water to the lady. He instructed her to serve this water to her son regularly. Then he prepared an amulet for her son to wear all the time. He assured her that he would visit her place soon to perceive the condition of her son.

The lady returned home and began serving holy water to her son as explained by The Sant. Gradually the intensity of aggressiveness of her son had toned down and he would not yell that much. There was a marginal improvement in his condition. His mother now had a ray of hope for her son.

Unexpectedly one day The Sant along with two other followers arrived at my home. I was amazed by their unanticipated arrival. Before I could ask anything, The Sant asked me to get ready immediately. Within no time we were on the way to Kila Raipur. When we reached there, we could sense from outside the house that the mad man was out of control. As we entered the house, his mother was helplessly watching his weird movements. She was frightened but when she saw us, felt a bit relieved.

The Sant briefed the lady that her son was under the hex of a very perilous and potent spirit. He told the lady that today he would encounter the spirit and she should not be frightened. He also mentioned that he would not harm her son. He signalled us to be prepared to clutch the mad man.

The Sant directed me, "Natha Singh, you grip the mad man firmly by the hair on his head but be careful not to strike his head at all as his head is like a raw earthen pot. If he is hurt on his head, he would collapse."

I gripped him by his hair and the other two followers clasped his legs and arms but the madman remained beyond control. I could not believe his ferocity and strength. The Sant attempted to converse with the mad man but he did not respond. The Sant closed his eyes and murmured something for a short time and soon his face began gleaming with a strange aura. The Sant opened his eyes, looked directly at the mad man and questioned him in a demanding tone, "Who are you? Who has asked you to seize this man?"

This time we noticed that the mad man had cooled down a bit and appeared to respond to The Sant. The Sant thunderously commanded again, "Speak now, who has ordered you to seize this man? I order you to renounce him."

At this time the mad man responded in a very garbled croaky voice to The Sant, 'you are ordering me to forsake this man but my Bengali master had taken a vow from me never to leave this person.'

The Sant questioned him again, "Who are you? What do you want?"

The same heavy voice came over and said his name in a distorted voice. He finally replied, 'I would obey only my master and keep this man under my siege.'

At this point The Sant indicated to release the mad man. He directed the lady to carry on serving holy water to her son. The Sant promised the lady that her son would be normal but he needed more time to tackle this case. The lady profusely thanked him as all her hopes relied on him now.

At the next monthly function The Sant discussed the condition of the mad man with us. He described to us that the spirit is backed by an extremely potent force. That force is the real power house of the Bengali. He would communicate directly with the source itself and not with the Bengali. He told us that the source is very tough and powerful but he would be able to crack it. He asked me to fix the date and directed his close followers to be geared up for this mission.

The Sant reached with his other three followers on the fixed date and I joined them from my village. When we landed in Kila Raipur, this time the mad man was comparatively calm and as usual his mother looked worried. The Sant mentioned to the lady again not to be worried much. The Sant seemed to be fully geared up for the final encounter. This time he had asked us to hold the mad man. We were sitting and The Sant observed silence for a few moments. Perhaps with his spiritual powers he directly communicated with the main force which was supporting the Bengali. The Sant had a strange radiance on his face now and feverishly looked at the mad man. The Sant certainly had more dominant spiritual powers than the Bengali and he was capable to summon that main force. He ordered the madman to respond immediately. In a short time a grumpy voice came over this mad man and asked The Sant, 'Why have you summoned me? I was supposed to appear only on doomsday but I cannot defy your order.'

The situation was fully under the control of The Sant. He dictated, 'This man is under my protection now. I conceive that the Bengali is dependent on your power. I wish you to quit.'

There was silence for a few moments. Now there was anguish in the tone when the mad man responded again with heavy croaky voice, 'I cannot repudiate your order. I would instruct the Bengali to spare this man. I would not support him anymore in this case.'

This conversation was over in a short duration and we were stunned to witness this dialogue between the two spiritual forces. The mission was not yet complete. Then The Sant summoned the Bengali through the mad man with his spiritual powers and ordained, 'Bengali, now unshackle your seize or be prepared to face the consequences.'

The Bengali had no other alternative but to surrender. The Bengali reacted with a heavy voice through the mad man, 'I would liberate this person now as my master has declined to support me. I will withdraw my seizure from this man.'

The Sant was enormously relieved now and gradually returned to his normal self. We all were watching this live scene and there was complete silence except for the communication between The Sant and the other spirits through this mad man. This appeared like a clash of the colossal giants but The Sant prevailed over his opponent. I could never envisage that The Sant had such gigantic spiritual powers. The people like The Sant are rare in this world. Now I have practically witnessed the confrontation between the positive and the negative spiritual forces. The mother of the mad man was contented that her son would soon return to normal. The Sant asked the lady to continue serving the holy water to her son. By all means The Sant felt satisfied and we departed from there.

Once The Sant had told us that his 'Guru' had especially blessed him that no negative evil forces would be able to stand in his way.

After a few months this lady was in tears at one monthly function at The Sant's place. She was cursing her fate and recounted the disastrous story of her son.

As luck would have it she and her son travelled to Calcutta because her son wanted to get into the business again. She was confident that her son had recovered now. She considered staying with her son for some time in Calcutta. During her stay there, she had a long conversation with her old lady friend about her son's arduous period. She expressed her happiness that her son was back to normal. Her friend was over enthusiastic when she listened to this episode. She immediately reacted, 'Well, you do not worry about it. I am acquainted with one master Tantric here who would protect your son from eveils in the future.'

The mother of the mad man unwittingly agreed to her friend and advised, 'Then let's go to that Tantric. I need protection for my son.'

Unfortunately, that lady ushered her to the same Bengali Tantric. The mother of the mad man described the condition of her son to the Bengali. The Bengali promptly assured her and remarked, 'There is nothing to worry about. I will sheild your son. You administer this water and ash in the food, nobody would be able to harm forever.'

She happily came back home and acted as advised by the Tantric. The moment her son consumed the stuff, he began returning to his madness again. The lady realised her grave blunder but it was too late. Her husband refused to keep his son there. Ultimately she brought her son back to the village.

When The Sant listened to her foolishness, he was really fuming at her. He was in no mood to listen to her any more. He regretted at her stupidity and said, 'I do not wish to listen to you anymore. You may leave now.'

*   *   *

People do seek the assistance from tantrics or black magic practitioners to harm their opponents. The powers of tantrics are said to vary according to their recitation of mantras, to hunt for control over the rival forces. They undergo exhausting meditation while rehearsing mantras with bizarre ways and means. Once they are able to gain control over the evil forces, then they exploit them mainly for evil purposes. When someone approaches the tantrics to take revenge on his rival, they would choose various methods to execute the evil effects with their skills. Some of them would provide some stuff to mix in any kind of food or drink. This stuff has to be served to his opponent by hook or by crook. Once it is consumed, the rival is said to be under a bizarre effect and starts behaving as if he was out of his mind. He could turn out to be aggressive or calm down in his daily activities, depending on what kind of evil effect has been imposed over him. Such categories of evil people would apply many means to implement their malevolent designs.

Every black magic practitioner or the tantric has his own methods of encountering the evil forces to nullify the impact on the affected person. It is believed that when the tantric would physically torture the affected person, the evil force would respond through the seized person. The tantric would neutralise the effect by administering some holy water to drink or any other method. Sometimes he would administer smoke to the person until the evil force submits. He could apply this practice in different sessions to exorcise the evil force.

It is said that when physical torture is applied to a person to compel the evil force to submit, surprisingly the person does not remember or experience the after-effects of the physical torture. It would appear that nothing had happened to the concerned person after the evil force had submitted and vanished. The whole process would affect the evil force only but not on the individual.

Sometimes ladies would employ such designs to restrain their men and keep them under their command. The man would behave as demanded by her. The time span of such an effect may vary from a couple of years to a permanent one.

The holy men like The Sant would never exercise their positive spiritual powers to ruin anyone but always attempt to unshackle the person from the clutches of the evil forces. When the holy man would begin treating a person, through his vision he would first gauge the powers of his contender. He would weigh up whether he had the capacity to encounter the evil force or not. If he is unable to match the influence then he would decline to lay his hands on the case. Consequently if his rival is more dominant than him, the evil force could impair him personally.

I had personally witnessed some people under the influence of evil spirits at The Sant's place. It may give an absurd impression that in this modern age such things still exist in this world and possibly may continue as long as the human race exists.

*　　*　　*

Risking for a Friend

S usan and I were rather surprised when my father revealed the many unknown momentous incidents in his life. Had he not narrated this story to us we would never have known that he took a great risk for his close friend. He had gone out of way to facilitate his friend who desperately needed his help. The following episode reflects another side of his courageous yet a distinctive character.....

"Once my old time school classmate, Gurdev Singh, was assigned as a Deputy Superintendent for the board examination of class ten in a nearby high school. There were two sessions for the exam; one was in the morning and the second one in the afternoon. After the evening paper was over, the Deputy Superintendent had the responsibility to count and pack the answer sheets and seal it with his stamp on the package. Then this parcel was to be dispatched by post to the head office of the education department. According to the directives, if the answer sheets had to be retained overnight due to unavoidable circumstances, then the Deputy Superintendent would break open the seal of the parcel the next morning and recount the sheets in the presence of his senior officer, reseal it and then dispatch it by post.

Since I was in-charge of the post office, Gurdev Singh approached me in the school and explained his intricate problem coming up ahead. Sensing this problem he wanted to make pre arrangements to avoid last minute hassle. He straightway said, "Look Natha Singh, the exam would conclude by four o'clock and your daily mail dispatch is also released at the same time. Hence under normal circumstances it would not be feasible for me to forward the answer sheets by mail on the same day. Only you can save me from this laborious exercise of recounting the answer sheets every day till the exams are over."

I understood his dilemma and he was now banking on my help. He expected some solution from me. I asked without any formality, "Gurdev Singh, what do you expect from me?"

He had a genuine plan in his mind and it entirely depended upon me whether to agree or not. He thoughtfully suggested, "Natha Singh, I want you to withhold the dispatch for me and take the parcel every day in the evening. It would consume some time after the exam was over to arrange the answer sheets and make a parcel of it. I would seal the package and deliver it to you to forward in the mail bag. I think this is the only possible way."

Initially I was hesitant because it was too precarious to hold the mail bag. But Gurdev Singh was my school classmate and I had the inclination to oblige him. He had accosted me for the first time for any help. I thought about it for a while before giving my consent. I was familiar that our post office in Kila Raipur would transport the mail bags by train to Ludhiana every morning only. As a routine our delivery man would pick up the incoming mailbag every morning from the post office there. Thus there was a feasibility that he could pick up the outgoing mail bag from me in the morning instead previous evening.

I decided to facilitate Gurdev Singh with my workable solution. I advised him, "Gurdev Singh, I am prepared to assist you but under certain conditions."

Gurdev Singh was slightly shocked, "Conditions?"

I said, "Yes, this arrangement should remain a top secret as I am risking my job. Secondly, nobody should ever know that the answer sheets stay with me overnight."

"Natha Singh, your conditions are acceptable to me. I promise that this arrangement would remain absolutely confidential in all respects. You can trust me." Gurdev Singh replied instantly.

Then I further added, "Gurdev Singh, I would confirm this arrangement only after I discuss it with the Postman. It would depend upon him to carry the mailbag from my home every morning."

Gurdev Singh was ready to wait till the postman also agreed. Gurdev Singh left on this note hoping that the Postman would. I was aware that my plan would not be executed without the co-operation from the Postman. I had to take him into full confidence for such a serious issue and explain the entire plan to him.

The next day I had a word with the Postman and described the entire situation to him. He was very considerate and consented to help us. He replied, "Masterji, I don't mind doing it if you are prepared to shoulder this responsibility."

I explained my line of operation to him, "You know keeping the mail bag overnight in the post office would be dangerous. I would rather carry it home in the evening. Opening the post office early in the morning would unnecessarily create suspicion."

The Postman being an open minded person, confidently said, "Masterji, I would pick up the mail bag from your home instead of the post office, it will not make any difference to me."

I informed Gurdev Singh that he should not worry as the whole process was in place. He was extremely happy about it.

I had explained to Gurdev Singh how to compute the amount of government service stamps required per kilogram and any fraction of it thereafter. The exams had begun and after the paper would get over, he would weigh the package and affix the government service stamps accordingly. In the evening I would wait for the parcel in the post office. Gurdev Singh would hand over the parcel and I would just mark the parcel number on it and cut a receipt for it. I would seal the mail bag in the post office and carry it home.

This system of despatching the exam papers was functioning efficiently.

The Post office had exclusive 'On Government of India Service', OGIS, stamps which were used for all types of government documents. The government departments had no need to buy regular postal stamps to mail anything. The concerned offices would maintain the account of such stamps.

One day during the exams, Gurdev Singh unexpectedly appeared at my house early in the morning. He seemed a bit perturbed and I sensed that some trouble was at hand. Generally he would not visit my place like this. Before he could utter a word, I enquired, "Gurdev Singh, what brings you here so early in the morning? Is there any problem?"

He wretchedly answered, "Natha Singh, I must send a money order of one rupee."

I was amazed by this atypical request from him because I had finalised everything the previous evening and sealed the mail bag. How could I modify the records now? I replied, "Well, Gurdev Singh, you know that it is not possible now. I have closed the accounts yesterday and the mailbag is ready for despatch. I am waiting for the Postman to come and pick up the bag."

Gurdev Singh was absolutely tense after I refused to help him. He was more worried and asked me, "If you can't do it then I would be behind bars."

He seemed to be crestfallen now. I enquired, "How have you landed in such a critical situation?"

He related the story to me, "Yesterday one student came late for the exam and he was fined one rupee. I collected the one rupee from him and accounted for it in the records. As per the rules I must deposit that fine with the government treasury office within twenty four hours. Otherwise I would be penalised."

"But why have you not done it yesterday? I could have adjusted it before closing the accounts," I quizzed Gurdev Singh.

"Unfortunately I failed to account for it being occupied with other sundry jobs after the exam and it struck me only after I reached home. I was helpless then," Gurdev Singh replied.

Now I could pulse the gravity of his situation. I had to search for a way out to protect him. I assured him, "Gurdev Singh, if this is the case, then I am prepared to open the post office and see what could possibly be done now."

With my assurance he seemed to be a bit relieved now and we went to the post office together. But on the way I made it very clear to him, "Gurdev Singh, if I have to strike through any entries in the record, then I will not do it. If there is a space for an entry then apparently I would oblige you. Whatever I am doing, is for the sake our friendship only."

To his good luck, when I opened the records in the post office, there was a space to add the one rupee amount without striking out any entry. I could comfortably add one rupee in it. I then accounted for his one rupee money order."

For all this Gurdev Singh was extremely thankful.

*   *   *

Panth Problem

"My second son was born on 23rd August, 1951 when I was still teaching at Machhiwara village. He studied in the village primary school and finished his higher secondary education from Khalsa Higher Secondary school in Mehma Singh Wala. The Principal Harnam Singh was a retired District Education Officer and my son had a good rapport with him. After he concluded his higher secondary education, I was keen that he should seek admission in the teachers training course like me. I had a word with my son regarding this. As he had a high percentage of marks there would have been no difficulty in getting admission and the Principal would have easily accepted him. But when my son consulted the Principal, he counselled my son with a very valuable advice. He suggested that since there was a college in our village he should not hurry for any professional training so early but instead look forward to study further atleast up to graduation. Once one better qualified then he would have better prospects for good professional courses.

My son came back and informed me his discussion with the Principal.

I had no reason to deny my son an opportunity to study in the village college. He would be able to attend college with bare minimum expenses except those of his fees and books. We could somehow cope up with this expenditure. I willingly encouraged my son, "I believe that your Principal has truly guided you. You should pursue your studies in the college. I had no chance to dream about it but you have this opportunity to so. You can go ahead for admission."

During his college days he would do physical labour in the fields along with his uncles. I knew that he was passing through a rough time but he never resented this struggle. He passed out from the college as a Science graduate. After graduation he joined a professional course for a degree in the Bachelor of Education in Chandigarh and became a qualified Science teacher. He had applied for various jobs during that time. In the mean while he joined as a Science teacher in village Mehma Singh Wala for a short time. After two-three months, he got an excellent opportunity to join an International Airline in Delhi.

Since my son was highly educated now, again my brothers-in-law were enthusiastic to propose their daughters in marriage to him. I plainly conveyed to them that my son intends to marry an educated girl but unfortunately their girls were uneducated. They would now refrain to talk about this issue any more. When my son was studying in the second year of college, a man from my in-laws was the panchayat secretary in Malaud village. He belonged to the Jat community and I would often meet him when I visited there. A Sansi from Malaud had an educated girl and he was in search of an educated boy for her marriage. He approached the Panchayat secretary to have my opinion about this proposal.

When I next visited my in-laws, the secretary came to me. He was an open minded person and without any hesitation he asked me, "Natha Singh, Baru in Malaud is serious about marrying his educated daughter to your son. What do you think about this proposal?"

I was not surprised about this proposal because I had heard about Baru's daughter. She was undergoing Staff Nurses training course. As there was a serious hindrance about the Panth, Baru had avoided contacting me directly. I replied, "Secretary Saab, this proposal is feasible but my son has not finished his graduation as yet. Secondly, this proposal has another serious drawback concerning Panth."

The Secretary was not well versed with the hitches of the Sansi community regarding the Panth issue. It appeared a straightforward case for him to decide about this proposal. He inquisitively asked me, "Natha Singh, I cannot visualise any impediments in this case but can you elucidate them to me?"

Without searching for any excuse I forthrightly replied, "There is a problem with the real brother-in-law of Baru. In the Sansi community a Panth is running in his name.

I cannot join hands with Baru to be blemished in the community for no reason. Hence I cannot endorse this proposal."

My succinct explanation was beyond his comprehension and he looked confused. He wisely avoided asking any further question but assured me, "I would coney this message to Baru that because of the Panth problem you cannot accept this proposal. There is no point for me to grasp the complexities of your community."

He thus informed Baru that I did not concur because of the Panth glitch. This matter ended without any further progress at that time.

More than two years had passed after Baru had asked the Panchayat Secretary about his daughter's marriage proposal to my son. One evening my brother-in-law and a relative of Baru arrived in the evening. They had consumed some alcohol and were high in spirits. Obviously they avoided coming to my place but stayed with my cousin for the night. The next morning my brother-in-law and the relative approached me when I was getting ready for school. My brother–in-law asked me, "Masterji, we have come to discuss some important issue with you."

I was in a hurry and did not want to get delayed for school. I informed them, "Look I am available only for half an hour otherwise I would be late for school. We can discuss your issue within this half hour."

My brother in-law lost no time and straightway came to the point and said, "Masterji, we have come with a proposal of Baru's daughter for your second son. Baru is voluntarily willing to accede to any of your demands unconditionally."

I highlighted the core issue without any formality, "What about his brother-in-law's Panth problem?"

Both of them responded in unison and replied, "The Panth issue would not be a hindrance anymore. For the sake of his daughter Baru and his family have decided to distance themselves from his brother-in-law. As per the law of the community he is primed to pay the penalty for crossing the Panth."

I realised if the core issue was resolved then it was a suitable match for my son. My son now had a permanent job and this was the perfect time for him to get married. I asked my wife about her opinion and she also had no qualms about this proposal now. Ultimately we agreed and I said to my brother-in-law, "In principle we are ready to accept this proposal, please inform Baru to personally visit us and resolve this Panth matter."

My brother-in-law and the other relative were thrilled that I had given my assent to this long awaited proposal for my son. They were ecstatic as if they had won the battle. As the real brother-in-law of Baru was directly involved in the Panth, the other Sansis in the area had their own speculations about this proposal whether he would cross over the Panth for the sake of his daughter or not.

After a week, Baru and his real brother-in-law visited us and thrashed out all the issues related to the Panth. He had already agreed to follow the principles of the community regarding the Panth issue. I was not in favour to compel him to accept my condition. I candidly asked him, "Baru, are you willing to follow the principles of our community regarding Panth?"

He was determined and instantly replied, "Nathu, I would abide by the laws of the community."

I appreciated his ingenuousness as he had no guilt in his mind about distancing himself from his real brother-in-law. I decided to reciprocate in my own style and proclaimed, "Baru since you are so straightforward with me and I would not inflict any penalty on you at this stage. I would be more than satisfied with your 'promise' on a ror, a pebble, that if anybody in the community questioned me about the Panth issue then you will be answerable for it at any place."

Baru and his brother-in-law could not believe my startling proclamation. Had I collected any penalty now and subsequently agreed to this proposal, then he would have been condemned in the community to openly renounce his real brother-in-law. His brother-in-law was also extremely pleased with my suggestion. The token penalty is always a blot on the concerned person. Otherwise the Sansis would not negotiate anything devoid of collecting the penalty first. Then Baru cheerfully answered, "Nathu, I swear to stand by my 'promise' and would never back out under any circumstances."

His word was more than enough for me.

After settling this Panth issue they happily returned home. In the due course of time we settled the various issues regarding the marriage. The engagement and marriage ceremony was completed together to avoid any unnecessary expenditure on both sides. On the wedding day they cordially welcomed the marriage party in a big way. Generally at the time of 'Milni' the father and grandfather are honoured but in our case, they honoured each of my cousins too with a Mohar, a gold coin. The marriage was solemnised according to the Sikh traditions. They had no objection in performing the 'Anand Karz'.

My all six children were educated and later on finished their professional courses as well. Subsequently they got jobs and settled in their lives.

*   *   *

Transfer from Narangwal

"I had been at the primary school for precisely nineteen years and twenty five days before I was moved to the Girls' High School. I was assigned to teach the fifth grade students in the high school.

In 1966, the Education Department reviewed the manpower in each school throughout the State. As a consequence it was established that there were four surplus teachers in the Girls' High School. Since I had recently joined the high school, I was reckoned as one of the surplus teachers.

The then State Education Minister was said to be cheesed off with the government school teachers. He had an opinion that the teachers were not favourable towards him during the recent State Assembly elections. He was furious with the teachers. The survey regarding the surplus teachers had landed on his table. He considered it a golden opportunity to execute his design now. He released a directive to the education department that all teachers eligible for transfers should be transferred at least thirty miles away from their present location.

Now the transfers were inevitable but I endeavoured to search for some convenient station within that range. I got in touch with my childhood friend, Harbans Singh, as he was posted in a school in Ludhiana. He suggested to me that we should approach the DEO, District Education officer for this purpose. The next day we headed for the DEO's office and observed that a man and lady were already having a conversation with him on the subject of transfers. We just waited outside his office but could overhear their conversation. The DEO was regretting that the Education Minister had really played havoc with the transfers of the teachers. He expressed his helplessness to the couple saying that he had received strict instructions from the Education Ministry, not to transfer any teacher less than thirty miles from his original place.

The DEO said that he phoned the Education Secretary and advised him that such strictness would adversely disrupt the system hence he should reconsider his decision regarding the minimum limit of thirty miles. But the Secretary emphasised that this was an order from the Minister and had to be executed accordingly. He had confronted the Secretary stating that he would go ahaead strictly to follow his orders however later on he would not exclusively favour any teacher on his recommendation.

The DEO finally concluded his discussion with the couple and added, 'That's why I am not interfering with these transfers. I would strictly follow the orders.'

We had the reply from the DEO so there was no point meeting him

I was transferred to the middle school in Ajner village near a town called Khanna. This place was certainly over thirty miles away from Narangwal. I joined there and introduced myself to the headmaster. He assigned me the charge of class five. In the beginning, I temporarily rented an accommodation in the Khanna town before I could find another suitable place.

A teacher from Narangwal referred me to his classmate teacher posted in this school. When I handed over the reference letter, he was delighted and did his best to help me. The headmaster and other teachers were concerned about my daily commute to and from Khanna. They discussed among themselves to make arrangement for my accommodation in the school itself. They finally managed to allocate one room for me in the school. I really appreciated their gesture. With this a lot of inconvenience of travelling was avoided. But now there was another major problem of my food. Unfortunately there was no 'Dhaaba' in the village.

The headmaster and the teachers were committed to help me to any extent. They were now sincerely working as how to resolve my food problem. They suggested a novel proposal to me, "Natha Singh, if you are willing to teach extra time to the students after school hours, then the students will arrange food for you every day from their homes."

I could not believe such a benevolent offer coming from them. There was hardly any work for me after school hours so I could easily take extra class to teach the students. Before I decided to give my consent to their proposal, a few doubts cropped up in my mind. My food problem should not create an unsolicited burden on anybody. What would the parents of the poor students do, when they could hardly feed their own children? I sceptically responded to my companion teachers, "Friends, I would accept your proposal on certain conditions."

They were surprised, "Conditions? What conditions?"

"Yes, I would accept food from the farmers' children or other people who could comfortably afford it. I have no intentions to be a burden on any family."

The headmaster and the other teachers appreciated my opinion. They replied, "You have a convincing point but we would ensure to arrange the food only from the well-to-do families."

But I further added, "Secondly I would teach the whole class. Later on those families who will provide food should not protest that the students from the poor families also study extra time, so they should also provide food. If this is acceptable only then I am willing to go ahead."

They assured me to consider these points before they would put the arrangement in place. At first they asked selected children to obtain the consent from their parents. After confirmation, they fixed the rotation of each student to fetch food for me. With this rotation a student would get a chance to bring food almost once in a month. I commenced taking extra classes. The students would carry breakfast, lunch and dinner for me without any disruption. Their parents would send really delicious food. The arrangement was working efficiently. The parents were happy that their children were getting tuitions without making any cash payment and I was glad that this facility had worked out well to solve my food problem.

There was a public place beside the school where people would gather to expend their leisure time. Sometime they would pass a comment, 'Look, all the other teachers have gone home and only this teacher is dedicated and taking extra classes to teach the students.'

Their remark would really amuse me.

There was one student who belonged to the backward class. One day he said to me, "Masterji, my mother has voluntarily opted to send food for you. As my father is posted in the army we can easily afford it. Would you please allow me to bring the food?"

I judged his feelings and it was hard for me to turn down his sincere request. I did not wish to discriminate against any student yet offer equal opportunity to those students who could comfortably provide food. I contentedly said, "Well, if you insist then you may bring the food."

There was no difficulty in Ajner except being away from my family. I would visit my village after a fortnight or sometimes go directly to participate in the monthly gathering of The Sant. During this period my efforts were on to seek a transfer back closer to my home. One of the Teacher's union leaders played a key role in my transfer from Ajner. He managed to obtain my transfer order for a high school called Tahli Saheb. I was in Ajner for twenty two months."

* * *

Retirement

"The High School Tahli Saheb is situated between three nearby villages. This school is about five kilometres away from my village. It is eminent because of its religious background. In the olden times our tenth Guru had blessed this place and planted a twig of a tahli tree which had flourished into a full grown tree then. Later on people had built a gurudwara there which was named as Gurudwara Tahli Saheb in the memory of our tenth Guru. In addition they also built this high school which is within the proximity of the Gurudwara.

I reported to the headmaster in Tahli Saheb when I joined there. I was acquainted with some of the teachers who were already working there. The headmaster called me to allocate my working periods. He assigned me two sections of class eight to teach mathematics and one section of class six to teach the Punjabi language. I was a bit uptight when he said, Punjabi. The headmaster looked at me in astonishment and said, "Natha Singh, I am allotting your periods within the prescribed limit. I would not allocate any extra periods."

I remained quiet but actually what I meant was that teaching Punjabi was not my cup of tea. Anyway I began taking classes and somehow managed to teach the Punjabi language. In the beginning of the new session in the second year, the headmaster enquired from me, "Natha Singh are you comfortable with your subjects or do you desire me to make any changes in it?"

I appreciated his concern about me and I eagerly requested, "Sir, mathematics is my favourite subject, but teaching Punjabi is a bit cumbersome for me."

Before I could utter a word, he straightway posed a question to me, "Natha Singh, would you be comfortable to teach mathematics to one section of class seven then?"

I was contented with his offer and immediately replied, "Yes, I would be grateful to you. I would prefer to teach mathematics instead of Punjabi."

During the new academic year, the education department had introduced two new chapters of geometry in the syllabus of class seven. There were three sections of this class and I taught mathematics only to one section. I personally brushed it up before I taught these chapters to the students. Unfortunately the teachers of the other two sections had ignored to teach those new chapters to their classes.

Now the annual exam was approaching and no mathematics teacher was prepared to write the mathematics question paper for class seven. The headmaster was fully cognizant of the fact that the two new chapters had not been taught to the other two sections of class seven. One day by chance I went to meet the headmaster for some work but before I could say anything to him, he took out two sheets of plain paper and handed it over to me. I was astonished and asked the headmaster, "Sir, I have come to meet you for a different purpose but why are you giving me these two blank sheets?"

He smiled and requested me to sit down. He directed me, "Natha Singh, I wish you to set the annual mathematics question paper for class seven."

I looked at him with surprise and remarked, "Sir, you know that I teach mathematics to this class and as a principle the class teacher is not supposed to prepare the final question paper. There are other mathematics teachers who could be assigned this responsibility."

The headmaster listened to me but replied, "Natha Singh, before you suggest anything to me, I have already requested the other two teachers but they have declined to set this paper. Now you are my last option."

I had no alternative except to accept this assignment."

While preparing the question paper, first and foremost the issue was whether to cover the whole syllabus or not. If I prepared the question paper without covering these two new chapters, then primarily it would be wrong not to cover the whole syllabus during the annual exam. If I considered the full syllabus then two thirds of the students would be at a disadvantage because their teachers had not covered those two new chapters. It would be sheer injustice to those students. I could not instantly visualise any solution to this problem.

After school, in the evening when I was walking back home, this problem kept gnawing my mind. Then suddenly this idea popped up that I should create the total number of questions from all the other chapters except the two new chapters which had not been covered by all the students. To cover the syllabus completely I should add an alternative question with the 'or' option from those two new chapters. I reached home and arranged for a mathematics book to set the annual question paper on those guidelines. I selected all types of questions for the brilliant as well as for the dull students. I was glad when this question paper was ready that evening. The next morning I went to see the headmaster and handed over the question paper. He looked at me with a gloomy face perhaps he assumed that I had approached him with some bad news about the paper. He looked at me but the next moment he could not hide his bewilderment and asked, "Natha Singh what is this?"

In amusement I replied, "Sir, this is the mathematics question paper for class seven."

He was stunned, "What! Have you prepared it so quickly?"

"Yes Sir", I replied.

Curiously he spread the sheets and observed the 'or' option between the questions from the new chapters. After he evaluated the full paper, he was very delighted and said, "Fantastic, this is a brilliant idea to cover the whole syllabus. Natha Singh, you have indeed done an outstanding job!"

I was contented that my hard work to teach the new chapters to my section was fruitful.

The teachers who taught mathematics to the other two sections were petrified when they received the information that I had set the annual question paper for class seven. They were frightened that their students would not able to answer most of the questions.

On the exam day, the other mathematics teachers seemed visibly nervous while the students awaited their question paper. I asked the teachers to go through the question paper to find out if there were any mistakes in it so that we could rectify it before delivering it to the students. They were hesitant even to open the package. I coerced them to have a quick look at it. Unwillingly they opened the packet and noticed the questions with the 'or' option between the two questions. They patiently told the students not to panic because there were adequate questions for everybody to answer.'

The teachers and students heaved an enormous sigh of relief.

As my superannuation was nearing the headmaster had deputed another teacher to take charge from me. The departmental formalities were being processed for my retirement. On my retirement day, the headmaster had invited the Block Education Officer to grace the occasion. During the function the headmaster and some teachers highly appreciated my services and expressed their sentiments. To honour me, they presented a blanket and one 'gutka', a small religious book.

In my farewell speech among other things I specified that during my tenure of thirty years of service, I had seldom squabbled with anybody in the school.

The BEO was astonished at my remark and appreciated it. He specifically added in his citation, 'I am amazed to hear from Natha Singh that during his thirty years of service, he had not disputed with a single person in the school. He is an ideal teacher.'

My last working day in the school was 30th June, 1979."

*   *   *

Pilgrimage

During his life time my father never had an opportunity or the money to travel on any pilgrimage or long vacation. Most of his life revolved around attending school or visiting The Sant every month. As far as I remember he had seldom expressed his desire to go out and enjoy himself alone or with his family. The core reason was the financial limitations which prevented him to think about it. He struggled to run his family all the time. After his children were able to manage their own families, he heaved a sigh of relief. Following his retirement, now he had leisure time and his own money from his pension. With his limited needs, his life was comfortable now.

In the old times the people in the villages had a similar lifestyle like my father. I had hardly ever heard of any family in the village who had ventured on a picnic irrespective of being rich or poor. At the most if any family organised a short trip then their destination would invariably be to some historical religious place. People did not have surplus money to spend on themselves. Mostly they would put aside money to be utilised for satisfying their family needs or social demands. The financial conditions hardly permitted them to expend any money for personal pleasure. Their main aim remained to save money to cope up with any eventuality in their lives.

Now my father was old and had no demanding liabilities in life. He would often visit the village Gurudwara. A young man from the village organised a pilgrimage to a Sikhs' religious place and openly invited one and all to join. Perhaps my father had an unrevealed desire in his heart which he could not accomplish in his early life. Now he spotted an opportunity to undertake this holy pilgrimage. Conceivably this trip was his ultimate pilgrimage and he earnestly described this holy journey with great enthusiasm.....

"Every month there is a religious gathering in the Gurudwara which is on the bank of our village canal. In 1989, I had gone to attend one congregation there and after the religious ceremony was over, it was announced that a group from our village would be undertaking a pilgrimage to Sri Hemkunt Saheb, a sacred place of our tenth Sikh guru, Sri Guru Gobind Singh. Those individuals, who wished to join this holy trip, should enrol their names and contribute three hundred rupees towards the journey expenses. This programme was chalked out at least fifteen, twenty days in advance. Manohar Singh was the tour organiser of this pilgrimage.

Instantly a deep desire arose in my heart as I had never endeavoured to undertake any pilgrimage during my whole life. Now why should I not take advantage of this magnificent opportunity? A strong urge propelled me and I went to meet Manohar Singh.

He was delighted to see me and enquired, "Masterji, please tell me what can I do for you?"

I directly asked him, "Manohar Singh, I yearn for this holy pilgrimage, I am keen to know if old persons like me undertake this journey?"

He positively responded, "Yes, Masterji why not, you can undertake this journey unless you have a problem with your knees or chest."

I further added, "Manohar Singh, I presume it must be a hilly region where one had to climb up and down. I am unsure if I would be able to climb the hills. I would not like to be an impediment to the whole group and make them halt because of me."

He laughed and to clear my misgivings, he said, "Masterji, in the first place the hills are not there throughout the journey. Secondly there are alternative modes of transport for those who cannot climb up the hills themselves. There is hardly any point for you to worry about this."

I gained more confidence from his encouragement and enquired, "How many sets of clothes would be sufficient for the journey?"

"Two, three sets would be adequate but I suggest that you carry some warm clothes too. It would be pretty cold up in the hills."

I was contented with his explanation and made up my mind to join the group. I deposited the money for the trip.

I informed my family about this pilgrimage and began collecting necessary belongings for my trip. I was pleased that finally a dream journey of my life was going to take place.

The group had expanded to a fairly large number of thirty seven men and twenty seven women. Two trucks were arranged for transportation. One doctor was accompanying our group to provide any medical assistance. On the day of departure, we all assembled and prayed at the village Gurudwara.

In each truck there was an exclusive group to sing the holy hymns, accompanied by a harmonium and 'tabla', a pair of drums. During the journey they continued chanting holy hymns and we followed them in singing. On the way to Chandigarh we made our maiden halt at the Gurudwara in Lawani Ghat. We had food there from the 'Langar', community kitchen. After finishing our lunch we were briefed that our next stop would be at the Gurudwara Ponta Saheb for an overnight stay. We arrived there by evening and settled down in the Gurudwara. This Gurudwara is situated on the bank of the river Jamuna. There is a location near the Gurudwara where our tenth guru would assemble with the other poets to compose the verses.

On one occasion one of the bards of the Guruji, Sri Guru Gobind Singh, had expressed his apprehensions regarding the noise from the waves. He pointed out, 'Guruji, here the river Jamuna is too close and its waves may create some disturbance whenever we gather here.'

The Guru calmly presaged, 'Don't worry; the river will always remain calm here.'

We were amazed to observe that there was no thud or sound from the waves near the Gurudwara. We could hear the noise of waves away from this place but it was absolutely serene here.

The next day we headed for Srinagar and Manohar Singh had prearranged our stay in a Gurudwara there. We were provided gratis accommodation like all other Gurudwaras' with sufficient beddings and blankets for everybody. Free food was generously available in the community kitchen.

In 1989 terrorism had its ominous shadow spread over Punjab and Kashmir. The security forces were vigilant from any threat from the people entering Srinagar. They would demand authentic details of every individual visiting there. Manohar Singh had sensibly procured sufficient copies of the detailed list of our group in advance and handed over a copy at the army check post.

Our departure was fixed for four o'clock in the morning from Srinagar. Most of our members woke up at two o'clock to avoid getting delayed and finished their morning ablutions. After a few hours of our journey, the sun was coming up and Mother Nature had pushed aside the curtain of darkness to view her abundant beauty in its full glory. This mesmerising splendour stirred deeply in our hearts. We all appreciated the Creator. After a fairly long journey we reached Rishikesh. Our accommodation was in the Gurudwara which is sprawled in an enormous area. For our stay the Gurudwara people opned up a hall for us. We had no difficulty in obtaining as many bedding as we required. From Rishikesh we headed for Math Saheb. On the way we passed by a gigantic stone which resembled an elephant. Nobody could judge from a distance whether this was a real elephant or of a stone.

Somebody informed us that the way up is clear, so we hurriedly leapt into the trucks and arrived at Gobind Ghat. The trucks and buses could reach up to this point only. Manohar Singh had made special arrangements there for us as the members of the Gurudwara were waiting to receive us. The weather had suddenly changed a lot as chilly winds welcomed us there. Gobind Ghat Gurudwara is like a fort in a large area. Here again they allotted a big hall to us for our overnight stay. They provided us with four blankets each to keep us warm and cosy in the night.

Before I retired for the night a young man arrived with a bundle of blankets and said, "Masterji, Manohar Singh has sent four additional blankets especially for you."

I was flabbergasted but replied, "Young man, I already have four and there is no necessity to take anymore."

The young man insisted, "Masterji, I am following the instructions of Manohar Singh and I must hand them over to you. You keep it and just return it tomorrow morning."

There was no point in insisting any more but I admired Manohar Singh who had specially considered my well being and genuinely took care of my comfort during the cold night. I slept well that night.

From Gobind Ghat, we had to walk or search for an alternative means of transport. We were asked to deposit our main luggage here and only to carry a few absolutely necessary belongings. We were advised of our assembly point in Gobind Dham which was about thirteen kilometres from there. Some members of our group preferred to ride on horses or mules but I confidently walked with the others to Gobind Dham. Manohar Singh had departed late from Gobind Ghat for some reason and hired a horse to join us. He met us on the way after we had gone about five-six kilometres. He enquired from everyone if everything was well. He exclusively asked me, "Masterji, how are you getting along? Are you comfortable walking?"

"Manohar Singh, so far I am all right," I replied enthusiastically.

He smiled and encouraged me, "Masterji, for you this journey should not be arduous as you have walked a lot in your life."

He informed us that a tea stall would be coming up ahead and our group could enjoy tea and snacks there. After a kilometre we reached the tea stall, rested there for a while and sipped tea. When Gobind Dham was within striking distance one old lady and I felt exhausted. We rested for some time and somehow we arrived at Gobind Dham Gurudwara. They opened a foyer for us and we settled down comfortably. Everybody was weary after this tough journey and our leg muscles had stiffened. To provide some relief to the weary muscles, some young men and women began massaging the legs of the whole group. The ladies assisted among themselves. A young man approached me to massage my legs but I rebuffed to get it done. Manohar Singh observed this and resented my refusal. He personally came over and asked me, "Masterji, you being a member of our group, why did you decline this massage? You should not have objected to it. This is for your benefit; I will now personally do it for you."

I yielded to Manohar Singh because he was determined to take exclusive care of me. I presume in a way he had undertaken the responsibility when he had encouraged me to join this pilgrimage. In fact I was a bit embarrassed when he began massaging my legs because nobody had pressed my legs openly like this in a group. He sensibly remarked, "Masterji, we do not apply full weight on the legs but just within tolerable limits. Please inform me when it is unbearable to you."

He massaged my legs for almost twenty minutes and I felt relaxed.

The distance of six kilometres from Gobind Dham to Sri Hemkunt Saheb, is a very strenuous journey. Before we retired for the night they enquired from each member if they required horses tomorrow for the climb to reach Sri Hemkunt Saheb. I was the first one to raise my hand. Some other members also requested to hire horses. The standard rate was one hundred rupees per horse for a return journey. The different modes of transportation available were ponies, horses, mules and basket carriers etc.

The next morning when we were about to set out on our journey suddenly it rained for a short time. Most of the members of our group preferred to march. But the transporters augmented their rates from one hundred to one hundred and thirty rupees per horse.

Manohar Singh seemed anxious and asked me, "Masterji what shall we do now?"

I had the money to pay for the increased rates for renting a horse. I assumed that there may not be any transport accessible in transit hence without any hesitation I was firm on renting a horse. I candidly concurred and replied, "Manohar Singh, there is no problem, I will pay one hundred and thirty rupees."

Another member and I agreed to hire the horses from one man, he had only one horse and one mule. My companion selected the mule named Hero and I opted for the black horse named Kalu. We set out on our journey. The animals were well trained and obeyed the commands of their master. On the way a small packet of glucose and two tablets were supplied to each of us in case any member underwent fatigue or uneasy feelings. The meandering way took considerable time from Gobind Dham to Hemkunt Saheb.

When we were nearing Sri Hemkunt Saheb, we could clearly glimpse the five symbols of Sikhs' from a distance. Before we were about to approach the Gurudwara the horse keeper enquired from me, "Saab, what would you do for your return journey?"

I realised that it would be gruelling for me to walk back on this hilly terrain. I firmly demanded from the horse keeper, "I would certainly return on your horse."

Then horse keeper was pleased and informed me, "Then I will charge you only a hundred rupees for the entire trip. In the meanwhile I am going down the hill again to pick up more passengers and when you are ready to return, you wait for me in this same place."

Ultimately we all gathered in the Gurudwara. I had an urgent task at hand. Some people from our village had wished to offer Prasad there on their behalf and handed over their money to me. The total amount was more than one hundred rupees. They have a custom there that if anybody offered Prasad of more than one hundred rupees, they would offer him a Siropa, a robe of honour. I offered the Prasad there and was honoured with a Siropa. I then walked around the Gurudwara and prayed there. After this I took a bath there but to my surprise the water was not very cold. In the community kitchen they served a glass of special tea. This tea had a marvellous boosting effect on me. I had forgotten my tiredness and felt invigorated and absolutely fresh.

After worshiping in the gurudwara for some time our group gradually began descending back to Gobind Dham. For various reasons nobody was permitted to stay up there overnight. I came back to my designated place and waited for a long time for the horseman but there was no trace of him. Ultimately I began walking down but I noticed that the horseman was waiting some distance away.

He rushed to me and wondered, "Oh Saab, where were you? I was looking for you here."

I retorted, "But you had asked me to wait there."

He apologetically replied, "No, no, I asked you to be here in this place."

This time he asked me to ride the mule. When we were about to move, an old lady hurriedly came running asked the horse man to hire the horse. He was pleased to have one more passenger. She had hardly travelled a short distance when she requested him to offload her. She was too scared to ride on the horse. Her fear made me uncomfortable too and I requested the horseman, "If there is any place where the mule cannot easily cross over then you can ask me to get down, let the mule pass and then I will ride again."

But he laughed and assured me, "Don't worry there is no need for you to get down. My animals are well trained for such terrains."

One by one all our members returned to the Gobind Dham Gurudwara for an overnight stay.

The next morning we returned to Gobind Ghat on foot. When we were about one and a half kilometre away, I felt exhausted again but somehow managed to reach there. I asked Manohar Singh if some more money was required for our contribution. He said, "Masterji, don't worry we will settle the accounts after we reach our village."

We returned to Ponta Saheb and most of our group members dispersed from there on their own. I purchased one bamboo walking stick from Ponta Saheb as a souvenir. With this wonderful and satisfying pilgrimage, I felt more at peace in my life."

*   *   *

EPILOGUE

*M*y American friend Susan and her family landed in our village in the early seventies and lived across the road. Her husband was The Director of Rural Health Research programme. They had three young children who pursued their studies at home. Gradually I became friendly with this family. I was studying in the higher secondary school at that time. I would often visit them in the evenings and had a keen interest in reading books as they had a big library in their house. Susan would often visit our home and spend some time there. My mother was very pleased to meet her whenever she came over. Unfortunately that health project was closed down and they moved to Bangla Desh. We remained in touch and Susan would often visit Delhi with her children and I would join them there for a few days.

When Susan and I were tape recording my father, I perceived that the most important phase of his life was veiled to me. I had witnessed his life only from my childhood days when he was already teaching in the village primary school. The most striking segment of his life was before he was employed as a permanent teacher. We being his children had a far better life than what he had encountered in his childhood and youth. When we began listening to the story of his life which was full of jerks and jolts, the beauty was that he remained firmly rooted to the bottom of life.

My childhood experience in school was no longer akin to my father. I had friends from all castes, rich and poor. We would play together devoid of any ill feelings. My clothing was comparatively less inferior to the well-to-do boys but it never became a reason for any disparity. I had studied in a co-education higher secondary school but my Sansi caste never turned to be the cause of any humiliation even from the girls of the Jat families. I would converse with them without any restraint. In the school the other low caste boys were also considered at par devoid of any prejudice by our teachers. Inside or outside the classroom the teachers never addressed any high or low caste students by their caste. During my college days an almost identical situation was true. Yes, I never encroached into the sanctum sanctorum of any religious places. I had apprehensions that I might be restricted to cross that line where they would feel offended but otherwise I would freely enter the religious places. This thought never crossed my mind that I was a Sansi and should lie low. Life was much more liberated now than in my father's time.

At that time in general, life in the village was different. In a few particular cases I had experienced where the high caste people felt candidly offended and their detestation had instantly surfaced. They used loathing language reminding me that I belonged to a low caste. When I used to work in the fields or in the village with my uncles, we would always carry our own utensils for food. This practice continued even when I was studying in the college. Sometimes we would work in the fields of my childhood Jat friend but he would never permit us to utilize our own utensils. He would sit and eat the same food with us and join us in the work.

One family in our neighbourhood vehemently hated Sansis and other low castes. Their condition was like when something boils over in a vessel, it burns its own brim. The best way was to ignore and avoid bestowing any undue deference to them. There was no point to get into a mêlée with these petty minded people. We were not reliant on them anymore.

Two highly educated Jats from my village envied me when I would frequently visit Susan's family in the evenings. One of them was a college principal and the other one a retired army officer. Infrequently both of them would also *drop by her house. It was hard for me to deduce what was cooking in their minds. One day both of them stopped me on the road and advised me not to visit her family. I was perplexed and avoided demanding any elucidation; however I still continued visiting Susan's family. I could infer that they had conspired something against me but she had never revealed it to me at that time. After that incident I noticed that if both of them appeared at her house for a social visit while I was already there, she would not invite them to come inside her visitor's room. On the contrary I perceived that Susan's family had a deeper association with me now and sometimes they would take me along on short vacations. My basic point is the mean mindset of even the highly educated people had not changed ever since my father's time. I have concluded that there would never be a genuine equality between the low and high castes; it would always fluctuate on the basis of one's financial status. This would perhaps never happen in the villages for a long time to come.*

There was another personal incident to expose this deep rooted superiority complex in the minds of the Jats towards the low castes. My college mate from our village had invited me to attend the marriage of his sister and help in running errands, which is a common practice in the villages. I was involved in various jobs there for the whole day. After the departure of the wedding party everybody felt relaxed and my friend accompanied his sister to her in-laws. Within no time one educated Jat ordered me, "Hey, Sansi, you fetch some eggs, I want to make an omelette."

I felt appalled at the way he had addressed me and I refused to obey him. Probably he had not anticipated refusal from a Sansi that too in front of the others. He gazed scornfully at me but dared not utter a word. I immediately left that place instead of picking up a brawl with him. I avoided it for the sake of my friend.

I had a few clothes when I completed my higher secondary education. My father had given me his permission to join Govind National College in my village. I was utterly ignorant about the norms of the college. One day I visited the college to obtain the prospectus to apply for my admission. I was dressed in a simple shirt and pyjama. One of the older students first smiled at me and then remarked, "Friend, look this is a college and your simple shirt and pyjama would not be befitting attire."

I was awe struck but did not mind his advice about the dress code in the college. Then I had to request my parents to purchase a pair of trousers for me. There were hardly any ready-made clothes available at that time. Somehow my mother managed to get one pair of pants for me. Just like my father got his first pair of shoes in the fifth class, I had my first pair of trousers when I joined college.

The true sacrifice of my grandfather to rescue his son by quitting smoking and giving up non-vegetarian food had borne fruit now. This transformation had guided the family to a reformed upbringing. Our family became vegetarian after my father had shunned meat and drinks at the behest of The Sant. We had also developed religious sentiments, recited holy hymns at home and followed Sikhism. My mother also encouraged her grandchildren to recite the holy mantra at home.

My father had an amazing knowledge about the social network of the Sansi community. This regular update had facilitated him when he had arranged the marriages of his children. He had never supported or favoured to execute the marriages of his educated children outside the Sansi community. He chose to remain aloof yet kept his roots deep in the community. In the village people would often approach him to seek his advice as he was the most senior person in the Sansi community. Sometimes people would find it hard to digest his outlook but he would not desist from verbalizing his honest opinion. The Sansis respected him more because he belonged to the older generation and they usually address him 'Baba'.

When I was young, I would accompany my father to his in-laws and observe that the Sansis there had an enormous admiration for him. He would ensure to call upon each Sansi family there and would not refrain at all from *sitting on their heavily soiled bed. They were delighted to see him and hastened to spread a good sheet for him. Even if they insisted to spread it, he would just take that sheet and keep it aside. He had not forgotten his old days of poverty. Later on when I was in college and visited there on my own, then I too would not mind at all sitting on their depleted cots or soiled beds. They would try to offer whatever best they had. Like my father, I would mingle with them without any qualms and even have food with them. Their fondness would drench me with warm feelings and I would create a comfortable atmosphere around, where they could identify that I was one of them. They appreciated me being educated, but I would make them feel that being educated does not mean that I cease to belong to them anymore.*

As the population of the Sansis had expanded, they spread over in different villages. The Sansis in Ludhiana district have their own close social network. They transformed the different areas of our district into three zones, termed as 'Des'. 'Des' literally means 'country'. Narangwal is in Tihara Des. The other two are Pehalhaddi and Peerokhanno. Tihara Des is subdivided into five 'deras'. Narangwal is in Kirtiya dera along with two other villages, Chhota Narangwal and Lohgarh. The second dera is Sabuke, containing Katani and Gill village and others. The third dera is Chitte Ke, enclosing the villages Mullanpur, Dakha, Lalton. Gurderke dera consists of villages Pakkowal, Andloo, Basrawan and others. Fathuke dera includes villages Dehlon, Aassi, Kila Raipur, Jodhan and Mandiani. Each dera has its Lumberdar, headman, to control the area.

For various reasons the covert language of the Sansis has ceased to pass on from generation to generation like in the old times. This language does not have any written script and in the old times the Sansis main aim was to avoid the other people understanding their conversation. My uncles talked in Sansi language at rare occasions. There were hardly any unlawful activities because the local circumstances have drastically changed. New generations have lost its touch because their parents have not passed it on to their children. I had seldom heard my parents speaking this language at home. I picked up some words only from my uncles but I am unable to speak or understand it. Interestingly when we were looking for a match for my sister, we went to meet the boy's family. My brother and I had a tough time to deal with that Sansi family. They asked us something in the Sansi language and we were totally blank about it. We just gazed at each other curiously. Luckily our uncle had accompanied us and he translated the meaning to us.

This language was more popular among the illiterates. The people from the 'Jungle' area especially would communicate in this language in daily life except with the outsiders.

They passed on this language from one generation to the next. There is nothing which could be taught but learnt merely by speaking. I am sure that my father must have been speaking this language in his childhood and youth. My mother would seldom utter a few words but my uncles and their families would communicate with each other in the Sansi language sometimes. With the awareness of education among the Sansis, the base of the Sansi language has eroded to a great extent. The young people are unable to learn it due to negligible usage in daily life. I knew a few words when my uncle Gurdial and Jeet sometimes spoke to me while working in the fields. They assisted me by explaining the following words and other covert ways and means of the Sansis.

For example, farmers are called 'kaja', cobblers are 'chinua', and the sweepers are called 'bukla', carpenters are called 'lukhian', potters are 'lumba', water carriers, 'jhewers', are called 'beungla'. They devised these words for their own secret use, so that nobody else could understand it. For farmers there were more words than 'Kaja' meaning the same thing. In addition to the words, there were some sounds, like clicks. These were mainly used during the night operations when they used to go stealing. There was a sound like the howling of a jackal. If there was another group, they would also growl or howl the same way, so it was understood that they were their own people. If during the night operations for some reason the group got scattered, they would growl to be together again.

The wanderers like the Sansis, the Baurias, the Harnias and the Gadianawalas, those who kept chariots, also used the same language. In Barnala and Sangrur districts they still speak the same old language. As long as people remained illiterate, they would carry on the usage of this language especially in the backward areas. But when people become educated, they stopped using it.

These are some example of short sentences. 'Nappi le' means hide it. 'Podi ja' means run away. 'Tiara ayee goga' means 'the farmer is coming'. 'Naukhi le' means see it. 'Nupp kari jasar' means be quiet. 'Loogi gaya' means 'the person has died. Sansis would instantly create new words according to the situation, which would be understood by his or her other companion.

My father and his cousins had a good rapport with each other. Both my uncles had dropped out from school after second or third grade. My eldest uncle, Gurdial was very intelligent and witty. We would always have fun with my younger uncle when we worked together in the fields. Generally my eldest uncle and I would pair together and younger uncle would pair with somebody else. We played tricks with him most of the time. My younger uncle would often get irritated with us and at times it would lead to *minor squabbles. But by the evening we would disregard everything and never carry home any ill feelings. My uncles never complained to my father against me. Sometimes we would indulge in making fun of the gullible farmers too.*

One day we were working in the fields of one farmer whose relative was a member of the State Assembly. My uncle Gurdial cooked up a story and informed the farmer that the State Government was considering issuing licenses to the farmers to grow poppy. Everybody was aware that the poppy crop was highly profitable. He instigated the farmer to contact his relative to put up his recommendation to acquire the license to grow poppy. The farmer assumed this information to be true and the next day he contacted his relative and requested for his recommendation. His relative informed the farmer that there was no such scheme. But the farmer insisted and upheld that it was true. Finally the famer got annoyed and accused his relative, 'All right, if you do not wish to favour me, it is a different matter. But I did not expect such a response from you.' His relative made an effort to pacify him that somebody must have played a joke on him.

When the farmer returned, we were still working in his fields. He was feeling embarrassed and asked my uncle, 'Gurdial, yesterday I visited my relative and asked him for the recommendation to get the license to grow poppy. But he informed me that there was no such scheme.'

My uncle was unperturbed when the farmer narrated the whole story to us. After the farmer finished his story then my uncle shrewdly modified his statement, 'You have misunderstood me completely. I had informed you that the government may consider growing poppy in the State under license and the farmers may require a license for it. You have not listened to me properly.'

The poor farmer really felt very embarrassed and we all heartily laughed at him. There are hundreds of jokes and stories like this which we would play with the illiterate farmers.

My uncles always maintained an excellent relationship with the neighbours. There were two carpenter brothers living near our house but their families lived separately. The younger brother was an open minded person and had a very good affiliation with the Sansi families. On the contrary the elder carpenter brother was orthodox in nature and considered himself to be highly religious. He always hated the Sansis. Once the younger brother's son was getting married and he asked my younger uncle Jeet to accompany the wedding party for any assistance. When they arrived at the brides place, the older brother could not digest the presence of my uncle. He got infuriated and burst out at his younger brother, 'Why do you always keep the Sansis around on every occasion? They also shamelessly join us. I cannot bear the presence of a Sansi here.'

The younger brother firmly replied, 'He is my neighbour and the Sansis stand with me in every crisis. I do not understand what your problem is with them. If you cannot tolerate his presence then you are free to depart if you wish.'

The elder brother got extremely cheesed off with this acrimonious remark and departed in a huff.

My eldest uncle Gurdial dropped out from school after fourth grade. He had attained some proficiency to read and write in Urdu and do basic mathematical calculations. While attending the court cases against him in old times he had become conversant with some of the Indian Penal Codes (IPC) with his sharp mind. He had memorised many Indian Penal Codes by heart for various crimes. Whenever there was any dispute in the village he would advise people which IPC would be applicable to file the case and guide them how to draft an application and to whom it should be addressed etc. Such things are important in legal matters. Without charge he had virtually become an unofficial legal adviser in the village. Sometimes he would accompany the family when they got involved in some court case. In his late fifties he had acquired a permanent membership in the Communist Party of India. This membership had boosted his image in the party circles. He took an active part in the village politics and contested in the village Panchayat elections. Finally he was unanimously elected as a Panchayat member in the village. This way he had gained a better say in the police station and other government offices.

* * *

When I was reproducing this book from the recordings, Susan went back to the USA to see her family. Unfortunately she fell sick there. Even though she had the best medical facilities available there, the cause of her illness could not be diagnosed. Her husband was a highly qualified surgeon and made all possible efforts from his side. It was too late when she was diagnosed with leukaemia. The cancer had quickly spread throughout her entire body and she passed away soon after.

I was occupied with the responsibilities of my job which consumed most of my time. This project remained pending for very long for the want of time. In the meanwhile my father was also not keeping too well. He died on the 28th May 2001. After my father's death, my both uncles also expired one after the other.

I resumed this project after a long break when I retired from my job. Susan had initiated this project and now I could finally accomplish it.